WHEN MYSTIC MASTERS MEET

Towards a New Matrix for Christian-Muslim Dialogue

WHEN MYSTIC MASTERS MEET

Towards a New Matrix for Christian-Muslim Dialogue

Syafaatun Almirzanah

BLUE DOME

Published by Blue Dome Press
244 Fifth Avenue #2HS
New York, NY 10001

www.bluedomepress.com

Library of Congress Cataloging-in-Publication Data Available

ISBN: 978-1-935295-12-9

Printed by
Görsel Dizayn Ofset Matbaacılık Tic. Ltd. Şti. Istanbul / Turkey
Tel: +90 212 671 91 00

Contents

ACKNOWLEDGMENTS

I wish to thank several people, communities, and institutions who made it possible for me to embark on this *journey*. Throughout my studies in Catholic Theological Union, Lutheran School of Theology and the University of Chicago, Dr. Scott Alexander, my *ustadz* (teacher), my advisor, provided the rare combination of strong intellectual support and friendship. I would like to express my deep gratitude to him. If this work has any important insight at all, I owe it to his guidance. Philip Yampolsky, Sheila McLaughlin, Dr. Barzinji, Dr. Bernard McGinn, Dr. Rob Worley, Fr. Anthony Gittins, Fr. Robert Schreiter, Fr. Edward Foley, Dr. Mark Thomsen, Dr. Harold Vogelaar, Dr. Jo e Rodriguez, provided much needed support and advice during critical stages of my PhD career. The Ford Foundation, The Bernardin Center at Catholic Theological Union, Lutheran School of Theology, and International Institute of Islamic Thought provided grants for my study in Chicago.

I want to thank my colleagues and friends in Catholic Theological Union, Lutheran School of Chicago, and the University of Chicago (especially Xaverian, SVD Communities, and May May Latt) for their friendships and supports.

My deepest gratitude goes to my family and community of true friends, especially my mother, Siti Amanat, my father, H. Z. A. Aljufri (may God have mercy on you) and my brothers, Muhammad Jamaluddin and Hussein al-Kholiq, and sisters, Khusnul Khotimah, Ahadiyah Nurul Qamar, and Siti Nur Laela, for caring for me and supporting me in the most crucial ways, and enabling me to have strength of mind and spirit. My love and thanks go to my beloved son, Muhammad Hasnan Habib, whose passion and understanding during our living and study in Chicago deepened my understanding of what life is all about.

I dedicate this work to all the people who have helped me since I first began my journey in this world. With admiration and hope.

EDITOR'S NOTE

Ibn al-ʿArabi and Eckhart are two giants of the history of mysticism in the traditions of Islam and Christianity, respectively. Mysticism, by its very definition, speaks of realms that are beyond the phenomenal world. Thus, its themes are intangible as they surpass the physical boundaries to which we are bound in our worldly realm. Mystics—in this case Ibn al-ʿArabi and Eckhart—more often than not voice the experiences of their spiritual journeys from non-phenomenal spheres. Ibn al-ʿArabi, for instance, lived along the farthest horizons of spirituality. For him the real life was when he was in a transcendental state during which this world was more like a vision. Probably he felt like he went into a state of dreaming when from our perspective he was just waking up to our level of life. His works feature complicated themes in varying colors, with frequent ups and downs. In order to attain and encourage deeper contemplation, at times he consciously uses provocative expressions, followed by an explanation. He prefers to dive into the deep oceans—unlike many of us who may drown in a pond—and he does not want to reach the shore, if there is a shore.

It is important to be aware of this condition before one starts reading the works of these giant figures of mysticism. We, thus, recommend readers to keep the mystic's viewpoint always in mind to avoid a possible risk of being mislead by some of the sayings and commentaries of these masters quoted in this volume that are not easy to reconcile with the doctrines of their respective religions.

ABBREVIATIONS

This work was originally submitted as my PhD dissertation to the Lutheran School of Theology in Chicago; thus, it is a product of my academic research. Nevertheless the text is intended not only for specialists but primarily for general readers, and I have refrained from having too many footnotes. The interested readers can find the information and additional information about the subject either in the Bibliography or the *Encyclopedia of Religion*, the *Encyclopedia of Islam*, and *New Dictionary of Catholic Spirituality*. The following frequently cited works are abbreviated in the footnotes:

BW   Ibn al-ʿArabi, *The Bezels of Wisdom*, translation and introd. by R.W.J. Austin; pref. by Titus Burckhardt, New York: Paulist Press, 1980.

DW   Eckhart, *Meister Eckhart: Die deutschen und lateinischen Werke,* ed. Josef Quint; 5 vols.; Stuttgart: Kohlhammer Verlag, 1936-

ESC   Meister Eckhart, *The Essential Sermons, Commentaries, Treatises and Defence,* ed. by Edmund Colledge and Bernard McGinn, New York: Paulist Press, 1981.

Fut.   Ibn al-ʿArabi, *al-Futuhat al-Makiyya,* ed. ʿUthman Yahya, Cairo: al-Hayʾat al-Misriyat al-ʿAmma li al-Kitab, 1972-1989.

IW   William Chittick, *Imaginal Worlds: Ibn al-ʿArabi and the Problem of Religious Diversity,* Albany: State University of New York Press, 1994.

LW   Meister Eckhart, *Die deutschen und lateinischen Werke,* ed. Josef Quint; 5 vols.; Stuttgart: Kohlhammer Verlag, 1936-

MP   Reiner Schurmann, *Meister Eckhart: Mystic and Philoso-pher: Translation with Commentary*, Bloomington: Indiana University Press, 1978.

QRS   Claude Addas, *Ibn 'Arabi, ou, La quete du sourfre rouge (Quest for the Red Sulphur: The Life of Ibn 'Arabi)*, translated from the French by Peter Kingsley, Cambridge: Islamic Texts Society, 1993.

SDG   William C. Chittick, *The Self-Disclosure of God: Principles of Ibn al-'Arabi's Cosmology*, Albany: State University of New York Press, 1998.

SPK   William C. Chittick, *The Sufi Path of Knowledge: Ibn al-'Arabi's Metaphysics of Imagination*, Albany, N.Y.: State University of New York Press, 1989.

ST   Meister Eckhart, *Sermons and Treatises*, translated and edited by M.O'C. Walshe, Shaftesbury, Dorset, England: Element Books, 1978, 1987.

TP   Meister Eckhart, *Teacher and Preacher*, ed. by Bernard McGinn, Classics of Western Spirituality, New York: Paulist Press, 1986.

VNR   Claude Addas, *Ibn 'Arabi: The Voyage of No Return*, Cambridge: Islamic Texts Society, 2000.

FOREWORD

Though Muslims and Christians account for the majority of the world's population, share many religious beliefs, values, and interests in common, Muslim-Christian relations have too often been marked by mutual stereotypes, ignorance, fears, and conflict. Historically, Muslim and Christian theologies of exclusivism and triumphalism as well as Muslim and Western political expansion and imperialism have too often demonized the "other" and cast it as a theological and political threat. And yet, Christians and Muslims have rich theological and spiritual resources for developing contemporary models of religious pluralism and tolerance grounded in mutual understanding and respect.

Christians and Muslims' shared beliefs include: recognition and worship of the one God, Creator, Sustainer, and Judge; share a belief in common prophets (Adam, Abraham, Moses, Jesus) and in divine revelation (the Torah and Gospels); belief in moral responsibility and accountability, the last judgment and reward and punishment. The Qur'an proclaims, "We believe what has been sent down to us, and we believe what has been sent to you. Our God and your God is one, and to Him we submit," (28:46) and "We have sent revelations to you as We sent revelations to Noah and the prophets who came after him; and We sent revelations to Abraham and Ishmael and Isaac and Jacob and their offspring, and to Jesus and Job... and to Moses God spoke directly" (4:163-164). Similarly, Peter, preaching in Jerusalem shortly after Jesus' death, declared that,

"The God of Abraham and of Isaac and of Jacob, the God of our fathers, glorified

His servant Jesus, whom you delivered up and denied in the presence of Pilate" (Acts 3:13-14).

Both religious traditions affirm an ethical monotheism, based on the belief that God possesses a moral nature that demands justice, righteous anger, and, at the same time is to be worshipped as a God of mercy, compassion, and forgiveness. Both proclaim the Golden Rule, found in "Do unto others as you would have them do unto you" (Luke 6:31) and in "No man is a true believer unless he desires for his brother that which he desires for himself" (Prophetic Tradition or hadith recorded in *Sahih Muslim*).

The impetus toward greater pluralism today is fueled by a variety of factors. While past approaches of religious exclusivism have tended to highlight theological differences, advocates of dialogue have emphasized shared beliefs, commonly held values and concerns: the moral breakdown of societies as well as recognition that power and wealth, rather than religion, tend to guide both national and international affairs. The impact of globalization, the communications revolution, and immigration increasingly have brought people of different faiths and cultures into daily contact. Modern multi-religious nation states require a national unity and notion of equality of citizenship that rooted in an inclusive society of peoples of diverse faiths and no faith.

Modern interfaith or multi-faith dialogue and relations emerged in the mid-twentieth century and has grown globally. However, most often the primary emphasis has been on theological dialogue. Despite significant progress, too often Christian-Muslim dialogue, as Syafa notes, gets "stuck" on irreconcilable theological propositions. Thus there is a need for a *new* matrix, one that, while acknowledging distinctive differences, is firmly rooted in shared spiritual experiences. Though dialogue at the level of spirituality and mysticism has existed, it has been underutilized as a resource in Christian-Muslim dialogue and relations.

This important volume fills a major gap, focusing on two great medieval mystic masters, one Muslim, the other Christian: Muhyi al-Din Ibn al-ʿArabi, the Sufi teacher often referred to as "The Greatest Master," German Dominican mystic and theologian whose status as "master" has become a part of his name—Meister (master) Eckhart. This study covers their teachings that have significant implications for addressing issues of religious diversity and interfaith dialogue. It will then place "the mystical discourse of these two masters in conversation with one another for the purposes of articulating "conversation points" between the two discourses."

The spirituality of Ibn al-ʿArabi and Eckhart share an emphasis on the Oneness of Being/God and distinction between the God and Godhead. The God of theology and doctrine is the creation believers and religious institutions use as a human construct in their finite, limited language to describe the ineffable. Though useful, it must be distinguished from the godhead, the true nature of the divine that transcends the grasp of human language and categorization. Refocusing on the Oneness of God takes us beyond the limitations of God language and human formulations of doctrine and lets "God be God," enabling us to base our understanding, worship and service of God on that unity which underlies our difference and diversity both within and across religions. This shared vision and experience provides a common bond that can lead to greater appreciation of our own faith as well as that of others. It enables us to be better Christians and Muslims, to be better human beings and practitioners of our faith, to work together to build a more just society and world order based on faith and social justice. Thus, the measure of faith and realization of God's will is based not on a religious exclusivism but inclusivism, not on the assertion that one religion is superior to others but on service based on Love of God and Love of Neighbor (not just members of one's own faith but all humanity): working together to help, feed, educate, provide healthcare, work to end conflicts and war, to save and protect the environment.

John L. Esposito
May 2010, Washington, D.C.

INTRODUCTION

This work is a study of the role mystical discourse and experience can play in Christian-Muslim dialogue as a subset of interfaith dialogue in general. It will concentrate on the work of two great medieval mystic masters, one Muslim, the other Christian. The Muslim is the Sufi teacher known to centuries of admirers as *al-shaykh al-akbar* or "The Greatest Master"—Muhyi al-Din Ibn al-'Arabi. The Christian is the great German Dominican mystic and philosophical theologian whose status as "master" has become a part of his name—Meister Eckhart. The dissertation will begin by discussing the life and legacy of each mystic master, and then move on to identify a principal theme in each of their teachings that has significant implications for addressing issues of religious diversity and interfaith dialogue. It will then proceed to its main objective: placing the mystical discourse of these two masters in conversation with one another for the purposes of articulating "conversation points" between the two discourses which might serve as "nodes" for a possible new matrix for Christian-Muslim dialogue.

The selection of Ibn al-'Arabi and Meister Eckhart was based, in part, on the fact that, although their greatness has been duly recognized, for several centuries each was forgotten by those outside the mystical schools of their traditions, and, to a significant degree, each was vilified as heretical by those who feared that their teachings posed a threat to their respective orthodoxies and orthopraxies. All in all, however, both demonstrate a thorough grounding in the mainstream thought and practice of their traditions. Yet they also both demonstrate a visionary boldness which impels them to attempt to broaden, renew, and reconstruct the theological worldviews in which they steadfastly locate themselves. Both are also thinkers whose writings exhibit an intersection of some of the dominant mystical, theological, and philosophical discourses of their day. Finally, the work of both Ibn al-'Arabi and Meister Eckhart is so rooted in canonical scripture that at times they appear to be writing quranic and biblical commentaries.

The methodology of the project is an under-explored mode of comparative mysticism which brings into contextualized conversation with each other the thought and related experiences of Meister Eckhart and Muhyi al-Din Ibn al-'Arabi. The aim of this methodology is *not* to reduce or ignore important differences between the two mystics, but rather to identify the ways in which the teachings of each speak to the content, context, and experience of the other. The point here is not to argue that Rudolf Otto and others who followed him were right: that there is a common pre-linguistic experience of "the holy" at the core of all religions. This is a topic for an epistemological and philosophical discussion all its own.[1] Rather, it is to suggest that the process of comparing ideas about any aspect of human experience, assumes a basis of commonality—however narrow—upon which a common discourse of analysis can be built.

The motivating premises of the research are three. First, because so much of Christian-Muslim dialogue gets "stuck" on irreconcilable theological propositions, a *new* matrix for the dialogue is necessary – ideally one that focuses on ways of looking at the cosmos that are rooted in distinctive and different, but nonetheless shared spiritual experiences. Second, many people in the world today—both Christians and Muslims—are becoming more disposed toward dialogue as a way of reducing conflict in our increasing number of "global villages." One obstacle in advancing the dialogue, however, is the alienation of practitioners from the rich intellectual resources of their respective traditions which can be drawn upon to legitimize, support, and encourage dialogue. Third, if practiced with intelligence, sincerity, and care, dialogue and encounter with people of other faiths can significantly enrich the identity of the religious individual as he or she articulates, in a plu-

---

[1]   See the debate between the likes of Walter T. Stace (*Mysticism and Philosophy*, 1960) and Ninian Smart ("Understanding Religious Experience" in Katz, ed. *Mysticism and Philosophical Analysis*, 1978) on the one hand, and Wayne Proudfoot (*Religious Experience*, 1985) and Steven Katz ("Language, Epistemology, and Mysticism" in his *Mysticism and Philosophical Analysis*, 1978) on the other.

ralist context, just what it means to be a Muslim, a Christian, or the adherent of any other religious tradition.

Before concluding this introduction with an outline of each chapter, I would like to address the question: *Why speak about a new "matrix" for Christian-Muslim dialogue?* According to *Webster's Dictionary*, the English word "matrix" comes from the Latin for a "female animal used for breeding," or a "parent plant," and is related to the Latin *mater* for "mother." Its broadest meaning is "something within or from which something else originates, develops, or takes form." In geological terms, it refers to "the natural material (as soil or rock) in which something (as a fossil or crystal) is embedded."[2] By proposing that the goal of this dissertation is to move *toward* the development of a new "matrix" for Christian-Muslim dialogue, I am proposing that this project will yield a set of ideas *from which*—if accepted by living communities of faith— a new genre of Christian-Muslim dialogue may emerge. It is important to note that I do not see the dissertation itself as the "matrix" or "mother" of this dialogue, but rather as providing some of the material from which the matrix might be formed. In particular, I am speaking here about the five "conversation points" or "nodes" of the proposed matrix that are enumerated and articulated in chapter five and further discussed in chapter six.

Chapters one and two will describe the historical context in which each of the mystic masters lived and worked. They are designed to help the reader to understand their methods and ways of thinking, as well as provide some insights into how their work was interpreted, and why. Specifically, knowledge of their historical contexts will assist the reader in appreciating the thought of Ibn al-'Arabi and Meister Eckhart from the point of view of its intended use, thus cultivating a deeper understanding of the masters' respective intellectual and spiritual agendas. In addition, these two chapters will review the historical legacy of the two masters addressing the question of how their teachings were received by the tradition, both during their lifetimes and long after they died.

---

[2] See *Merriam-Webster's Online Dictionary*, "Matrix"; http://www.m-w.com/dictionary/matrix; visited on July 24, 2007. Also see *The Concise Oxford Dictionary of Current English*, ed. Della Thompson, ninth edition (Oxford: Clarendon Press, 1995), 841.

Chapters three and four deal with the essential teachings of each master. The aim of these chapters is to articulate clearly the somewhat difficult concepts at the center of their teachings, being careful to point out, when necessary, common oversimplifications, misunderstandings, and misrepresentations of their teachings. These chapters are not intended to be exhaustive analyses of every aspect of the works of these two highly prolific thinkers, but rather as an exercise in highlighting, around one central theme (the "Self-disclosure of God" for Ibn al-'Arabi and "Detachment" for Meister Eckhart), the teachings of the masters that have the most relevance for thinking about some of the challenges presented by religious diversity and interfaith dialogue.

Chapters five and six are the most synthetic in that they attempt to construct (chapter five) and interpret (chapter six) a comparative mystical conversation between the thinking of these two masters. The objective of chapter five is not so much to identify "similarities" in the teachings of each master, but rather "points of conversation" in which we find the teachings of both men to be "deeply analogous." The difference here lies in the recognition that each of the masters is working within distinct theological and philosophical frameworks which, in some respects overlap, but which, in other respects, are quite incompatible. The objective of chapter six has two major dimensions. The first is to interpret the five points of conversation outlined in the previous chapter as potential "nodes" for the proposed "new matrix" for Christian-Muslim dialogue. The second is to demonstrate that this process can be one of genuine "re-discovery of tradition" in which these key teachings of the masters, so relevant to questions about religious diversity and interfaith dialogue, can be celebrated as deeply rooted in Christian and Muslim orthodoxy and orthopraxy. The ultimate intention of this chapter—and indeed of the entire work—is not to present my proposal as some prepackaged remedy to the problems we face in our attempts to advance Christian-Muslim dialogue. Rather, it is to invite readers who value the dialogue to help develop this new matrix by engaging in a critical evaluation of my claims within the context of their own experience.

Chapter I

IBN AL-'ARABI:
HISTORICAL CONTEXT, LIFE,
AND LEGACY

IBN AL-'ARABI: HISTORICAL CONTEXT, LIFE, AND LEGACY

1. Historical Context

According to Mahmoud al-Makki, the Islamic conquest of the Iberian Peninsula marked a very significant moment in the history of the beginning of the Middle Ages. "For it was in this corner of the earth, named al-Andalus by the Arabs," writes Makki, "that there arose the first Arab-Islamic state on the continent of Europe."[3] After escaping from the Abbasids who had seized power from the Umayyads in Damascus, and after spending five years traveling across North Africa's desert as a fugitive, Abd al-Rahman ibn Mu'awiya (755–788) arrived at al-Andalus. Supported by many people, he soon conquered Cordoba and laid the foundations of what would become, for nearly eight centuries, one of the most luminous of Islamic societies. Like Baghdad and Damascus, al-Andalus began to develop its own particular brand of Islamic civilization which took shape in a symbiotic relationship to the pre-existing European culture out of which it emerged.

For eight centuries, al-Andalus or Andalusia, as it was eventually to be known, was among the most densely inhabited, culturally sophisticated, and economically vital areas in all Europe. In fact, it had no rival in commerce. It was also culturally and religiously very diverse. For example, the number of Jewish communities in Andalusia greatly increased under the new Umayyad caliphate in sharp contrast to the previous period of Christian rule during which Jews were

---

[3] Mahmoud Makki, "The Political History of Muslim Spain (92/711–897/1492)," in S. K. Jayyusi, *The Legacy of Muslim Spain*, Vol. I (Leiden: Brill, 2000), 3.

persecuted and the growth of Jewish communities severely restricted. One early twentieth-century European historian describes the distinctive tolerance of the Umayyad regime for cultural and religious diversity as follows:

> Side by side with the new rulers lived the Christians and Jews in peace. The latter rich with commerce and industry were content to let the memory of their oppression by the priest-ridden Goths sleep, now that the prime authors of it had disappeared. Learned in all the arts and sciences, cultured and tolerant, they were treated by the Moors with marked respect, and multiplied exceedingly all over Spain; and, like the Christian Spaniards under Moorish rule – who were called Mozarabes – had cause to thank their new masters for an era of prosperity such as they had never known before.[4]

Indeed, the harmonious living between Jews and Christians under Umayyad Muslim rule grew to be one of the legendary hallmarks of medieval Andalusian society, to the extent that the tenth-century Saxon nun, Hroswitha of Gandersheim, dubbed Andalusia to be "the ornament of the world."[5] Regardless of the fact that the Muslims understood Judaism and Christianity to be corrupted forms of true Abrahamic faith, and thus superceded by Islam, the Muslim rulers of Andalusia allowed Jews and Christians to preserve their possessions, beliefs and practices, and thus to continue their ways of life within the framework of this new society.

It was the Cordoban caliph al-Hakam (796–822) who set the tone for the distinctiveness of Andalusian society. He was known to be a tolerant ruler who respected the counsel of his advisers and who loved learning. In addition to expanding what was to become the great mosque of Cordoba, al-Hakam was responsible for founding the very first university in Andalusia, which would eventually rank with the Nizamiyyah University and the Bayt al-Hikma of Baghdad, as well as

---

[4]　See for further explanation, Martin A. S. Hume, *The Spanish People: Their Origin, Growth, and Influence* (New York: D. Appleton and company, 1914, c1901).

[5]　See Maria Rosa Menocal, *The Ornament of the World: How Muslims, Jews, and Christians Created a Culture of Tolerance in Medieval Spain* (Boston: Little, Brown & Co., 2002), 12.

Qayrawan of Fez. While so much of Western Europe was in a transitional phase to which some erroneously refer as the "Dark Ages," Cordoba rose to the status of the greatest center of learning in Europe.

Since the final quarter of the fifth/eleventh[6] century, al-Andalus was subject to rulers of Maghribi origin: first the Almoravids (*al-murabitun*), who took control with the aim of defending Cordoba against the threat of a Christian reconquista; and then the Almohads (*al-muwahhidun*) who replaced the Almoravids, taking control of Andalusia from 540/1145 until 609/1212 when, after the defeat by Christian forces at Las Navas de Tolosa, the Almohads abandoned Spain. Under the Almohads, certain local rulers who were part of the Almoravid regime were reinstated as governors of certain regions. One of the most important examples of this—especially with an eye to the life of Ibn al-'Arabi—was Ibn Mardanish of Murcia who reigned from 542/1147 to 568/1172 and for whom both Ibn al-'Arabi's grandfather and father served as high-ranking military officers and high-level administrators. In terms of their interpretations of Islam and their impact on the societies over which they ruled, the Almoravids were very successful in ensuring, both in the Maghrib and in al-Andalus, a strict observance of Islamic law based on a very conservative interpretation of the Maliki School which had been the dominant Sunni law school in North Africa since the third/ninth century.[7] Meanwhile, in the East, new intellectual and religious trends were emerging and shaping interpretations of Islam based on a synthesis between, strict observance of the Shari'a, on the one hand, and the emphasis on the more affective and somewhat subjective dimensions of religious experience, on the other. This latter emphasis was reflected in the teachings and activities of the

---

[6] Dates are *anno hegira*, or Islamic calendar / common era.

[7] The official adoption of Maliki was due to the amir Hisham I (172/788-180/796) and and his son al-Hakam I (180/796-206/822). Amir Hisham was notable for a number of religious foundations; he took an interest in Islamic sciences, encouraged the training of *ulama'* in the East and kept in touch with the development of religious discipline there. Al-Hakam I very quickly made it clear to the members of the hierarchy around him that they should give their juridical opinions (*fatwa*s) and their judgments solely according to the school of Malik. See Dominique Urvoy, "The '*Ulama'* of Al-Andalus," in S. K. Jayyusi, *The Legacy of Muslim Spain*, 852.

numerous Sufi brotherhoods (i.e., *tariqa*, sing.) which, at the time, were beginning to multiply throughout the Muslim world. In fact, it was in this context that the famous Sunni Imam Abu Hamid al-Ghazali (d. 505/1111), became one of the principal figures associated with this synthesis and whose works enjoyed immense and immediate success, receiving support from both intellectuals and rulers alike.[8]

Among the many important Muslim thinkers who emerged out of this rich context of intellectual debate and exchange was Ibn Hazm (384/994–456/1064), who identified himself as a Zahiri and thus opposed certain Maliki methods of legal interpretation. Ibn Hazm was born in Cordoba on 7 Ramadan 384/November 7, 994. He had an extraordinary career as a historian, an excellent jurist, and a great writer with a wide-ranging command of philosophy. During the *fitna*, or a civil unrest following the death of the 'Amirid ruler of Valencia, 'Abd al-Malik al-Muzaffar, Ibn Hazm was imprisoned and exiled. Exhausted and weary of polemics Ibn Hazm then retired to Huelva, where he died in the summer of 455/1064.[9] Among his literary legacy are such well-known works as *Tawq al-hamama, Kitab al-fisal fi al-milal, Kitab fi maratib al-'ulum,* and *Kitab al-tarqib li-hudud al-kalam.*

Another important Muslim thinker in the history of al-Andalus who helped shape the intellectual ethos into which Ibn al-'Arabi was born was Muhammad b. Masarra (d. 319/ 931). Ibn Masarra was initiated into the Isma'ili and Mu'tazili systems of thought by his father, 'Abd Allah b Masarra (d. 266/899), who had acquired this knowledge over the course of his studies in the East.[10] Among Ibn Masarra's many accomplishments was the founding of "a small retreat for friends and companions in the cave of Sierra de Cordoba, where prayer, penitence, and other forms of asceticism were practiced."[11] As alluded to above,

---

[8] See, Piere Guichard, "The Social History of Muslim Spain from the Conquest to the End of the Almohads Regime," in S. K. Jayyusi, *The Legacy of Muslim Spain*, 697.

[9] Menocal 2002, pp. 112-118.

[10] Miguel Cruz Hernandez, "Islamic Thought in the Iberian Peninsula," in Jayusi, *The Legacy*, 777.

[11] Ibid. See also Maribel Fierro, "Opposition to Sufism in Andalus," in *Islamic Mysticism Contested, Thirteenth Century of Controversies and Polemics,* eds. Frederick De Jong and Bern Radtkey (Leiden: Brill, 1999), 180. See also Miguel Asin Palacios, *Ibn al-'Arabi,*

Ibn Masarra's thought is a synthesis of Muʻtazili doctrine on the unity of God, divine justice and free will, and of Sufi theory and practice as developed by Dhu'l-Nun al-Misri and al-Nahrajuri.[12] For Ibn Masarra, God is that Essence to which unity pertains *per se*. Likewise, God can only be truly known through ecstatic union. Ibn Masarra's teaching became the principal root of the dialectical thought of the Sufis of al-Andalus, and was very dominant within what Asin Palacios called the "School of Almeria."[13] In his *Futuhat*, our Shaykh al-Akbar refers to some idea of Ibn Massara's philosophical system.[14]

There is one remaining intellectual giant of the medieval Andalusian scene who should be mentioned in any sketch of the intellectual ethos into which Ibn al-ʻArabi was born and worked. He is none other than the great Aristotelian *faylasuf* Ibn Rushd (520/1126–595/1198)—known in the Latin West as Averroes. Though he was the son and grandson of Cordoban *qadi*s (i.e., religious "judges") of the Almoravids, Ibn Rushd "openly supported the Almohads" and in fact "was very close to them, both as a physician to the sultan and as the person officially responsible for making known the works of Aristotle."[15] In addition to composing many scientific and philosophical works, he also wrote a very important treatise on jurisprudence, *Bidayat al-mujtahid wa nihayat al-muqtasid*, which, according to

hayatuhu wa-madhhabuh, tr. 'Abd al-Rahsan Badawi, from *El-Islam Christianizádo; estudio del "sufismo" a través de las obras de Abenarabi de Murcia* (Cairo: Maktabat al-Anjlū al-Miṣrīyah, 1965).

[12] Fierro 1999, p. 178. On Ibn Masarra, see Miguel Asín Palacios, *The Mystical Philosophy of Ibn Masarra and His Followers*, transl. [from the Spanish] by Elmer H. Douglas and Howard W. Yoder (Leiden: Brill, 1978).

[13] Palacios 1946, p. 144, cited by Claude Addas, Ibn 'Arabi, ou, La quête du sourfre rouge (*Quest for the Red Sulphur: the Life of Ibn 'Arabi*), (hereafter abbreviated as QRS), translated from the French by Peter Kingsley (Cambridge: Islamic Texts Society, 1993), 57.

[14] Ibn al-'Arabi, *al-Futuhat al-Makiyya* (hereafter abbreviated as Fut.), ed. 'Uthman Yahya, (Cairo: al-Hay'at al-Misriyat al-'Amma li al-Kitab, 1972- 1989), I, 149; II, 581.

[15] Dominique Urvoy, "The Ulama' of al-Andalus," in S. K. Jayyusi, *The Legacy of Muslim Spain*, 870.

Dominique Urvoy, "embodies Almohadism's ideal of rationality".[16] Many consider this book to represent the culmination of the Andalusian contribution to Islamic jurisprudential theory (i.e., *usul fiqh*). Among its distinctive characteristics is its somewhat phenomenological approach, describing with great objectivity the opinions of a variety of different Muslim legal schools while at the same time offering his own interpretation of the law.[17] At the height of his juridical career, Ibn Rushd was appointed *qadi al-qudat* of Seville, then of Cordoba, and again of Seville, and finally again in Cordoba where at the same time he was a physician to the sultan. Toward the end of his life, however, in the context of the threat from the Portuguese and discontent among the *fuqaha'*, Ibn Rushd was subjected to an inquisition in 592/1196. Like Ibn al-'Arabi and Meister Eckhart after him, this is just one of many examples of the nearly unavoidable quality of controversy when it comes to the work of the most brilliant and creative of minds—especially in the arena of religion.

2. Life

Ibn al-'Arabi, whose full name is Muhammad b. Ali b. Muhammad b. al-'Arabi al-Ta'i al-Hatimi is acclaimed to be one of the greatest Sufi masters of all time. By all informed accounts, he was "a towering figure in human spirituality"[18] and thus came to bear the *laqab* or honorific epithet of *al-shaykh al-akbar* or "the Greatest Master." He was born on 27 July 1165 /17 Ramadan 560, or, according to other sources, 6 August/27 (Ramadan)[19] in the beautiful township of Murcia, inland

---

[16] Dominique Urvoy, "The Ulama' of al-Andalus," in S. K. Jayyusi, *The Legacy of Muslim Spain*, 870.

[17] See Averroes, *Bidayat al-mujtahid wa nihayat a`muqtasid*, Muhammad Salim Muhaysin and Sha'ban Muhammad Ismail, eds. (Cairo: Maktabah al-Kulliyat al-Azhariyah, 1970-1974).

[18] Stephen Hirtenstein, *The Unlimited Merciful, The Spiritual Life and Thought of Ibn 'Arabi* (Oxford: Anqa Publishing, 1999), ix.

[19] Cf. Khalil ibn Aybak Safadi, *al-Wafi bi al-Wafayat*, Weisbaden, 1966, vol. 4, 178. See also Al-Muhadarat, I: 34 (Cairo, 1906), where Ibn al-'Arabi said: "I was born in Murcia when it was under sultan Abi 'Abd Allah Muhammad ibn Mardanish's reign, in Andalus, cited by Asin Palacios, *Ibn al-'Arabi*, 6.

from the Mediterranean Costa Blanca between Valencia and Almeria, in the *qiblah* (prayer direction) of Andalus, at the beginning of the Almohad reign. As mentioned above, his father exercised military duties in the service of Ibn Mardanish,[20] ex-Christian warlord.

Ibn al-'Arabi's family was related to one of the oldest, noble and pious[21] Arab lineages in Spain of the time—the lineage of the Banu Ta'i. Ibn al-'Arabi himself states, "I am al-'Arabi al-Hatimi, the brother of magnanimity; in nobility we possess glory, ancient and renowned."[22] As asserted by Addas, Ibn al-'Arabi's family belonged to the *khassa* of his society, meaning the cultural "elite" that consisted of the ruling class and the highest officials in the Andalusian administration and army.[23]

The Almohads rule over al-Andalus less than a hundred years. Like their predecessors, the mission of the Almohads was to purify Islam. But unlike their Berber predecessors, the Almoravids, the Almohads rooted their agenda in a strong emphasis on "the transcendence and oneness of God, the supremacy of Qur'an and hadith over the law schools, and the need for moral reform."[24] Taking direction from the founder of the movement, Muhammad b. 'Aballah b. Tumart (b. between 471/1078 and 474/1081), the Almohads championed Ash'arite theology, denounced crude anthropomorphism, and denounced many pagan customs, especially those involving music. According to Ira Lapidus, the puritanism of both the Almoravids and the Almohads, engendered the development of a "new form of Sufism, based on both Spanish and eastern teachings" led by Abu Madyan al-

---

[20] Muh. B. Sa'd b. Muh. B. Ahmad Ibn Mardanish.

[21] Ibn al-'Arabi has at least two uncles who were on the Path (Zahid). Ibn al-'Arabi said in *Futuhat*, "One of my family who was zahid, or who withdraw from the world, was from Tunis. He used to stay in the mosque praying for God and his tomb was a place for *ziyarah* (visit)." See *Fut.* II, 23.

[22] Ibn al-'Arabi, *al-Diwan al-akbar*, Bulaq, 1271H, 47, cited by *QRS*,17.

[23] See *Fut.* I, 506, 588-9; cited by Claude Addas, *Ibn 'Arabi: The Voyage of No Return* (hereafter abbreviated as VNR) (Cambridge: Islamic Texts Society, 2000), 11-12; see also *QRS*, 48-49.

[24] Ira M.Lapidus, *A History of Islamic Societies* (Cambridge: Cambridge University Press, 1988, second edition, 2002), 306.

Andalusi (d. 1197), a mystical teacher who, though they never met, had great influence on Ibn al-'Arabi.[25] In fact it appears that the intellectual ethos into which Ibn al-'Arabi was born was a fairly complex one, shaped as much by classical Almohad puritanism as it was by a "new Sufism"[26] which began to call into question some of the more absolutist dimensions of Almohad thinking.

As known before, the Almohads entrusted Ibn al-'Arabi's father with what seems to have been a major post. Addas points to some details regarding his father's death which suggest that he was one of the *awliya'* or saints.[27] Indeed, there is documentary evidence that at least three of Ibn al-'Arabi's uncles – Abu Muhammad 'Abd Allah b. Muhammad al-'Arabi al-Ta'i on his father's side, and Abu Muslim al-Khawlani and Yahya b. Yughan on his mother's – were distinguished for their spiritual aspirations. In the *Futuhat al-makiyya*, Ibn al-'Arabi says,

> My maternal uncle Abu Muslim al-Kawlani was one of the greatest of their kind. He would stay standing in prayer all night long, and when his strength started to fail him he would hit his legs with sticks which he kept specifically for this purpose and say to them: "you deserve more blows than my horse does. If the companions of Muhammad believe they will have the prophet all to themselves then, by Allah, we will push them up around him until they realize they left behind them men (*rijal*) who are worthy of the name."[28]

One of the greatest difficulties involved in sketching a critical biography of Ibn al-'Arabi is the attempt to isolate the various intellectual and spiritual influences that shaped his persona. One of the reasons why this is a difficult process is because the intellectual and spiritual atmosphere of Ibn al-'Arabi's youth in Andalusia was a rich soup of some of the most important and complex scientific, religious, and philosophical ideas of the day. One technique which can help simplify this process somewhat is to divide Ibn al-'Arabi's life into phases. In

---

[25] Lapidus, *A History of Islamic Societies*, 309.

[26] Lapidus, *A History of Islamic Societies,* 309.

[27] *QRS*, 18. She even says that he was "more precisely among those who have realized the 'Dwelling-place of Breaths' (*man tahaqqaqa bi manzil al-anfas*)."

[28] *Fut.* II, 18. 9, see also Addas QRS, 24.

what follows, I am borrowing the three-fold typology of Toshihiko Izutsu.[29] Izutsu's three phases are: 1) the phase of preparation and formation for his spiritual and intellectual journey as a Sufi; 2) the phase of development (incuding his spiritual experience around the Ka'ba; and 3) the phase of spiritual and intellectual maturity as a Sufi.

A. Preparation and Formation

Ibn al-'Arabi's family moved to Seville after the fall of Ibn Mardanish and the conquest of Murcia by the Almohads. At the time, Ibn al-'Arabi was eight years of age and schooled in the traditional Islamic sciences including Qur'an, quranic exegesis, hadith, jurisprudence, *adab* (Arabic grammar and composition), *kalam* (dialectical theology) and scholastic philosophy.[30] Under the tutelage of the best Andalusian *ulama* of his time, the young Ibn al-'Arabi quickly mastered all the major fields of Islamic knowledge. By all accounts, this studious Andalusian youth had a fairly "carefree childhood."[31] As the first and only male child, he seemed to have been a source of great happiness to his parents, and as a young boy he liked to chase animals and, in "imi-

---

[29] Izutsu, "Ibn al-'Arabi" in *Encyclopaedia of Religions*, ed. Mircea Eliade (New York: MacMillan, 1987), 553-558.

[30] Izutsu, "Ibn al-'Arabi" in *Encyclopaedia of Religions*, ed. Mircea Eliade, 553; Ibn al-'Arabi, *The Bezels of Wisdom* (hereafter abbreviated as BW), tr. and introd. by R.W.J. Austin ; pref. by Titus Burckhardt (New York : Paulist Press, c1980), 1. Addas indicates, Ibn al-'Arabi "seems not to have attended the local Qur'an school, where, according to Ibn 'Abdun, the teachers were ignorant and the teaching mediocre." As a child of social privilege and relative wealth, it is likely that Ibn al-'Arabi had "private tutors in his own home." In fact, the sources indicate that "he studied Qur'an with 'a man of path,' Abu 'Abd Allah al-Khayyat, to whom he would always remain deeply attached." As Ibn al-'Arabi himself testifies in the *Ruh*: "When I was a child I studied the Qur'an with him [i.e., Abu Abdullah al-Khayyat] and had a great affection for him; he was our neighbor. . . . Of all the spiritual men I have met since returning to the Path, there is no one of them I have wanted to be like –except for him and his brother." (Ibn al-'Arabi, *Risalat ruh al-quds fi muhasabat al-nafs*, Damascus : Mu'assasat al-'Ilm lil-Tiba'ah wa al-Nashr, 1964, 9 and 10, 93; Ibn al-'Arabi, *Sufis of Andalusia: the 'Ruh al-quds' and 'al-durrat al-fakhirah' of Ibn al-'Arabi*; tr. with introd. and notes by R. W. J. Austin; with a foreword by Martin Lings (London, Allen and Unwin, 1971), 92, cited by *QRS*, 30.

[31] *VNR*, 15.

tation of his father, he entered the army."[32] It appears that as he pursued his education in this first phase of his life, Ibn al-'Arabi had an intuition of some kind of spiritual destitution although according to him he was uncertain to undergo a necessary action to address them. It was this period of his life to which Ibn al-'Arabi would eventually refer as his *jahiliyya*,[33] a period in which he kept driving a wedge between his craving for this ungodly phenomenal world, and his longing for God. Ibn al-'Arabi writes,

> As the night drew to an end my wicked companions and I went off to get some sleep because we were exhausted after all the dancing. We would go off to our beds just as the hour for the dawn prayer was approaching. We would then perform the smallest possible ablution and might perhaps go to the mosque. But most of the time on such occasions we chose instead to perform the prayer at home by reciting the *Surat al-Kawthar* and the *Fatiha*. . . . Occasionally, when I was feeling better disposed than the others, I would perform my ablutions and go to the mosque. If when I got there I was told that the prayer had finished, that gave me no cause to sorrow; precisely to the contrary. . . . If I happened to arrive in time to perform the prayer behind the imam, one of two things occurred. Either I was completely absorbed in thinking about the marvelous night I had just spent listening to an excellent musician declaiming some fine verses: In this case I would spend the entire prayer reviewing the same thoughts over and over again until I no longer knew what the imam was praying or which prayers he has recited, but simply saw people doing something and imitated their gestures. . . Alternatively sleep would start to overcome me, and in that case I would keep watching the imam to see if he had finished the prayer; the lengthy recitation became unbearable and inside myself I would start cursing him: "There he goes, off the *Surat al-Hashr* or the *al-Waqi'a*! Couldn't he have made do with *al-Infitar* or the *al-Fajr*? Didn't the Prophet himself recommend that prayers be kept short?"[34]

---

[32] *VNR*, 15.

[33] *Jahiliyya* is the term used in Islamic historiography to refer to the "Age of Ignorance" in pagan Arabia before the rise of Islam.

[34] Ibn al-'Arabi, *Ruh al-quds*, tr. Asin Palacios (Damascus, 1964), 42, cited by *QRS*, 31-2.

In addition to its status as a great intellectual center, Seville was also an important center of Sufism, with a number of outstanding Sufi masters in residence. It was not surprising that Ibn al-'Arabi was attracted by their mode of living and their teachings. As we mentioned above, his family's Sufi heritage also appears to have predisposed him to cultivate an interest in the Sufis' very special brand of Muslim piety. Before turning to the accounts of what led the master to the Sufi way, we should pause to make some important observations about the form that most of these accounts take.

What is interesting about Ibn al-'Arabi's foray into Sufism is the nature of the narrative material we have about his experiences. Not only are they decidedly hagiographical, as one might suspect, but they are auto-hagiographcal. In other words, the large percentage of the material at the center of Ibn al-'Arabi's hagiographical portrait comes from the pen of the master himself. The significance of this is not entirely clear. One might imagine, for example, that such attestations about oneself might bring more scorn and derision than admiration and adulation. If so, it would not be the first time that a Sufi has sought to engender the scorn of potential admirers. Indeed, the entire tradition of the Malamatiyya is based on the performance of antinomian acts as an effective means of acquiring the public derision necessary to keep the ego (i.e., *nafs*) under tight control. At the same time, these accounts are celebrated and carefully preserved for posterity. Perhaps Ibn al-'Arabi's auto-hagiography is a way of grounding the admiration for the master among those who recognize his gifts and are open to his teachings, while simultaneously working to dismiss those who are closed to what he has to offer. In any case it is also clear that this genre of auto-hagiography which we find in the writings of Ibn al-'Arabi, seems closely linked with the fact that Ibn al-'Arabi understands all of his writings, not to be the product of his own isolated consciousness, but rather as revelations which he receives in visions and for which he cannot take any ultimate credit. Henri Corbin argues that this is all part of Ibn al-'Arabi's imaginal[35] epistemology according to which abstract intellectual distillations of mystically perceived truths are even farther from the Real than the visions of the imagination.[36]

One of the many visionary events that is part of the narrative of how the young Ibn al-'Arabi became a Sufi occurs in his teens, when he heard a voice from heaven commanding him to abandon his ungodly ways and to convert to a life radically devoted to the service of God. The story relates that, as was his custom, Ibn al-'Arabi was attending one of the many nightly parties that took place throughout his native Seville. As usual, in Andalusia, wine was served after the meal. Just as Ibn al-'Arabi lifted the wine cup to his lips, he heard a voice calling to him, "O Muhammad, it was not for this that you were created!"[37] It was after this event that he withdrew from the world and went into retreat in a cemetery, where he started to practice the invocation (*dhikr*). It was there that he had his vision in which he met, and received instruction from Jesus, Moses, and Muhammad—an illumination that simultaneously started him upon the spiritual way and established him as a master of it. "When I returned to this Path," Ibn al-'Arabi declares as he begins his account of the cemetery experience, "it was accomplished through a dream vision (*mubashira*) under the guidance of Jesus, Moses, and Muhammad."[38] Ibn al-'Arabi goes on to write:

> "I lived like this until the Merciful turned His care toward me, sending Muhammad, Jesus, and Moses to me in my sleep, may the grace and peace of God be upon them! Jesus urged me to take up a life of asceticism and renunciation, Moses gave me the 'disk of the sun' and told me that from among the science of 'Unicity'

---

[35] I borrow the term "imaginal" from William Chittick (see his *Imaginal Worlds*) who uses it as an alternative for "imaginary" primarily because the latter connotes a sense of the false or unreal in colloquial English. By "imaginal" Chittick is coining an adjective used to describe a phenomenon closely connected to the imagination, but which is understood to be uniquely real.

[36] Henry Corbin, *Creative Imagination in the Sufism of Ibn 'Arabi* (Princeton, NJ: Princeton University Press, 1969), 377.

[37] *QRS*, 36.

[38] *Fut.* IV, 172. 13; *QRS*, 42.

(*Tawhid*) I would obtain 'knowledge from God' (*al-'ilm al-Laduni*). And Muhammad commanded, 'Hold fast to me and you shall be safe!' I awoke in tears and devoted the rest of the night to chanting the Qur'an. Then I resolved to dedicate myself to God's Path ....."[39]

From this point on, Ibn al-'Arabi made his decision to serve God, a status defined by the quranic verse that he so often quoted, "O men! You are indigent in the face of God!" (35:15). Thus, Ibn al-'Arabi went into retreat of which he later declares, "I began my retreat before dawn and I received illumination before sunrise [....] I remained in this place for fourteen months, and I obtained secrets about which I later wrote; my spiritual opening, at that moment, was an ecstatic uprooting."[40] In Addas's words this experience entailed a "tremendous metamorphosis." [41] Of his renunciation of worldly affairs, Ibn al-'Arabi says:

"Since the moment I attained this spiritual station [that of 'pure servitude'], I have not owned any living creature; nor do I own even the clothes that I wear, for I wear only what is lent to me and what I am allowed to use. If something fell into my possession, I would immediately get rid of it by giving it away, or, in the case of a slave, by freeing him. I took this upon my self when I chose to aspire to supreme servitude in God's eyes. And then it was said to me, "That will not be possible for you so long as one single being has the right to claim something from you!" I replied, "God Himself could claim nothing from me!" In response to this I was asked, "How can this be?" And I answered, "One claims only from those who recognize (it); one claims from those who maintain that they have rights and goods, not of those who declare, 'I have no right, anywhere, to anything!'"[42]

According to Addas, the account of the encounter in the cemetery has two tightly interwoven threads of significance. One thread alludes to the central Islamic doctrine that Muhammad represents the

[39] Ibn al-'Arabi, *Diwan al-Ma'arif*, (MS. Fatih, 5322), 36b, cited by *VNR*, 20.

[40] *VNR*, 17, William C. Chittick, *The Sufi Path of Knowledge : Ibn al-'Arabi's Metaphysics of Imagination* (hereafter abbreviated as SPK) (Albany, N.Y.: State University of New York Press, 1989), xiii; *QRS*, 36-7.

[41] *VNR*, 19.

[42] *Fut.* I, 196, cited by *VNR*, 29, See also *QRS*, 41.

"seal" of prophetic revelation as it has been transmitted through the ages—through prophets and messengers as great as Moses and Jesus ("founders," as it were, of Judaism and Christianity). The suggestion here is that, just as Muhammad is the "seal" of the prophets and messengers of God, Ibn al-'Arabi is being commissioned as the "seal" of the *awliya'* (i.e., "friends" of God, or "saints"). Another thread is that the story signifies "the universal quality of Ibn 'Arabi's teaching."[43] It suggests that Ibn al-'Arabi's mystical experiences of the Truth reveal the one common source from which all three of the Abrahamic traditions spring. According to Addas,

> From the perspective of Ibn 'Arabi's hagiology, the Muhammadan Seal is the inheritor *par excellence* of all the prophets and, therefore, of these three Messengers. It would appear to me that there is no doubt that this vision refers to the status of the Muhammadan Seal as *warith*, the inheritor of the prophets, and particularly of Muhammad, Jesus, and Moses. But it also suggests, albeit discreetly, that the three communities – Muslim, Christian, and Jewish – represented by these three prophets are more particularly concerned with his ministry. Everything takes place as if, in Ibn 'Arabi's eyes, the Muhammadan Seal's vocation – the counterpart to the support that these messengers gave to him – was to help their respective communities, most notably by preserving, through his teaching, the essential and immutable truths that were the basis of the traditions to which they were connected.[44]

Unlike Christian asceticism, which traditionally has entailed vows of lifelong celibacy (particularly in the church of the Latin West), the ascetic dimensions of the Sufi path did not usually require celibacy, and when they did, they were for specified period of time. According to some sources,[45] Ibn al-'Arabi married a young woman from a prominent family, named Maryam bt. Muhammad b. 'Abdun al-Bija'i,

---

[43] *VNR*, 20, see also *QRS*, 41-4.

[44] Claude Addas, "The ship of stone," *The Journal of the Muhyiddin Ibn 'Arabi Society* (1996), Volume XIX, in the special issue entitled, "The Journey of The Heart," 1.

[45] Asin Palacios, for example, says that the master was married at an early age to Maryam bt. Muhammad 'Abdun, see Palacios *Ibn al-'Arabi, hayatuhu*, 37. According to Addas, however, "this is neither stated nor even suggested in any source at all or in any text of Ibn 'Arabi. (see *QRS*, 40).

whose father was a man of great standing and influence. Not only is she said to have come from the best family, but Maryam also had a reputation as a pious wife (*al-mar'at al-salihah*). Her spiritual aspirations were very much in harmony with those of her new husband. Ibn al-'Arabi makes reference to this sharing of common spiritual aspirations and values when he writes of his wife:

> My saintly wife Maryam bint Muhammad bin 'Abdun al-Bija'i said to me: "In my sleep I saw someone who often comes to visit me in my visions, but whom I have never met in the world of sense-perception. He asked me: 'Do you aspire to the Way?' I replied: 'Most certainly yes, but I don't know how to reach it!' He said: 'Through five things, namely trust (*al-tawakkul*), certainty (*al-yaqin*), patience (*al-sabr*), resolution (*al-'azima*) and sincerity (*al-sidq*).'" Thus she offered her vision to me and I told her that it was indeed the method of the folk. I myself have never seen one with that degree of mystical experience. However, my wife, Maryam bint Muhammad Abdun, once told me that she had seen such one and described his state to me, knowing him to be one who had this experience. Nevertheless she did mention certain states of his which gave indication of a lack of strength in him.[46]

In fact, it may well have been due to the influence of his wife that Ibn al-'Arabi decided formally to enter the Sufi path. According to some,[47] his experience with illness—at some time in his teens or earlier—seems to have had an effect, especially because of the vision that accompanied his rather miraculous recovery:

> One day I became seriously ill and plunged into such a deep coma that I was believed to be dead. In that state I saw horrible-looking people who were trying to harm me. Next I became aware of someone—kindly, powerful, and exhaling delightful fragrance—who defended me against them and succeeded in defeating them. "Who are you?" I asked. The being replied to me: "I am the sura Ya-Sin; I am your protector!" Then I regained consciousness and found my father—God bless him—standing at my bedside in tears; he had just finished reciting the sura Ya-Sin."[48]

---

[46] *Fut.* I, 278 and III, 235. 14; cf. *QRS*, 86.

[47] Miguel Asin Palacios, *Ibn al-'Arabi, Hayatuhu,* 10.

[48] *Fut.* IV, 648, cited by *QRS*, 20.

At one point in the *Futuhat*, Ibn al-'Arabi declares:

> I used to dislike women and sexual intercourse as much as anyone
> when I first entered this Path. I stayed that way for about eighteen
> years until I witnessed this station. Before that, I had feared the
> divine displeasure because of this, since I had come across the pro-
> phetic report that God had made women lovable to his Prophet.[49]

Hirtenstein concludes that this must mean that "until he arrived in
Mecca, Ibn 'Arabi was almost certainly still single."[50] Hirtenstein is
interpreting Ibn al-'Arabi's stated "dislike" for women and intercourse
as an indication that the master remained unmarried until his journey
to Mecca. But such an interpretation conflicts with Ibn al-'Arabi's own
testimony about his earlier marriage to Maryam (mentioned above). It
is more likely the case that, although Ibn al-'Arabi did marry Maryam
well before his journey to Mecca, neither he nor Maryam enjoyed sexual intercourse with one another. This would certainly fit with the pattern of a marriage between two Sufis who may agree that, after con-
summation, the couple would mutually embrace celibacy.

Though, according to his own recollection, Ibn al-'Arabi says he
was twenty years old when he formally began to pursue the Sufi path
(in the *Futuhat* he clearly states, "I reached this [beginning] state in
the path in the year 580[/1184]"), it is nonetheless clear, especially
from his writings on his spiritual teachers, that he used to accompany
Sufis and learned their teaching since he was very young.[51] One can
conclude that, from a very young age, Ibn al-'Arabi experienced
advanced states of spiritual awakening long before his formal "con-
version" in 580/1184. Indeed no event from the accounts of his youth
is as well known as his legendary meeting with the great philosopher
Ibn Rushd, when the former was still a beardless youth. [52]

About this encounter, Ibn al-'Arabi tells us the following:

---

[49] *Fut.* IV, 84. 29; cf. *QRS*, 40, and Hirtenstein, *The Unlimited*, 149.

[50] Stephen Hirtenstein, *The Unlimited Mercifier*, 149.

[51] Cf. Ibn al-'Arabi, *Sufis of Andalusia: 'the Ruh al-quds' and 'al-Durrat al-fakhirah' of
Ibn al-'Arabi*; tr. with intr. and notes by R. W. J. Austin; with a foreword by Martin
Lings (London, Allen and Unwin, 1971).

[52] *Fut.* I, 153. 34, *SPK*, xiii.

One fine day I went to Cordova to visit the Qadi Abu l-Walid Ibn Rushd (Averroes). He wanted to meet me, as he had heard of the illumination which God had granted to me during my retreat (*ma fataha llah bihi 'alayya fi khalwati*); he had expressed amazement on learning what he had been told about me. My father was one of his friends, and accordingly sent me to him on the pretext of doing some errand or other, although his real purpose was to allow him to speak with me. At that time I was still just a boy (*sabi*) without any dawn on my face or even a moustache (*ma baqala wajhi wa la tarra sharibi*). As I entered, the philosopher rose from his seat and came to me, showing me every possible token of friendship and consideration and finally embracing me. Then he said to me: "Yes." I in turn replied to him: "Yes." Then his joy increased as he saw that I had understood him. But next, when I myself became aware of what it was that had caused his joy, I added: "No." Immediately Averroes tensed up, his features changed colour and he seemed to doubt his own thoughts. He asked me this question: "What kind of solution have you found through illumination and divine inspiration? Is it just the same as what we receive from speculative thought?" I replied to him: "Yes and no. Between the yes and the no spirits take flight from their matter and necks break away from their bodies." Averroes turned pale; I saw him start to tremble. He murmured the ritual phase, "there is no strength save in God," because he had understood my allusion.[53]

It is difficult exactly what to make of this story. On one level, it sounds utterly fantastic—would the great jurist and philosopher really be set aback by the linguistic cleverness of a precocious teen? On another level, it conveys an important theme in the thought of Ibn al-'Arabi—the theme of the limitations of reason and speculative thought when it comes to truly plumbing the depths of the Real. Whether or not we are meant to take this episode as an actual event and take Ibn al-'Arabi at his word—that he did leave the brilliant sage speechless and in cognitive distress—what we can take away from the story is that Ibn al-'Arabi may well have had keen and mystically influenced epistemological sensibilities from an unusually young age. For Izutsu, this story "allows us to put our finger accurately upon the nodal point of Ibn al-'Arabi's philosophical thinking and mystical experience,

---

[53] *Fut.* I, 153. 34, *SPK*, xiii-xiv, see also *BW*, 2.

showing how mysticism and philosophy were related to one another in his metaphysical consciousness."[54] Izutsu goes on to explain:

> It was not simply a matter of mysticism overcoming philosophy. His mystical-visionary experiences were most intimately connected with, and backed by, rigorous philosophical thinking. Ibn Arabi was a mystic who was at the same time a real master of Peripatetic philosophy, so that he could—or rather, he had to—philosophize his inner spiritual experience into a grand scale metaphysical worldview.[55]

One final important feature of this first phase of Ibn al-'Arabi's life is that it was during this phase that he met two holy women who eventually became his spiritual teachers, the masters of the master, so to speak. Their names are Shams of Marchena[56] and Fatimah of Cordoba, both of whom were Sufi women who had a strong influence upon their young mystic in training. Ibn al-'Arabi states, "Among the saints there are those men and women known as the sighing ones, may God be pleased with them. I met one of them, a lady of Marchena of the Olives in Andalusia, called Shams. She was advanced in years."[57] He also speaks of the celebrated Fatima of Cordoba,[58] a woman saint, who appeared to him in a vision, surrounded by a kind of heavenly aura. In his youth, Ibn al-'Arabi served her for about two years. [59] Here "serving" means that he became her spiritual son by recognizing her as a *shaykha*—his spiritual guide and teacher. "I am," Ibn al-'Arabi quotes her as saying, "your spiritual mother and the light of your carnal mother."[60] At the time Fatimah of Cordoba was a very old woman, over ninety years old, but, as Ibn al-'Arabi himself recalls, an unusual atmosphere of enchanting beauty seemed to surround her making her

---

[54] Izutsu, "Ibn al-'Arabi," in *Encyclopaedia of Religions*, 553. On the relation of mysticism and philosophy see, Chittick, "Mysticism versus Philosophy in Earlier Islamic History: The al-Tusi al-Qunawi Correspondence," *Religious Studies*, 17, 1981, 87-104.

[55] Izutsu, "Ibn al-'Arabi," in *Encyclopaedia of Religions*, 553.

[56] *Fut.* I, 186; *Sufis of Andalusia*, 25.

[57] *Fut.* I, 35; *Sufis of Andalusia*, 142-43.

[58] *Fut.* II, 347. 26.

[59] *Fut.* II, 347. 26.

[60] *Fut.* II, 348. 9; see also *QRS*, 87.

seem as if she were a girl in her teens. Her face was so pink and fresh that, whenever he was in her presence, the young Ibn al-'Arabi is said to have been unable not to prevent himself from blushing.[61] In his *Ruh al-quds*, Ibn al-'Arabi says that "she was a mercy for the world."[62] In his own words, Ibn al-'Arabi says,

> I served as a disciple of one of the lovers of God, a Gnostic, a lady of Seville called Fatimah bint Ibn al-Muthanna of Cordova. I served her for several years, she being over ninety-five years of age. . . . She used to play on the tambourine and showed great pleasure in it. When I asked her about it she answered, "I take joy in Him Who has turned to me and made me one of His Friends (Saints), using me for His own purposes. Who am I that He should choose me among men. He is jealous of me for, whenever I turned to something other than He in heedlessness (*ghaflah*), He sends me some affliction concerning that thing." . . . With my own hand I built for her a hut of reeds as high as she, in which she lived until she died. She used to say to me, "I am your spiritual mother and the light of your earthly mother." When my mother came to visit her, Fatimah said to her, "O light, this is my son and he is your father, so treat him filialy and dislike him not."[63]

In sum, Fatima of Cordoba (or Seville) played the guiding saint role and spiritual teacher for Ibn al-'Arabi. Among other things, what this means is that Ibn al-'Arabi was not embarrassed to learn from her, or to surrender to her leadership, or to stand as a *murid* (i.e., Sufi "novice") before her. "This is a practical proof of Ibn al-'Arabi's declaration that a woman can be a shaykh and a spiritual guide, and that men are allowed to be among her disciples."[64]

Among the other Sufis whom Ibn al-'Arabi knew as a youth, was Abu 'Ali al-Shakkaz. According to Addas, Shakkaz "was closely linked in friendship with Ibn al-'Arabi's paternal uncle, Abu Muhammad al-'Arabi, and would subsequently become one of [the former's] spiritual

---

[61] *Fut.* II, 347. 27; *QRS*, 87.

[62] Quoted by *QRS*, 87.

[63] *Fut.* II, 347. 26-348. 9; Cf *QRS*, 87; see also Sufis of Andalusia, 25-26.

[64] Souad al- Hakim, "Ibn al-'Arabi's twofold Perception of Women," in *Journal of The Muhyiddin Ibn al-'Arabi Society*, volume xxxix (2006), 5.

teachers."[65] In fact, Addas, refers to Ibn al-'Arabi's first Sufi Shaykh, or *murshid al-awwal* (first teacher), as Abu Ja'far al-'Uryabi, "whom Ibn al-'Arabi mentions most frequently in the *Futuhat*."[66] It is impossible to say, however, what this exactly means. "This master," Ibn al-'Arabi writes referring to Abu Ja'far al-'Uryabi, "came to Seville when I was just beginning to acquire knowledge of the Path. When I met him for the first time I found him to be one devoted to the practice of Invocation [*dhikr*]. He knew immediatelty [after] he met me, the spiritual need that had brought me to see him."[67] At the time of their meeting, Ibn al-'Arabi described this shaykh, who by then was at the end of his life, as being of the spiritual heritage of Jesus.[68]

B. Development

When he was nearing his mid-thirties (in the year 590/1193), Ibn al-'Arabi traveled across the Iberian Peninsula and spent much of his time in Tunis, where he studied *Khal' al-na'layn* (*The Doffing of the Sandals*) with its author Ibn Qasi who was a student of Ibn Masarra and who was the Sufi leader who fought against the Almoravids in the Algarve.[69] Eventually Ibn al-'Arabi wrote a commentary on it.[70] During his stay in Tunis, Ibn al-'Arabi also visited and had consultations with other Sufis, such as 'Abd al-'Aziz al-Mahdawi to whom he would later send a copy of *Ruh al-quds,* and al-Khamis al-Kinani al-Jarrah, al-Mahdawi's teacher, and Abu Madyan's disciple.[71] Indeed it was in Tunis that, according to Ibn al-'Arabi's own testimony, he met

---

[65] *Ruh,* 12, 96-8, where Ibn al-'Arabi states that he continued to visit him from the time of entering the path down to Abu 'Ali al-Shakkaz's death, in *QRS*, 30.

[66] Cf, *Fut.* I, 186; III, 539. 26, where he is called Abu al-abbas, See *QRS*, 61.

[67] Ibn al-'Arabi, *Sufi of Andalusia*, 63, Cf. *QRS*, 49. He was well-known for his being engaged in dhikr whether he was awake or asleep (Sufis, 68).

[68] *Fut.* I, 223. 20-1, See also *QRS*, 51 and *Fut* III, 208. 27 (*wakana shaykhuna Abu al-'Abbas al-'uraby 'ala qadami 'Isa 'alaihi al-salam*).

[69] *BW,* 4 and 88, Cf. *VNR*, 53, also see Sufis of Andalusia, 26.

[70] *BW,* 4 and *Sufis of Andalusia,* 26.

[71] Ibn al-'Arabi, *Sufis of Andalusia*, 27, See also *QRS*, 115.

his spiritual counselor, al-Khidr,[72] a transhistorical figure who looms large in Sufi cosmologies and whom Ibn al-'Arabi mentions frequently in the accounts of his spiritual visions. The master writes:

> I was in the port of Tunis, on a small boat at sea, when I was gripped by a pain in stomach. While the other passengers slept I went to the side of the boat to look out at the sea. Suddenly, in the light of the moon which on that particular night was full, I caught sight of someone in the distance who was coming towards me walking on the water. As he drew level with me he stopped and lifted one foot while balancing on the other; I saw that the sole of his foot was dry. He then did the same with his other foot, and I saw the same thing. After that he spoke to me in a language which is unique to him; he then took his leave and went off in the direction of the lighthouse which stood at the top of a hill a good two miles away. It took him three paces to travel the distance. . . . Possibly he went to visit shaikh Ibn Khamis al-Kinani, one of the great masters of the way who lived at Marsa 'Idun and from whose place I was returning on that particular evening.[73]

When Ibn al-'Arabi was thirty-three, he was taken on one of the most extraordinary journeys of all: an "ascension" (*mi'raj*)[74] which mirrored the Prophet Muhammad's famous Night-Journey (*isra'*) and Ascension (*mi'raj*). Like the Prophet did in his ascension, Ibn al-'Arabi traveled a similar path. He explained on the journey:

> God does not transport His servant so that he can see Him, but in order to show him some of His Signs, those that have not been seen by him. He has said: "Glory be to Him who caused His servant to travel by night from the Sacred Mosque to the Distant Mosque, the precincts of which We have blessed, so that We might

---

[72] "Khidr" is the name given to the mysterious "servant of God" (...*'abdan min 'ibadina ataynahu rahmatan min 'indina wa 'allamnahu min ladunna 'ilman*) who appears as the esoteric tutor of Moses in *Surat al-Kahf*, vv. 65–82. In Islamic lore, Khidr is an Elijah-like figure who has been granted quasi-immortality and who wanders the earth inducting the worthy into the deepest mysteries of the universe.

[73] *Fut.* I, 186, quoted by *QRS*, 116.

[74] On Ibn al-'Arabi's spiritual ascension, see James M. Morris, "The Spiritual Ascension: Ibn 'Arabi and the Mi'raj," pts. 1 and 2, *Journal of the American Oriental Society* 107, no 4 (1987), 108; no. 1, (1988), 69-77.

show him some of Our Signs"[75]. . . I have transported him only to
see the Signs, and not to Me, since no place can contain Me and the
relation of "places" to Me is identical. I am the One who is contained in the heart of My faithful servant, so how can I possibly
transport him to Me when I am next to him and with him, wherever he is?[76]

Beside encountering saints who were heirs of the Prophet Muhammad, peace be upon him, Ibn al-ʿArabi saw himself among the saints.
In fact, Ibn al-ʿArabi considered himself as the Muhammadan Seal of
Sainthood (or "Friendship," or "Nearness"). For this experience, Ibn
al-ʿArabi writes, "I became acquainted with the report (*ʿalimtu l-ha-
dith*) of this Muhammadan Seal in Fez in the lands of the Maghrib in
the year 594/1198 when the Real caused me to meet him (*ʿarrafani
bi-hi*) and gave me his distinguishing Sign (*aʿtani ʿalamatahu*), but I
shall not name him."[77] It is important to note that, taken within the
context of Ibn alʿArabi's wider cosmology, this declaration of sainthood is not a matter of arrogance. God welcomes into friendship
(*walaya*) and becomes the intimate guardian (*wilaya*) of the believer.[78]
Although Ibn al-ʿArabi's declaration to be the "Seal of Sainthood"
(just as Muhammad is the "Seal of Prophethood") seems like he is
claiming an extraordinary status, beneath such a declaration is the
fundamental realization of the self-disclosure of God in all things—especially the human heart—and thus the implication that all human
beings have the potential to be the "Seal of Sainthood."

Ibn al-ʿArabi's next journey was to Granada. He arrived just in
time to witness the burial of Ibn Rushd (i.e., Averroes), who died a

---

[75] Q. 17: 1

[76] *Fut.* III, 340. 23. On Ibn al-ʿArabi's spiritual Ascension (*miʿraj*), see also, Morris,
James M., "The Spiritual Ascension," 108, no. 1 (1988), 69-77.

[77] *Fut.* III, 514. 13, cf. 67, also cited by Michael Chodkiewicz in *Seal of the Saints:
Prophethood and Sainthood in the Doctrines of Ibn Arabi*, trans. Liadain Sherrard
(Cambrigde: Islamic Text Society, 1993), 121, cited also by Gerald Elmor, *Islamic
Sainthood in The Fullness of Time, Ibn al-ʿArabi's Book of the Fabulous Gryphon* (Leiden,
Brill, 1999), 59.

[78] For a fuller treatment of the relationship between *walaya* and *wilaya*, see Vincent
Cornell, *Realm of the Saint: Power and Authority in Moroccan Sufism* (Austin: University
of Texas Press, 1998).

short while earlier at Marrakesh, on 9 Safar 595/11 December 1198.[79]
Ibn al-'Arabi recounts his experience at the funeral as what appears to
be a lesson in the vanity of speculative schlolarship without true spiritual experience:

> His remains were taken to Cordoba, where he was buried. When
> the coffin containing his ashes [*sic.*] was loaded upon a beast of
> burden, his works were placed upon the other side to counter-bal-
> ance it. I was standing there, and with me was the jurist and man
> of letters Abu al- Husayn Muhammad Ibn Jubayr, scribe to [the
> Almohad] Prince, Abu Sa'id, and my companion Abu al-Hakam
> Ibn al-Sarraj, the copyist. Abu al-Hakam turned to us and said:
> "Have you not observed what serves as a counterweight to the
> master Ibn Rushd on his mount? On one side the master, on the
> other his works, the books he wrote!" Ibn Jubayr replied: "My son,
> indeed I observed—how well you have spoken!" I made a note of
> all this as a warning and as a reminder. May God have mercy upon
> them, I am the sole survivor of that group. I composed the follow-
> ing verse regarding this: "Here the master, there his works—would
> that I knew if his hopes have been fulfilled!"[80]

At the end of the year 597/1200, he experienced two visions. The
first vision was the highest degree attained by a saint which is *maqam
al-qurb* (lit., "the state of nearness" or "proximity") to God, and the
second was a calling to conduct a journey to the East. Ibn al-'Arabi
managed to go on pilgrimage (*hajj*) stopping at Cairo and Jerusalem.
This journey to the East was the beginning of the third phase of Ibn
al-'Arabi's life, where he eventually settled down in Damascus.[81]
Before moving to an analysis of this third phase of his life, however,
some observations need to be made about his pilgrimage experience.

During his pilgrimage, the head of a famous Iranian family, Abu
Shuja' Zahir b Rustam al-Isfahani, cordially welcomed Ibn al-'Arabi
to Mecca. Abu Shuja was himself a Sufi master, who came to the
Hijaz from Iran and who eventually took up a high position in Mecca.
As mentioned by Ibn al-'Arabi in his account, Ibn Rustam, who was

---

[79] *Fut.* I, 154, *QRS*, 171, Cf. *VNR*, 67.

[80] *Fut.* I, 153, Ibn al-'Arabi, *Sufis of Andalusia*, 33-36.

[81] Ibn al-'Arabi, *Sufis of Andalusia*, 35.

also well-known as a *muhaddith*, or transmitter of prophetic traditions, had a very beautiful, intelligent, and profoundly spiritual daughter, named Nizam. She was called *"'ayn al-shamshi wa l-baha'"* ("the shining splendor of the sun").[82] On this beautiful girl, Ibn al-'Arabi writes, "never have I witnessed a face that was more graceful, or speech that was so pleasant, intelligent, subtle and spiritual. She surpassed the people of her age in her discernment, her erudition, her beauty and her knowledge."[83] Admiring and longing for such amazing girl, Ibn al-'Arabi then expresses his feeling in his long poem, *Tarjuman al-ashwaq* (*The Interpreter of Ardent Longings*). He writes,

> When I began my stay in the year 599, I met there a group of the most eminent men and women, the elite of good behavior and learning. Although they were all people of distinction, I saw none more concerned with self-knowledge, more enamoured of observing the daily changes in his state, than the learned shaykh, imam of the Station of Abraham (*maqam Ibrahim*), a native of Isfahan who had taken up residence in Mecca, Abu Shuja' Zahir bin Rustam, and his elderly and learned sister, lady of Hijaz, Fakh al-Nisa' bint Rustam. . . . Now this shaykh had a daughter, a soft and slender girl of virginal purity, who captivated the gaze of all who saw her, whose presence was an ornament to our gatherings, giving pleasure to all present, bewildering all who contemplated her. Nizam was her name, and she was endowed with the title of "The Sun Itself and Radiant Splendor" ('*Ayn al-Shams wa'l-Baha'*), one of those who know and worship Him, a spiritual wanderer and renunciate [of other than God], mistress in the Holy Places and teacher in the Prophet's land. [84]

At first glance, *Tarjuman* appears to be a common erotic love poem. In fact, a majority of orthodox Muslims understand it this way, which led to accusations that Ibn al-'Arabi was antinomian. Sensitive readers, however, have noted that in this poem, Ibn al-'Arabi transforms the beautiful Iranian girl Nizam into an archetypal embodiment

[82] Asin Palacios, *Ibn al-'Arabi Hayatuhu*, 58.

[83] Ibn al-'Arabi, *Tarjuman al-ashwaq* (Beirut edition, 1961), 11, cited by *QRS*, 209, Cf. Hirteinstein, *The Unlimited Mercifier*, 148.

[84] Ibn al-'Arabi, *Tarjuman al-ashwaq*, 7-8; see also *Dakhair al-a'laq, sharkh tarjuman al-ashwaq*, (Beirut, 1895), 2, Cf, Sufis of Andalusia, 36.

of a theophanic figure, which some claim is analogous to Beatrice in Dante's *Comedia*. According to Izutsu, Ibn al-'Arabi's poem is "self-expression of a man who has just been initiated into what Corbin calls the 'sophianic religion of love.'" [85]

To clarify the issue, Ibn al-'Arabi himself later wrote a long commentary on the poem. This tract is crucial to the extent that it illuminates the most basic principles of Ibn al-'Arabi's approach to scriptural hermeneutics. The literal meaning of *ta'wil*, the word in Ibn al-'Arabi's writings that most closely approximates "hermeneutics," has the literal meaning of bringing something back to its ultimate point. In fact, the entire epistemology that Ibn al-'Arabi develops in the latter half of his life actually can be considered a product of this principle of hermeneutics which involved using his own visionary experiences as the lense for excavating what he believed to be the deepest meanings of the Qur'an and hadith. Indeed, the works of Ibn al-'Arabi, as Chodkiewiecz asserts, "is in its entirety a quranic commentary."[86]

It seems that *Tarjuman* marks another stage in Ibn al-'Arabi's discovery of the ways in which the divine self-discloses in the feminine—a stage associated with insights into the prophetic hadith, "Three things have been made beloved to me in this world of yours: women, perfume, and prayer."[87] On one occasion in the *Futuhat*, as mentioned, Ibn al-'Arabi confesses that for much of his life as a young man he disliked women and sexual intercourse. He feared that sexual desire and activity would distract him from his spiritual pursuits. This changes, however, when the master discovers the hadith mentioned above. Ibn al-'Arabi says he began to fear God's displeasure at the fact that he disliked what God Himself made loveable to the Prophet himself. In this case Ibn al-'Arabi writes:

> For [the Prophet] did not love [women], because of nature. He
> loved them because God had made them lovable to him. When I
> was sincere toward God in turning my attentiveness toward Him in

---

[85] Izutsu, Ibn al-'Arabi, in *Encyclopaedia*, 554, also see *QRS*, 209.

[86] Michel Chodkiewiecz, *Ocean Without Shore: Ibn Arabi, the Book, and the Law* (Albany, NY: State University of New York Press, 1993), 24.

[87] See *BW*, 269.

that, because of my fear of His displeasure—since I disliked what God had made lovable to His Prophet—that dislike disappeared from me. Praise belongs to God! He made them lovable to me. I am the greatest of creatures in care for them and the most observant of their rights. For in this I am "upon insight" [12: 108]. This derived from my being made to love. This is not a love deriving from nature.[88]

As a result of his discovery of the hadith of the "three things" beloved to the Prophet and thus the ways in which the divine self-discloses in the feminine, he decides to take a second wife[89] in the daughter of Meccan notable, Fatima bint Yunus b. Yusuf Amir al-Haramayn. From their union Ibn al-'Arabi received his first son, Muhammad 'Imad al-Din (d. 667 ah), to whom he would eventually hand on the first draft of the *Futuhat*.[90]

According to Addas, Ibn al-'Arabi's experience in Mecca was not just a common event, but "a kind of pact of allegiance in the tabernacle of Sainthood."[91] Addas insists that the master's time in Mecca was an "advent,"[92] in which Ibn al-'Arabi was meant to realize the role he would play with respect to sainthood or "friendship" with God in the tradition of the Prophet Muhammad, peace be upon him. Like the Prophet, who was first made to realize in Mecca that all the dimensions of prophethood would reach their ultimate fulfillment in him, Ibn al-'Arabi's sojourn in Mecca would be the time and place in which he would come to realize that all the dimensions of sainthood or "friendship" with God (*walaya*) were to be fulfilled in him. According to Addas, it was during his own Meccan period that Ibn al-'Arabi would come to know that "he is also. . . the source of all sainthood in

---

88 *Fut.* IV, 84. 32, see also Sachiko Murata, *The Tao of Islam, A source Book on Gender Relationships in Islamic Thought* (Albany: State University of New York Press, 1992), 186. Cf. Hirtenstein, *The Unlimited Mercifier*, 149.

89 One can only speculate, but it appears that Ibn al-'Arabi's marriage to Maryam—his first wife—was a marriage of 'spiritual convenience' in which no conjugal duties were expected to be fulfilled and which would afford Maryam the opportunity to pursue a celibate lifestyle in her husband's indefinite absence.

90 *Fut.* IV, 554. 1, *QRS*, 86, cf. Hirtenstein, *The Unlimited Mercifier*, 150.

91 *QRS*, 200.

92 *QRS*, 200.

just the same way that Muhammad or rather the Muhammadan Reality (*haqiqa Muhammadiyya*), always was the source of all prophecy from the very beginning of time, and always will be through to the fulfillment of the ages."[93]

Among the many interesting and important experiences the master had while residing in Mecca was a mysterious encounter, in close proximity to the Ka'ba, with "the Youth" (*fata*) whom he eventually understood to be the being who would reveal to him the text of his magnum opus: *The Meccan Revelations* or *al-Futuhat al-makiyya*.[94] About this encounter, he writes:

> ...[A]s I was standing in a state of ecstasy in front of the Black Rock I encountered the Evanescent Youth, the Silent Speaker, He who is neither alive nor dead, the Simple Composite, He who envelopes and is enveloped. When I saw him perform the ritual circuits around the Temple, like a living person revolving round a person who has died, I recognized his true reality and his metaphorical form, and I understood that the circuit around the Temple is like the prayer over a corpse. . . . Then God revealed to me the dignity of this Youth and his transcendence with regard to "where" and "when." When I recognized his dignity and his descent (*inzal*), when I saw his rank in existence and his state, I embraced his right side, wiped away the sweat of revelation on his forehead and declared to him: "Look upon him who aspire to your company and desires your intimacy!" He replied to me using signs and enigmas he had created so that he would never have to speak except in symbols: "When you recognize, understand and realize my symbolic language, you know that it can never be grasped either by the most eloquent of orators or by the most competent of rhetoricians" . . . He gestured to me and I understood. The reality of his Beauty unveiled itself to me and I was overcome with love, I became powerless and was instantly overwhelmed. When I recovered from my swoon, my sides shot through with fear, he knew I had realized who he was. . . . He said to me: "Observe the details of my constitution and the disposition of my form! You will find what you ask of me written upon me, because I neither speak nor converse, I

---

[93] *QRS*, 200.

[94] *Fut.* I, 47-51, see also, Chodkiewiecz, Michel, *Ocean Without Shore*, 28.

have no knowledge apart from the knowledge, the Known and the
Knower: I am Wisdom, the Sapiential Deed and the Sage!"[95]

Citing Ibn 'Abbas, Chodkiewiecz identifies this mysterious Youth
as "'the umbilicus of the earth'—thus a visible image of the supreme
spiritual center, is 'the manifest prototype,' or the 'explicit model' (*al-imam-al mubin*): a quranic expression to refer to the Book in which
'all things are numbered' (6: 38)."[96] Ibn al-'Arabi sometimes associ-
ates *al-imam al-mubin* with "the guarded Tablet (*al-lawh al-mahfuz*),"
at other times with "the Perfect Man (*al-insan al-kamil*)," and still at
other times, with the Qur'an itself.[97] By Ibn al-'Arabi's own account,
the Youth told him to write down the insight he received from this
encounter, and this was the genesis of his book the *Futuhat*.[98] It can
be said that, besides being a personal testimony to his own destiny
and his own visionary experience, *Futuhat* is also a faithful transcrip-
tion of all the things he was inspired to contemplate on that day of
encounter. Ibn al-'Arabi gives a full account of this encounter:

> 'I am [the Youth said to me] the ripe orchard and the full harvest!
> Now lift my veils and read what is contained in my inscriptions.
> Whatever you observe in me, put in your book and preach it to all
> your friends.' So I raised his veil and read his transcriptions. The
> light lodged within him enabled my eyes to see the hidden knowl-
> edge which he contains and conceals. The first line I read, and the
> first secret with which I became acquainted, is what I will now
> record in writing in the second chapter.[99]

If, according to Islamic tradition, the Qur'an was revealed to the
Prophet Muhammad, peace be upon him, by the angel Gabriel, so the
Futuhat, Hirtenstein says, which "explains the esoteric meaning of the

---

[95] *Fut.* I, 47-51, Addas, *Quest*, 201-2, Cf. Hirtenstein, *The Unlimited Mercifier*, 151.

[96] Chodkiewiecz, Michel, *Ocean Without Shore*, 28-9.

[97] According to Ibn al-'Arabi the guardian Tablet and the Perfect Man are different
names for the same function of mediating between the universe and the enigma of
the divine Being. *Fut.* II, 394, Chodkiewiecz, Michel, *Ocean Without Shore*, 29.

[98] Chodkiewiecz insists that the *fata* indeed a book, but "a *mutus liber: mutakallim
samit*." Chodkiewiecz, *Ocean*, 29

[99] *Fut,* I, 51, *QRS*, 203.

Qur'an was revealed to Ibn al-'Arabi by the Youth with no name. And like the Qur'an, which is said to have descended in its totality upon the heart of the Prophet and then been revealed to him piece by piece, so the *Futuhat*, although present in its entirety within the Youth, would also take many years to write down."[100] Ibn al-'Arabi also mentions that while writing the *Futuhat*'s preface, he experienced another vision where he saw himself as two gold and silver bricks that completed the walls of the Ka'ba. "At that moment, Ibn al-'Arabi testifies," I was given the Gifts of Wisdoms, just as if I had received the Totality of the Words."[101] He writes:

> When I was in Mecca in the year 599, I had a dream in which I saw the Ka'ba built of bricks of silver and gold, placed alternately. The construction was complete, and there was nothing left to add. I contemplated it and admired its beauty. Then I turned to the side between the Yemenite and Syrian corners—near the Syrian corner I noticed there were two bricks missing, one gold, one silver, on two rows of the wall. The missing gold was on the upper row, the missing silver on the lower. I saw my self being put into the place of these two bricks. Then I woke up and gave thank to God, saying to myself: "I am to the followers of my kind, just as the Envoy of God is to the prophets."[102]

To interpret the symbolism of the "two bricks" is difficult, but it appears to be directly connected with Ibn al-'Arabi's mystical episte-mology. According to this epistemology, the fullness of knowledge only comes through the awareness of ignorance.[103] Because the mes-sengers of God receive the fullness of divine revelation, in and through the reality of their own encounter with God, they cannot see that there are some things that they cannot see. This is why, the Prophet himself only sees one brick missing and he becomes that one

---

[100] Hirtenstein, *The Unlimited Merciful*, 152.

[101] *Fut.* I, 3, and I, 43-6, cf. Hirtenstein, *The Unlimited Mercifier*, 153.

[102] *Fut.* I, 318-9 and I. 43-6, cf. *Fusus al-hikam*, 63, *BW*, 66, cf. *QRS*, 213.

[103] In the *Fusus* Ibn al-'Arabi maintains that "Some of us there are who profess igno-rance as part of their knowledge, maintaining (with Abu Bakr) that "To realize that one cannot know (God) is to know" (*BW*, 65).

brick, while Ibn al'Arabi sees two missing and becomes the two.[104] To depart briefly from the metaphor of the "bricks" and turn to the metaphor of light, for the messengers of God, the darkness surrounding and within the godhead is obscured by the bright light of revelation. This does not mean, however, that the messengers of God cannot perfect their knowledge by a realization of ignorance, but only that this ignorance can only be experienced through the saints.

Ibn al-'Arabi is emphatic that "this does not in any way diminish [the station of the saint]... since [the saint] is, in one sense, below the messenger and, in another sense, higher."[105] Although some may, and indeed have, taken such statements of Ibn al-'Arabi to be blasphemous, this is because the statements are taken outside of the context of his epistemology. From within this context, what the master seems to be saying is that the reception of revelation by those who are not prophets and messengers of God is as much a part of the revelatory process as the reception of the revelation by the prophets and messengers themselves. In fact, if revelation were fulfilled in the prophetic experience alone, it would lose its universal nature and intent. The point of Ibn al-'Arabi's metaphor of the "one brick" of the Prophet and his own "two bricks," is to validate and bring to fruition the revelation given to the Messenger of God (i.e., Muhammad), the way the Messenger of God validates and brings fruition to the revelation given to all those prophets and messengers who have come before him. For Ibn al-'Arabi, the greatest blasphemy would be to suggest that the revelatory process ends with the death of the Prophet. Although he would agree that the *wahy* or special revelation given to all prophets and messengers does reach finality in the Seal of the Prophets (i.e., Muhammad)—an important tenet of orthodox Sunni Islam—he has to dissent vehemently from any notion that the process of divine communication to creation ever comes to an end. To say this would be tantamount to saying that the "Breath of the Merciful" (to be discussed below in

---

[104] In the *Bezels*, unlike himself who saw two bricks, Ibn al-'Arabi says that as the Prophet, Muhammad saw the lack of one brick only and he was the missing brick (see, *BW*, 66).

[105] *BW*, 66.

chapter three) ceases—that God ceases to be. In order, however, to preserve the important orthodox elevation of the Prophet Muham-mad over all human beings, he cleverly intuits that what the Seal of the Saints contributes to the knowledge of the prophets is not "more knowledge," per se, but rather the ignorance that makes knowledge of the One complete. What may seem, at first glance—and certainly to the many adversaries of Ibn al-'Arabi who arose after his death—as a statement of arrogance is actually a strong expression of humility. What the Messenger of God, as Seal of the Prophets, comes to do is to reveal to humanity for one last time the fullness of *what* they do not know; what the Seal of the Saints comes to do is to build on this knowledge and complete it by telling humanity *that* they do not know. To put it in somewhat more direct terms, while the Prophet comes to end the arrogance that comes from ignorance of one's iden-tity as servant of God, Ibn al-'Arabi understands his task to be to bring the ignorance necessary to check the arrogance that arises from possession of this knowledge. Allow me to note here that this con-nection between Ibn al-'Arabi's theory of the role of the "Seal of the Saints" and the theme of epistemological humility in both Ibn al-'Arabi and Meister Eckhart will emerge in chapters five and six (below) as an important "node" of the new matrix for Christian-Mus-lim dialogue.

The year that Ibn al-'Arabi spent in Mecca was a very productive one. In it, he not only completed several works, such as *Mishkat al-anwar*, *Hilyat al-abdal*, *Taj al-rasa'il*, *Ruh al-quds*, and the beginning of his *Futuhat*, but he also continued to encounter many well-known Sufi figures from Konya and Malatya, including Majd al-Din Ishaq al-Rumi (died c. 1215).

In the years 606–7/1209–10 Ibn al-'Arabi was in Konya, where he continued writing and composing—or in his idiom, receiving the inspiration that resulted in—additional books. In Konya, the Seljuq ruler, Kay Ka'us and the people welcomed him with hospitality. "The king ordered for him," Osman Yahya asserts, "a house worth 100,000 dirhams. After he had been in it for a while a beggar passed by and asked him for alms, whereupon he told him to take the house, since it was all he had to give."[106] Here, in Konya, Ibn al-'Arabi also met Awhad al-Din Hamid al-Kirmani (c. 1164–1238), who, over the next twenty years, became close friends and companions. Together, Ibn al-'Arabi and Kirmani became the teachers of Sadr al-Din al-Qunawi who would one day become Ibn al-'Arabi's stepson and one of his most important disciples and expositors.[107] As Hirtenstein mentions, through his stay in Konya, Ibn al-'Arabi "established a profound and lasting influence upon the subsequent development of mystical and religious teaching in Turkey and beyond."[108] Indeed, while the extent of their interaction is either unknown, or the stuff of unsubstantiated legend, there is no mistaking in the influence of Ibn al-'Arabi's thought on the most celebrated mystic poet of all time, Mawlana Jalal al-Din Rumi (d.1273).

C. Phase of Spiritual and Intellectual Maturity as a Sufi

Ibn al-'Arabi stayed in Damascus, "the refuge of the prophets,"[109] for the final seventeen years of his life, where he was to remain under protection of the Ibn Zaki family of qadis until the day of his death,.[110] Here in Damascus, he continued writing, at least, he begun writing a synopsis of his teachings—*Fusus al-hikam*—which he composed in 627/1230, as a result of his vision of a visitation from the Prophet Muhammad in a remarkable dream in mid-December 1229. It was here in Damascus that he also completed his first draft of the great *Futuhat* (628/1231).[111]

---

[106] *Fut.* IV, 560. 28.

[107] R. A Nicholson, "Lives of 'Umar Ibni al-Farid and Muhyi al-Din Ibn al-'Arabi, *J. R. A. S.* (1906), 816, cited by Austine in his translation, Ibn al-'Arabi, *Sufis of Andalusia*, 40.

[108] Hirtenstein, *The Unlimited Merciful*, 190, also Sufis of Andalusia, 40.

[109] *QRS*, 245.

[110] Ibn Kathir, *al-Bidaya wa 'l-nihaya* (Cairo nd., xiii), 156; *Fut.* IV, 83-4; *QRS*, 254, Hirtenstein, *The Unlimited Mercifier*, 208.

[111] Hirtenstein, The *Unlimited Mercifier*, 213-15.

There are speculations for Ibn al-'Arabi's choosing Damascus as his last home. Ibn Zubayr called it the "paradise of the East."[112] But this city was besieged plenty of times, and, as Addas states, many people who visited this place brought their new ideas which may have been a source of unrest for people's minds. She says "during the troubled period, the doctors of law were having a hard time," and the ulama had had Suhrawardi of Aleppo executed "for professing a disquieting doctrine in which Plato, Zoroaster and Avicenna rubbed shoulders with Abu Yazid al-Bistami, Dhu al-Nun al-Misri and al-Hallaj."[113] But according to her, "Ibn 'Arabi did not suffer any persecution in Syria. On the contrary, he was on close and good terms with a number of eminent people in Damascus, especially with some of the city's most highly reputed jurists."[114] In fact, in the *Futuhat*, Ibn al-'Arabi himself mentions the reason for his stay in Damascus until the end of his life. "Live in the land of Sham if you are able," Ibn al-'Arabi writes, "because it has been established that the Messenger of God has said 'Take care of the land of Sham because it is the land for which God has shown His presence, and it is from there that He selects the elite of His servants.'"[115]

As stated earlier, in Damascus Ibn al-'Arabi composed his most celebrated work, *Fusus al-hikam*, a brilliant reflection on the nature of prophethood and religious belief, which became the object of attacks from certain jurists shortly after his death. And as mentioned, this book came from his vision in 627/1229, when "the Prophet came to find him and handed him the book of *Fusus al-hikam*, the Bezels of Wisdom."[116] Ibn al-'Arabi says:

> I saw the Messenger of God in a vision of a good omen that was granted to me during the final ten days of the month of Muharram in the year 627 at Damascus—may God protect her! In his hand

---

[112] Ibn Zubayr; *VNR*, 301, cited by *QRS*, 245.

[113] *QRS*, 248.

[114] *QRS*, 250.

[115] The hadith is from Ibn Hanbal, IV, 110; Abu Dawud, 553 in *Fut*. IV, 500. 29 as mentioned in *QRS*, 259.

[116] *QRS*, 277.

he was holding a book, and he said to me: "This is the book of the *Fusus al-hikam*. Take it and give it to humanity so that they may obtain benefit from it." I replied: "I hear you, and I obey God, His messenger and those among us who are the keepers of the commandments," as it has been prescribed (Qur'an 4: 59). So, I set about fulfilling this wish. With that aim in mind I purified my intention and my aspiration so as to make this book known just as the Messenger of God had assigned it to me, without adding anything to it or taking anything away. . . . I state nothing that has not been projected towards me; I write nothing except what has been inspired in me. I am neither a prophet nor a messenger, but simply an inheritor; and I labour for the future life.[117]

Indeed, Ibn al-'Arabi claims that his writings are inspired and not just the result of his long spiritual and intellectual experiences. He says "Everything I say in my intuition and in my works derive from the presence of the Qur'an and from its treasures, to which I have been granted the key of understanding."[118] In the case of *Futuhat*, Addas says, "he claims, divine inspirations determine not only the content of the message but also the form of its presentation: hence, he warns, the apparent incoherency in the ordering of the chapters."[119] In fact, when he compiled his *Fihrist* (i.e., "bibliography") for his disciple, Sadr al-Din al-Qunawi, he explains:

In what I have written, I have never had a set purpose, as others write. Flashes of divine inspiration used to come upon me and almost overwhelm me, so that I could only put them from my mind by committing to paper what they revealed to me. If my works evince any form of composition, it was unintentional. Some works I wrote at the command of God, sent to me in sleep or through mystical revelation.[120]

---

[117] Ibn al-'Arabi, *Fusus*, I, 47-48, cf. M Chodkiewicz, *Seal of Saints*, 49-50; *QRS*, 277; *BW*, 17.

[118] *Fut.* III, 334. 32, *QRS*, 204, see also *BW*, 13.

[119] *QRS*, 204, see *Fut.* II, 163.23.

[120] A. A. Afifi, "Memorandum by Ibn al-'Arabi of His Own Works," Introduction, in the *Bulletin of the Faculty of Arts* (Alexandria University, VIII, 1954), cited by Austin in his introduction in *BW*, 13.

Some of the themes in the *Fusus* have become the focus of attacks from the eighth century down to the present day, such as the unity of being, the notion of the pre-existence of the human soul, the final salvation of Pharaoh, the perfect man, and the non-eternity of infernal punishments—though they are not absent from the *Futuhat*. It was for this reason, Addas argues, that—"due allowance being made for the intellectual laziness of the jurists, who were generally happy simply to cite the 'condemnable propositions' already catalogued by Ibn Taymiyya—the *Fusus* lent themselves to criticism far more readily than the *Futuhat*."[121]

During the last years of his life, Ibn al-'Arabi was still active composing a number of works, revising the *Futuhat,* and teaching his disciples. One day God commanded him: "Tell your disciples: 'Make the most of my existence before I go!'"[122] It seems that it was what his disciples did; they never tired of gathering around the shaykh to study his works. In 22 Rabi' II 638 / November 1240, at the age of seventy-five, Ibn al-'Arabi passed away. "The pilgrim," Addas writes, "arrived at the end of his long terrestrial journey... the Shaykh al-Akbar left his disciples to perform a *mi'raj* from which there would be no return: one that would lead him to the Rafiq al-A'la, the Supreme Friend."[123]

3. Legacy

In Islamic history, though Ibn al-'Arabi is not considered to be the founder of Islamic mysticism, he is an extraordinarily prominent Sufi author. At the same time, he is the most controversial.[124] S.H. Nasr, one of the most prominent contemporary scholars of Sufism, refers to Ibn al-'Arabi as "the expositor par excellence of gnosis in Islam."[125]

---

[121] *QRS*, 278.

[122] *Fut.* I, 723. 14, *QRS,* 287.

[123] *QRS*, 287.

[124] William C. Chittick, "Ibn al-'Arabi and His School" in *Islamic Spirituality, Manifestation*, ed. by Seyyed Hossein Nasr (New York: Crossroad, 1991), 49, William Chittick, *Ibn 'Arabi, Heir to the Prophets* (Oxford: Oxford, 2005), 1, see also, John T. Little, "al-Insan al-Kamil: The Perfect man according to Ibn al-Arabi" in *The Muslim World*, vol. vii (1987), 43.

[125] S.H. Nasr, *Three Muslim Sages* (Delmar, New York: Caravan Books, 1970), 90.

According to Corbin, "the determining influence on Sufism and spirituality was not Ghazali's pious agnostic critique, but the esoteric doctrine of Ibn al-'Arabi and his school."[126] Indeed, certain corners of the Sufi tradition surely concur, for they have conferred upon Ibn al-'Arabi the epithet of *al-Shaikh al-Akbar* (The Greatest Master) of Sufism.

Although he left as his written legacy nearly three hundred books, his fame is due largely to the two we have already mentioned: *al-Futuhat al-Makiyya*, or *The Meccan Revelations*, and *Fusus al-Hikam*, or *The Bezels of Wisdom*.

A. Controversy and the Example of Ibn Taymiyya

As discussed earlier, much of Ibn al-'Arabi's works have triggered attacks from certain jurists. The question that must be addressed in any assessment of his legacy is *why* his teachings aroused so much hostility among certain Muslims toward him? In his monograph on the subject, Alexander D. Knysh presents a study of the disagreement within Islamic world over the legacy of Ibn al-'Arabi. He analyzes the intense theological and intellectual debates about Ibn al-'Arabi, including the doctrinal disagreement and factional differences among the ulama, whose interests were by no means identical with those of other strata of medieval Islamic society. According to Knysh, to understand the fierce disputes over Ibn al-'Arabi, it is crucial to understand the place and role of the ulama in medieval Islamic society.[127] Now, why was Ibn al-'Arabi condemned?

Fr. Paul Lachance—an internationally recognized specialist in Franciscan mysticism and spirituality and a teacher of mine at Catholic Theological Union—once said: "To be a mystic is to be on trial."[128] Focusing in more depth on the trouble certain mystics seem to get

---

[126] Henry Corbin, *Creative Imagination in the Sufism of Ibn al-'Arabi* (Princeton: Princeton University Press, 1969), 9.

[127] See Alexander D. Knysh, Ibn 'Arabi in the Later Islamic Tradition: The Making of a Polemical Image in Mediaval Islam (Albany: State University of New York Press, 1999).

[128] My interview with him in the library of Catholic Theological Union, Chicago, Illinois (fall, 2004)

themselves into, Carl W. Ernst maintains that "the circumstances of the persecution of mystics are [usually] hedged around with hagiographical interpretations that make it hard to evaluate precisely [what the source of the problem is], although it is clear that political considerations are always relevant in cases of religious persecution."[129] In his book *Words of Ecstasy in Sufism*, he says, concerning the trial of Abu Husayn al-Nuri, "the tense political situation in Baghdad doubtless contributed to an atmosphere in which government acted on accusation of heresy without delay."[130] Ernst goes on to point out that, "In Nuri's case the legal process depended entirely on the whims of the ruler and those who had his ear."[131]

In the cases of the execution of al-Hallaj, of 'Ayn al-Qudat Hamadhani, and the condemnation of Ibn al-'Arabi, just to mention some examples, there are many indications of power struggles either between governmental rulers or between different religious factions among the religious scholarly elite. Indeed, intra-Sufi power struggles are often times played out with the aid of certain governmental authorities and vice versa. The reason for 'Ayn al-Qudat's persecution, for example, was not of being a Sufi. In his time (as also in the time of al-Hallaj), we witnessed many other "politically correct Sufis wandering around Hamadan and Baghdad."[132] "He was killed because he assimilated the Sufi discourse into his personal narrative and reached for a personal account of a truth with which he could live—others could not."[133] In other words, 'Ayn al-Qudat's "crime" was not so much in what he was saying, but rather *how* he said it and what the popular response

---

[129] Carl W. Ernst, "Persecution and Circumspection in Shattari Sufism," in *Islamic Mysticism Contested: Thirteen Centuries of Debate and Conflict*, Fred De Jong and Bern Radke, eds. (Leiden: Brill, 1999), 417.

[130] Carl W. Ernst, *Words of Ecstasy in Sufism* (Albany: State University of New York Press, c1985), 101.

[131] Carl W. Ernst, *Words of Ecstasy*, 101.

[132] Hamid Dabashi, "Persian Sufism during the Seljuk Period," in Leonard Lewinsohn, ed. *The Heritage of Sufism, Classical Persian Sufism for Its Origin to Rumi (700-1300)*, Vol.I (Oxford: Oneworld, 1999), 149.

[133] Dabashi, "Persian Sufism during the Seljuk Period," 149; see also Carl W. Ernst, *Words of Ecstasy*, 115.

was. In the minds of his persecutors he was crossing the boundaries of legitimate theological, and perhaps—by implication—political discourse. The same seems to have been true in the case of al-Hallaj. Some of Hallaj's greatest adversaries were themselves Sufis who, either were envious of fearful of the potential inherent in Hallaj's charisma, or who legitimately believed that Hallaj endangered Sufism in general through the crime of "revealing the secret." This is all to say that controversies over the teachings of various Sufis are, more often than not, far more than they appear to be.

Still, that there are certain inherent tensions between Sufi claims to experientially-based authority and the exclusively text-based claims to authority of normative Islamic jurisprudence cannot be denied. According to Hamid Dabashi,

> [T]his hostility [between certain expressions of Sufsm and certain expressions of normative jurisprudence], which dates back to the earliest period of Islamic history, is ... a reflection of two fundamentally opposed interpretations of the quranic revelation and the Muhammadan legacy. The positive nomocentricity of Islamic law found the language of Islamic mysticism as quintessentially flawed in nature and disposition. The feeling was mutual. The Sufi, too, rejected the rigid and perfunctory nomocentricity of the jurists as quintessentially misguided and a stultification of the quranic message and the prophetic traditions. The metaphysical bipolarity had, of course, an active political component with both the mystic and the jurists seeking to manipulate the powers-that-be in their respective interest and advantage. The political power could, and would, alternate between the jurist and mystics as the culprits of effective legitimacy for their own rule. The Muslim philosophers and other men of science, the mostly quiet advocates of the rule of reason, the logocentric forces in the course of Islamic intellectual history, had to manoeuver their limited ways through these troubled and dangerous lands. [134]

In other words, the popularity of a certain brand of Sufism can have an "alarming effect" on both the scholarly and political authority of the

---

[134] Dabashi, "Persian Sufism during the Seljuk Period," *The Heritage of Sufism*, 150, See also H. Dabashi, *Truth and Narrative: The Untimely Thought of Ayn al-Qudat al-Hamadhani* (Richmond: Curzon Press, 1999).

jurists. Thus, "when the culmination of public sentiment towards mystical sensibilities appears to undermine the authority of the powers that be, the jurists [of the status quo] have [usually] reacted swiftly and effectively in eliminating their religious and political rivals."[135]

One thing is certain, however, in any highly politicized "heresy" trial, the politics of demonization and expediency take precedence and leave little room for a thorough, fair, and objective analysis of what it is the controversial mystic is actually saying. The Egyptian mystical poet Ibn al-Farid was charged with implying incarnation and a belief in the possibility of unification of the mystic with the divinity. According to Ibn Ilyas, however, who gives us a detailed report of the controversy which arose among the ulama of Cairo with regard to Ibn Farid, says "that the ulama who denounced the poet did not understand him."[136] The issue of a literal understanding of Sufi discourse, as opposed to what the Sufis are trying to communicate by way of metaphor is oftentimes the line of demarcation between those jurists who reject certain forms of Sufi discourse and those who accept them. A comment on Ibn al-'Arabi's book from a qadi for example says, "How clear and eloquent is God's book! The Arabic Qur'an is enough for us; we do not need this obscure book by Ibn al-'Arabi."[137]

In addition to the reasons for hostility toward Sufis mentioned above, the reference also should be made to the fact that there are Sufis who reject the claims to authority and authenticity made by other Sufis. Although it may sound simplistic, it may well have been Ibn al-'Arabi's disciples themselves who provoked the attack precisely by acknowledging him, among other Sufis, to be "the Greatest Master." Superlative claims such as this must have been seen by other

---

[135] Dabashi, "Persian Sufism," 150.

[136] Michael Winter, *Society and Religion in Early Ottoman Egypt, Studies in the Writings of 'Abd al-Wahhab al-Sha'rani* (New Brunswick: Transaction Books, 1982). 163; al-Sha'rani himself, an admirer of Ibn al-'Arabi, writes a book entitled *al-Tabaqat al-Kubra* (Cairo, 1954).

[137] Winter, *Society and Religion*, 164.

Sufi masters as, at best, tendentious, and at worst, a sign of the height of arrogance.[138]

No discussion of the controversial legacy of Ibn al-ʿArabi would be complete without the mention of the systematic attacks against Ibn al-ʿArabi and his school that culminated in the writings of the famous Hanbali jurist Ibn Taymiyya (d. 1328) who articulates one of the most scathing and subsequently influential critiques of Ibn al-ʿArabi and his teachings. That Ibn Taymiyya was a Sufi, there can be no doubt.[139] But as a conscientious Sufi, Ibn Taymiyya felt obliged to defend orthodox/orthoprax Sufism against corrupting innovations in Sufi belief and practice.

Contemporary scholarly assessments of Ibn Taymiyya's perspectives on the teachings of Ibn al-ʿArabi vary to a certain degree. Some, such as the work of Muhammad Umar Memon, are themselves polemical, echoing and even magnifying the negative sentiments of Ibn Taymiyya himself. [140]Others, such as the work of Alexander Knysh on this topic, are more balanced and insightful. Knysh is well aware that Ibn Taymiyya is the author of numerous tractates and legal opinions (*fatawa*) which rely on quotations from scripture, condemning the theses that he finds in Ibn al-ʿArabi's writing. He also notes that, while Ibn Taymiyya appears to have an excellent knowledge of the works he was refuting, curiously enough, his critiques are not aimed against Ibn al-ʿArabi's entire corpus, but rather against certain of the master's works, especially *Fusus al-hikam*. In this regard, Ibn Taymiyya writes:

> At first, I was among those who held a good opinion of Ibn ʿArabi and praised him highly for the useful advice he provides in his books. This useful advice is found in pages of "Revelations" [*al-Futuhat al-makiyya*], the "Essence" [*al-Kunh ma la budda minhu li*

---

[138] See the discussion of the challenges posed by the legacy of Ibn al-ʿArabi as *al-shaykh al-akbar* to al-Iskandari's attempt to advance al-Shadhili as the "divine Pole" or *qutb* of his age in Knysh, *Ibn ʿArabi*, 80-81.

[139] See George Makdisi, "Ibn Taymiyya: A Sufi of the Qadiriya Order," *The American Journal of Arabic Studies*, 1 (1973), pp. 118-129 quoted in Muhammad Umar Memon, *Ibn Taymiyya's Struggle Against Popular Religion* (The Hague: Mouton, 1976), x.

[140] Muhammad Umar Memon, *Ibn Taymiyya's Struggle Against Popular Religion* (The Hague: Mouton, 1976).

al-murid], the "Tightly Knit and Tied" [*Kitab al-amr al-muhkam al-marbut*], the "Precious Pearl" [*al-Durrat al-fakhira fi dhikr man intafa'tu bi-hi fi tariq al-akhira*], and the "Position of the Stars" [*Mawaqi' al-nujum*], and similar writings. At that time we were unaware of his real goal, because we had not yet studied the *Fusus* and suchlike books. [141]

Apparently, at one time or another, Ibn Taymiyya had an appreciation of Ibn al-'Arabi's thought. He obviously read the *Futuhat* and admired it. Sometime, however, between his reading of this and other of the master's works, Ibn Taymiyya's opinion changed. According to Ibn Dawadari, the change occurred in the year 703/1303 when Ibn Taymiyya receieved a copy of *Fusus* and found it to be highly problematic.[142] It appears that the issue here is not that Ibn al-'Arabi makes a perceived departure from orthodoxy in *Fusus* which one could not impute to the *Futuhat* as well. Instead, it seems that Ibn Taymiyya is reading *Fusus* through a distinctly different interpretative lens than he read the *Futuhat*. All indications point to the fact that this second "lens" through which Ibn Taymiyya read *Fusus* is that of what he perceived to be the dangerous combination of the popularization and concomitant distortion of the teachings of Ibn al-'Arabi, the proliferation of sectarian phenomena such as that of the Nusayriyya, and the bastardization of classical Sufism to include all manner of popular beliefs and practices having little to do with what Ibn Taymiyya understood to be orthodox Islam. Knysh writes:

> Using his notion of "correct Sufism" as his measuring stick, Ibn Taymiyya singled out what he viewed as Ibn 'Arabi's tendency to obfuscate the critical God-man demarcation as his main target and as the starting point of his antimonistic critique. In his view, this tendency put the Greatest Master amid the cohort of "heretics" and "grave sinners," responsible for such "vices" as the excessive influ-

---

[141] Ibn Taymiyya, *Majmu'at al-rasa'il wa l-masa'il*, four volumes, Muhammad Rashid Rida, ed. (Cairo: Matba'at al-Manar, 1922-1930), v. 4, 179, quoted in Knysh, *Ibn 'Arabi in the Later Islamic Tradition*, 96.

[142] Ibn al-Dawadari, *Kanz al-durar wa l-jami' al-ghurar* (Wiesbaden: Qism al-Dirasat al-Islamiyya, al-Ma'had al-Almani li al-Athar bi al-Qahira, 1960-1982), 143, quoted in Knysh, *Ibn 'Arabi in the Later Islamic Tradition*, 96.

ence on the Muslim state of its Christian and Jewish subjects, sug-
gestive female dress, popular superstitions, the game of backgam-
mon, the spread of the Mongol customs among the Mamluks, the
miracle-working of the dervishes, minor pilgrimages to saints'
shrines, Shi'i heresies, the exotic garments of wandering Sufis,
hashish-smoking, the chivalric cult of *futuwwa*, state control of food
prices, rationalist philosophy, and *kalam*.[143]

In simple terms, then, Ibn Taymiyya does not give us an "objective" and comprehensive review of Ibn al-'Arabi's thinking because he
does not see this as his task. Rather, he understands his role to be that
of a defender of orthodox/orthoprax Islam and orthodox/orthoprax
Sufism at a time when he understands both to be under a tremendous
pluralist cultural assault.

The premier aspect of Ibn al-'Arabi's teaching that is most trouble-
some for Ibn Taymiyya is his teaching on the "oneness of being" (often
referred to in Arabic as *wahdat al-wujud*,[144] although Ibn al-'Arabi never
uses this expression). Within this teaching, Ibn Taymiyya locates the
particular difficulty to lie in Ibn al-'Arabi's doctrine of *al-a'yan al-thabita*
or the "immutable entities."[145] For Ibn al-'Arabi, the Arabic word *'ayn*
refers to an "entity" whether existent in the created order, or in a state
of non-existent potentiality in the mind of God. The creative activity of
God occurs as God brings into existence any combination of the entities
which are established in the divine consciousness. According to this
schema, nothing which is brought into existence does not have its full
and complete origin in the Godhead. To say otherwise would, for Ibn
al-'Arabi, be tantamount to *shirk*. For Ibn al-'Arabi, God does indeed
create *ex nihilo*, but not in the sense that any reality is beyond God's

---

[143] Knysh, *Ibn 'Arabi in the Later Islamic Tradition*, 89.

[144] On *wahdat al-wujud*, see Chittick, "*Wahdat al-Wujud* in Islamic Thought," *Bulletin of
the Henry Martyn Institute of Islamic Studies*, 10 (1991), 7-27; Chittick, "Rumi and
Wahdat al-wujud," in Amin Banani; Richard G Hovannisian; Georges Sabagh, *Poetry
and Mysticism in Islam : the Heritage of Rumi* (New York: Cambridge University
Press, 1994): Chittick, "Sadr al-Din al-Qunawi on the Oneness of Being,"
International Philosophical Quarterly, 21 (1981), 171-184.

[145] This is Chittick's translation of *al-a'yan al-thabita* from *SPK*, 7 and *passim*. Knysh
also adopts this translation.

imagination and the scope of God's knowledge. Therefore the "nothing-ness" of everything that God brings into existence is not, for Ibn al-'Arabi, a literal no-thing-ness—as it is for Ibn Taymiyya—a void that has nothing to do with, and thus is the opposite of Being. Rather, for Ibn al-'Arabi the "nothingness" out of which God creates is the nonexistence or "pre-existence"[146] of all those myriad and unlimited "things" that are established in the mind of God.

Ibn al-'Arabi insists, for example, that the fact that God "sees all things" before they exist, does not in any way contradict the fact that He creates what exists out of nonexistence. In fact, the distinction between any type of "existence" on the one hand, and "thing-ness," on the other hand, is a crucial component of Ibn al-'Arabi's meta-physics. Another way of saying this is that, for Ibn al-'Arabi, the quranic equivalent of the Christian doctrine of "creation out of noth-ingness" can more precisely be glossed as "creation out of nonexis-tence." Of all things that ever have been brought into existence or ever will be, it is absolutely vital that Ibn al-'Arabi declare: "He [i.e., God] never ceases seeing it. He who holds that the cosmos is eter-nal," the master goes on to warn, "does so from this perspective [*but does so erroneously!*]. But he who considers the existence of the cosmos in relation to its own entity [or "thing-ness"] and the fact that it did not possess this state when the Real saw it maintains [*correctly*] that the cosmos is temporally originated."[147]

---

[146] All terms, like "pre-existent"—which are not direct English translations of an expres-sion used by Ibn al-'Arabi and thus depart significantly from his primary discourse— can be problematic. This is because, as Knysh points out, Ibn al-'Arabi's discourse is "deliberately crafted so as to obfuscate its essence" (9). This does not mean that Ibn al-'Arabi is being deliberately obscurantist, but rather reminds us that Ibn al-'Arabi recognizes the limitations of language in any attempt to describe the Real. In this particular instance, Ibn al-'Arabi is trying to distinguish between absolute no-thing-ness and the absolute non-existence out of which God creates the phenomenal world. Insofar as "pre-existence" suggests any type of "existence"—however *poten-tial* and not *actual* it may be—this is not what Ibn al-'Arabi is trying to evoke when he describes something as a truly nonexistent "thing." From Ibn al-'Arabi's perspec-tive, the danger of a term like "pre-existent" is that it makes his cosmology more susceptible to the charge that he is denying *creatio ex nihilo*.

[147] *Fut.* II, 666.34 in *SPK*, 85.

In sum, Ibn al-'Arabi intends his teaching with respect to *al-a'yan al-thabita* ("immutable entities") as an attempt to maintain fidelity to the quranic doctrine of the temporality of the cosmos alongside of an unqualified assertion that nothing—especially God's creation—can possibly be "new" or "alien" to God . Because of his historical context, however, and the vocation he embraces as a defender of orthodoxy and orthopraxy, Ibn Taymiyya does not receive this teaching in the mode in which it was intended. Instead he receives it as part of a larger threat to mainstream Islamic teaching in which Ibn al-'Arabi himself had no appreciable role during his lifetime. Speaking of Ibn al-'Arabi's teaching with respect to *al-a'yan al-thabita*, Ibn Taymiyya writes:

> ... [H]e brought together two [heretical] theories, namely the negation of God's existence, on the one hand, and the negation of His [status as the] originator of the creaturely world, on the other. Thereby he denies that the Lord is the maker [of the world] and affirms that there is neither the existence of God, nor the act of creation. In so doing, he invalidates [the quranic notion of] "the Lord of the worlds." [For him,] there exists neither the Lord, nor the world over which He holds sway. In other words, there is nothing but the immutable entities and the existence that sustains them.[148]

Despite such a strong condemnation of Ibn al-'Arabi's thought, it is interesting to note that Ibn Taymiyya refrains from the *ad hominem* attacks that could be found on the lips or flowing from the pens of so many of Ibn Taymiyya's disciples in subsequent generations. Of all those who profess what Ibn Taymiyya interpreted as being heretical doctrines of the oneness of being, Ibn Taymiyya says of Ibn al-'Arabi that the latter is

> ... the closest to Islam among them.... He at least distinguished between the manifest One and the concrete forms of His manifestation. Moreover, he affirmed the validity of Divine Command and Prohibition and the Divine Laws as they stand. He also instructed the travelers on the [mystical] path how to acquire high morals and the acts of devotion, as is common with other Sufis and their dis-

---

[148] Ibn Taymiyya, *Majmu'at*, vol. IV, 21-22 quoted in Knysh, *Ibn 'Arabi in the Later Islamic Tradition*, 102.

ciples. Therefore, many pious worshippers (*'ubbad*) have learned [the rules of] their path through his instruction and thus have greatly benefited from him, even though they sometimes failed to understand his [mystical] subtleties. [149]

By recognizing the moral and ritual rectitude of his fellow Sufi, Ibn Taymiyya is locating himself squarely within a mainstream Sufism which has always placed a premium on right behavior as an absolute sine qua non of the spiritual quest. Indeed, what impresses the great Abu Hamid al-Ghazali and draws him to Sufism during his years of searching for the truth is that the Sufis are those who teach about truth, first and foremost, by the example of their lives:

> Their life is the best life, their method the soundest method, their character the purest character; indeed, were the intellect of the intellectuals and the learning of the learned and the scholarship of the scholars, who are versed in the profundities of revealed truth, brought together in the attempt to improve the life and character of the mystics, they would find no way of doing so.[150]

Through his praise for Ibn al-'Arabi's lived example, it is obvious that Ibn Taymiyya holds the master in high esteem and realizes that—while the master's teachings may be (mis)interpreted as challenging the practical distinction between God and the world, paradise and hellfire, and threatening the rigorous observance of the Shari'a—in his own life, the master was a scrupulously pious Sunni Muslim. By the same token, Ibn Taymiyya's comment on the tendency for people to 'fail to understand [Ibn al-'Arabi's mystical] subtleties' should not be overlooked. In fact, I would argue that it is precisely these misunderstandings to which Ibn Taymiyya feels compelled to respond, and that Ibn Taymiyya by no means would countenance the *takfir* (i.e., declaring to be an unbeliever) of Ibn al-'Arabi that one finds among so many of Ibn Taymiyya's followers in today's world.

---

[149] Ibn Taymiyya, *Majmu'at*, vol. I, 183 quoted in Knysh, *Ibn 'Arabi in the Later Islamic Tradition* 98.

[150] Montgomery, Watt, *Muslim intellectual; a study of al-Ghazali* (Edinburgh, University Press, 1963), 60, see also Al-Ghazali, *Al Munqid min al-dalal* (Lahor: Hay'ah al-Awqaf bi-Ḥukumat al-Bunjab, 1971).

B. Lasting Influence

On the lasting influence of Ibn al-'Arabi, William Chittick attests to a large number of popular works which he found in India, and offers this find as one indication of the enormous impact that the Greatest Shaykh has had on Muslim societies worldwide.[151] Indeed, by looking at the books and articles being published on the great Sufis of Islamic history, such as al-Hallaj, Rumi, and especially Ibn Al-'Arabi, it is clear that Sufism has been recognized by a significant contemporary audience as a storehouse of spiritual and religious teachings which are still important in our own age. In fact, one of the many reasons for Ibn al-'Arabi's popularity is "His work, in distinction to all that preceded it. . . . has a distinguishing feature: . . . it has an answer for everything."[152]

Ibn al-'Arabi's ideas are very much alive and well in both in Sunni and Shi'i circles in the contemporary Muslim world. In many places, including Indonesia, my native country, we witness that Ibn al-'Arabi's style and insights have been passed down through the ages. What is interesting, however, is that if one were to ask an average Indonesian Muslim practicing a tradition heavily influenced by Ibn al-'Arabi, about Ibn al-'Arabi, this Muslim is likely to exclaim that Ibn al-'Arabi was a heretic. Thus, the Sunni ulama in Indonesia tend to ignore Ibn al-'Arabi in broad public settings while teaching his works in private circles. As Eric Winkel reminds us, "Founders of the Sufi paths were able to pass on complete systems of spiritual journeying by relying on the articulate foundation laid by Ibn al-'Arabi. Local shaykhs and Sufis gained access to Ibn al-'Arabi's works through his popularizers, like Sha'rani."[153]

Thus, although there are still ongoing polemics against Ibn al-'Arabi and his teaching, he is nonetheless very influential for the development of contemporary Sufism, in both its intellectual and popular

---

[151] William Chittick, "Note on Ibn Al-'Arabi's Influence in the Subcontinent," *The Muslim World*, Vol. LXXXII, No. 3-4 (July-October, 1992), 221.

[152] Michel Chodkiewicz, "The Diffusion of Ibn Arabi's Doctrine," *Journal of the Muhyiddin Ibn al-'Arabi Society* (1991), 51, quoted by Chitiick, "Notes on Ibn al-'Arabi's Influence," 218.

[153] Erick Winkel, *Islam and The Living Law, The Ibn Arabi Approach* (Oxford: Oxford University Press, 1997), 19-20.

forms. It should be noted, however, that differences of circumstance and context will determine not only the mode and scope of the dissemination of Ibn al-'Arabi's teaching, but also the ways of understanding it. On certain occasions—as we saw in the case of the causal factors behind Ibn Taymiyya's polemic—the doctrine of "the unity of being" (*wahdat al-wujud*), for example, has been interpreted in ways approaching monism or pantheism. Accordingly, some saw the mystic path as a personal striving to become one with the only Being—a striving that has no use for so-called "organized religion." Such relativistic and anti-religious[154] interpretations depart radically from the teachings of Ibn al-'Arabi in the way that they blur all distinctions between Islam and other religions (something Ibn al-'Arabi never did), and generally undetermined all legitimate notions of "heresy."

As the influence of the master continued to evolve, some groups of reformers came to stress other aspects of Ibn al-'Arabi's teaching. Certain groups emphasized a shift from "unity of being" to "the reality of Muhammad" (*al-haqiqa al-Muhammadiyya*), another important element in al-Shaykh al-Akbar's thought, signifying the Prophet's place in the one Being as the Perfect Man, through whom all creatures emanate and through whom they can draw near to God.[155] Thus, this new emphasis on the figure of the Prophet in mystical life offered a significant alternative to Sufi-inspired relativism by bringing the devout adherence to the Sunna so characteristic of classical Sufism, back to the center of Sufi life. This interpretation of Ibn al-'Arabi's teaching reflects the growing inclination among contemporary Muslims not to withdraw from the world but to be more involved in pub-

---

[154] Especially in the contemporary sense in which "spirituality" is set up in opposition to "religion."

[155] For the notion of the Muhammadan Reality in the Akbari teaching see Chodkiewicz, *Seal of the Saints*, 60-73; Hakim, *Al-Mu'jam al-Sufi*, 347-352; for the Perfect man see Reynold Nicholson, *Studies in Islamic Mysticism* (Cambridge, 1921), 77-142; Chittick, "The Perfect Man as a Prototype of the Self in the Sufism of Jami," *Studia Islamica* 49 (1979), 135-158; Toshihiko Izutsu, *Sufism and Taoism: A Comparative Study of Key Philosophical Concepts* (Berkeley, 1983), 218-283; Masataka Takeshita, *Ibn al-'Arabi's Theory of the Perfect Man and Its Place in the History of Islamic Thought* (Tokyo, 1987); Hakim, *Al-Mu'jam al-Sufi*, 158-168.

lic affairs, as exemplified by the Prophet, and to stress the distinction between Muslims, who accepted his mission, and followers of other religions, who rejected it. Along with this tendency, Muslims developed a renewed interest in the works of Ghazali.[156]

For many centuries now, the teachings and legacy of Ibn al-'Arabi have held a special attraction for those who strongly feel the mysterious dimensions of God's presence in all human experience. Many find Ibn al-'Arabi's spirituality—one of deep piety and moral conviction, on the one hand, and an expansive notion of what is True and Real, on the other hand—uniquely compelling, especially in a context where the importance of embracing cultural, ethnic, political, and religious plurality is only matched by the importance of rooting oneself in what it is one believes.

---

[156] Nehemia Levtzion, and John O. Voll, Introduction, in *Eighteenth Century Renewal and Reform Movement in Islam* (Syracuse: Syracuse University Press, 1987), cited by Itzchak Weismann, *Taste of Modernity, Sufism, Salafiyya, and Arabism in Late Ottoman Damascus* (Leiden, Boston, Koln: Brill, 2001), 147.

Chapter II

MEISTER ECKHART:
HISTORICAL CONTEXT, LIFE,
AND LEGACY

MEISTER ECKHART:
HISTORICAL CONTEXT,
LIFE, AND LEGACY

1. Historical Context

The mid-thirteenth and fourteenth centuries were marked by the collapse and transformation of economic, intellectual, and religious life in Europe.[157] This "calamitous" period, as Barbara Tuchman[158] refers to it, suffered from successive waves of the terrible Great Plague as it swept through Europe. The Plague, in turn, led to a serious undermining of society and its institutions at all levels.[159] It was also a time of war. "Externally the Mongols from the East and the Turks in Asia Minor threatened stability."[160] Richard Weber summarizes well the upheavals of the age:

> Two global wars, the overthrow of the western and Atlantic political, economic and social order, the erosion of faith in the postulates of liberal and rational western civilization, the rise of new power, new ideologies and a half century of violence, war and terrorism... [M]edieval civilization was shaped from within, assaulted from without, and a great culture began to die, a marvelous synthesis of faith and learning slowly unraveled and came apart. There were population problems, economic depressions, demands for reform and a merry dance of hedonists bent upon instant pleasure. It was

---

[157] Robert. K. Forman, *Meister Eckhart, Mystic as Theologian* (Shaftesbury, Adorset, 1991), 29.

[158] See Barbara W. Tuchman, *A Distant Mirror: The Calamitous 14th Century* (New York: Alfred A. Knopf, 1978).

[159] *The Rhineland Mystics: Writings of Meister Eckhart, Johannes Tauler, and Jan van Ruusbroec and Selections from the Theologia Germanica and the Book of Spiritual Poverty*, ed., intro., and trans. by Oliver Davies (New York : Crossroad, 1990), 6.

[160] Robert. K. Forman, *Mystic as Theologian*, 29.

a time when men and women began to think that the world was coming to an end.[161]

It was also a time of division within the church. As Richard Woods mentions, "the great edifice of Medieval Christendom was beginning to crumble."[162] In the greater Rhineland Valley, the medieval religious world was coming to an end rapidly. This rapid rise in institutional decadence, especially within the church, is described by Barbara Tuchman as follows:

> Avignon became a virtual temporal state of sumptuous pomp, of great cultural attraction, and of unlimited simony—that is the selling of offices. Diminished by its removal from the Holy See of Rome and by being generally regarded as a tool of France, the papacy thought to make up prestige and power in temporal terms . . . [.] Everything the Church had or was, from cardinal's hat to pilgrim's relic, was for sale . . . [.] To obtain a conferred benefice, a bishop or abbot greased the palms of the Curia for his nomination . . . [.] Money could buy any kind of dispensation: to legitimize children, of which the majority were those of priests and prelates . . . [.] Younger sons of noble families were repeatedly appointed to archbishoprics at eighteen, twenty, or twenty-two. Tenures were short because each preferment brought in another payment.[163]

By this time, monastic spirituality seems to have lost much of its earlier influence. The rise of new towns and cities created new needs and new ways of life, especially in Northern Italy, Western Germany, and the Netherlands. With these new ways of life came new problems and new attitudes of mind as the needs of increasingly prevalent urban societies began to clash with established agrarian culture and norms. This period also saw a decline in respect for the representatives of the church hierarchy and the loss of the church's credibility due to such increasingly common phenomena as "[f]lagrant concubinage, frequent

---

[161] Cited by Forman, *Mystic as Theologian*, 29.

[162] Richard Woods, OP, *Eckhart's Way* (Collegeville, Minnesota: The Liturgical Press, 1990), 25.

[163] Tuchman, *A Distant Mirror*, 26f, cited by Matthew Fox, *Breakthrough: Meister Eckhart's Creation Spirituality in New Translation* (New York: Image Books a division of Doubleday and Company Inc, 1980), 13.

illiteracy of local priests, and a widespread quest for wealth and political power" on the part of church officials."[164]

The life of Meister Eckhart marks a period of transition from the old to the new in which established social institutions were breaking down, but in which the emergence of a new order was not yet apparent. During this time, in the Rhineland valley where Meister Eckhart lived the population was increasing rapidly—especially in Strasbourg and Cologne.[165] Part of what this urban demographic expansion brought with it was an experience of the filthiness and degradation of widespread poverty which put strains on religious institutions both to minister to the poor, as well as to try to explain and address the reasons for such widespread suffering. Amidst all the challenges of these new urban contexts "certain facts of city life," says Forman, "tended to encourage religious experimentation."[166]

One of the new developments unfolding during this tumultuous period was the rise of popular religious movements seeking to meet the demand of a growing laity for more access to the structures of Christian life—such as educational privileges and prayer opportunities—which were, up until this time, restricted largely to predominantly male religious orders. The rationalizations which had developed out of and justified the ancient social institutions came increasingly under fire, thus, people were searching for a new identity. This movement for new forms of piety emerged in the form of distinct groups "of...disillusioned yet caring persons" such as "the Pastoureaux, the Beguines and Beghards, witches, mystical sects, and toward the end of the century, the religious reformers John Wycliffe in England, and Jan Hus in Bohemia."[167] Describing the Pastoreaux Tuchman writes,

> In 1320 the misery of the rural poor in the wake of the famines burst out in a strange hysterical mass movement called the Pastoureaux, for the shepherds who started it . . . the Pastoureaux spread the fear of

---

[164] Forman, *Meister Eckhart,* 30

[165] Matthew Fox, *Breakthrough,* 11.

[166] Forman, *Meister Eckhart,* 31.

[167] Fox, *Breakthrough,* 16.

insurrection that freezes the blood of the privileged in any era when the mob appears.[168]

It is not surprising that the many of the modes of piety which were developing among these groups were mystical in character. As Forman notes, "because mysticism is a new religious form which is independent of collapsing institutions and structures, yet also provides its adherents with a convincing system of meaning and belief, it becomes one other obvious alternative."[169] The Cathari of northern Italy, the Humiliti of Lombardy, the Waldensans and Albigensians of southern France, and the Beguines and Beghards of the Rhine valley are only the best known groups of hundreds of pious associations of laypeople who voluntarily dedicated themselves to a simple life of evangelical poverty and common ownership. As one might expect, these unofficial "grass-roots" associations developed its own leadership of ecclesiastically unauthorized lay preachers and missionaries whose main goals were the mass conversions of layfolk to a devout, but uncloistered life, thus challenging the shape of a type of traditional male monasticism that had been established as the primary spiritual tenor of medieval Christendom for hundreds of years.

According to some historians, the circulation of Eckhart's sermons marked a watershed moment in this context of newly emerging piety movements. In Southern's opinion Eckhart "was the first powerful [spiritual] voice of the northern towns,"[170] It was these people who formed the audience for Eckhart's sermons, in particular the growing number of women in religious communities, especially those of the Dominicans. Because of the freshness of their content and their obvious level of mystical insight, it is not difficult to imagine how exciting Eckhart's sermons had to have been for these religious women. In his sermons Eckhart seems to have always been bringing forth something novel, articulating his message "in a language which still gives the read-

---

[168] Tuchmann, *A Distant Mirror*, 40, 42, cited by Fox, *Breakthrough*, 16.

[169] Forman, *Meister Eckhart*, 32.

[170] R. W. Southern, *Medieval Humanism and Other Studies* (Oxford: Basil Blackwell, 1970), 22.

er a curious physical sensation of power. His language has the stamp of all later German eloquence."[171] As Schurmann points out, the master's predilection for preaching as his primary literary genre was not only in keeping with his Dominican charism, but also uniquely well suited to his times. "It is not accidental," Schurmann writes, "that he was a preacher."[172] In fact, one of the reasons for the popularity of his sermons was most likely because

> [h]is preaching urges our freedom to commit itself upon a path which, from the being of provenance or from the creatures' nothingness, leads to the being of imminence or to the Godhead's nothingness. Being as coming forth is encountered first of all in the preached word itself.[173]

It is not surprising, therefore, that many of the well-educated women entering Dominican convents, attracted to "the emphasis placed on study in the Order, together with the mystical character of its spirituality at that time"[174] would be particularly drawn to Eckhart's work. Of course Eckhart was not the only Dominican preacher, nor was he the only leading preacher in the formation of the mystical revolution of the fourteenth century; by most accounts, however, Eckhart was the greatest.[175] For one thing, Eckhart is the only figure who played double roles as professional theologian and mystical preacher and writer.[176]

Since the beginning of the fourteenth century, if not before, the diversity in both religious theory and practice characterized by the search for a direct relationship with God increased. For some, this diversity was both intended and perceived as a challenge to the very *raison d'être* of the church hierarchy, with the consequences, as Gordon

---

[171] R. W. Southern, *Medieval Humanism*, 21.

[172] Reiner Schurmann, *Meister Eckhart: Mystic and Philosopher: Translation with Commentary* (hereafter abbreviated as MP) (Bloomington: Indiana University Press, 1978), 89.

[173] *MP*, 89.

[174] Richard Wood, O.P., "In The Catholic Tradition, Meister Eckhart (1260-1328) Mystic under Fire," in *Priest and People* (November, 1994), 435.

[175] Wood, "In The Catholic Tradition," 435.

[176] According to McGinn, there is still a debate on the "fundamental nature of his teaching and preaching,' whether Eckhart is a 'mystic' or as a 'philosopher theologian." See McGinn, *Mystical Thought*, 21.

Leff, says, being a "gradual rejection of the church in its visible form as the one mediator between the individual and God, which was at the center of Luther's theology and had its outcome in the loss of the church's universality."[177] But for Leff, what is so remarkable about this diversity of "responses to the same desire for spiritual renewal is that they cut across the different divisions between reformer and heretic, mystic and ecclesiastic:"[178]

> The failure of the later medieval church and its institutional forms was not in any sudden moral failing; those with which it was charged—simony, pluralism, immorality, greed, apostasy—were common to most of the Middle Ages. It was a spiritual failure to meet the demands of a new spirituality that could no longer be contained within the existing structure and was not permitted new outlets under the latter's aegis. The consequences were precisely either a turning away from the church in the propagation of extra-ecclessiastical groups and individuals devoted to their own religious experiences, or the demand for the church's own spiritualization by restoring it to its apostolic purity.[179]

In fact, this demand for a new spirituality which eventually challenged the church authority was not something new. From the later eleventh century this movement was a constant issue. The Cathars, the Waldensians, and the Albigensians are examples, "all of whom preached and practiced forms of voluntary poverty, radical obedience to their leadership and an anti-institutional spirituality."[180] But it should be noted that the nature of the challenge was not ultimately an attack on the church, but rather a withdrawal from it. The opposition to the church was secondary to the search for a new mode of spiritual life; and "it was frequently the hostility of the Church—as with the

---

[177] "The Spiritual World," in Gordon Leff, The Dissolution of the Medieval Outlook, An Essay on Intellectual and Spiritual Change in the Fourteenth Century (New York: New York University Press, 1976), 118.

[178] "The Spiritual World," in Gordon Leff, *The Dissolution*, 120.

[179] "The Spiritual World," in Gordon Leff, *The Dissolution,* 120-1.

[180] Woods, *Eckhart's Way*, 31.

Waldensians and Spiritual Franciscans—which caused such a movement to become heretical."[181]

In fourteenth-century Europe, mysticism was "the most pervasive spiritual force"[182] because it was the one form of religious experience equally open to the lay, the illiterate, and the theologically uninitiated. And it was within this framework that Eckhart's speculative mysticism became the dominant influence as it took root initially "throughout the Rhineland and the Dominican houses in Germany, and directly inspiring the new school of Rhineland mystics of whom Henry Suso, John Tauler, and John Ruysbroec were the outstanding representatives."[183] "But beyond that," Leff insists, "Eckhart indirectly helped to give a new impetus to popular and unofficial piety which extended over the greater part of the Rhineland, Low Countries, and Central Europe during the fourteenth century."[184] Thus, Eckhart was regarded as a "spiritual father of the neo-Romantic mood of anti-institutional and subjective religiosity."[185]

2. Life

Not much is known about Eckhart's early life beyond speculation. Nothing is known of this Dominican preacher, theologian and mystic's family, birth, or childhood. But with the publication of Eckhart's Latin works in 1886 by Denifle,[186] a Dominican scholar, the long controversial question concerning Eckhart's origin was settled. The book states that he was born at Hochheim, most likely near Erfurt, in Thuringia,

---

[181] Gordon Leff, "Heresy and the Decline of the Medieval Church," in *Religious Dissent in the Middle Ages*, 103.

[182] "The Spiritual World," in Gordon Leff, *The Dissolution*, 121.

[183] "The Spiritual World," in Gordon Leff, *The Dissolution*, 121-122.

[184] "The Spiritual World," in Gordon Leff, *The Dissolution*, 122.

[185] Oliver Davies, *Meister Eckhart: Mystical Theologian* (London: SPCK, 1991), 15. This statement is not totally right. What Eckhart intend is that it is not an obstacle for God to be birth in the Soul by being attached to it, as will be mentioned in chapter four in this discussion.

[186] Henrich Denifle, "Meister Eckharts Lateinische Schriften und die Grundanschauung seiner Lehre" *Archiv für Literatur und Kirchengeschichte des Mittelalters* 2 (1886), 417-615.

in central Germany, at around the year 1260 to the old noble family, von Hochheim. Following a well-established pattern, Eckhart entered the Dominican Order[187] at about the age of fifteen and became himself the most celebrated preacher of his day.

At seventeen, in 1277, he attended the college of liberal arts in Paris, and some years later he started studying theology. Eckhart followed the Dominican route typical of the best students of his time and undertook his early studies of the Arts (grammar, logic, and rhetoric) either in his native Germany or perhaps in Paris, which was the principal center of medieval academic excellence. He received most of his education in the *Studium Generale* in Cologne which Albert the Great had founded in 1248. Here, it is debatable as to whether or not he came into contact with Albertus Magnus,[188] who taught there and was the teacher of Thomas Aquinas.[189] In any case it is certain that he was in Paris as 'a reader of [Peter Lombard's] *Sentences*' in the year 1294,

---

[187] Also called "Order of Preachers" (O.P.), one of the four great mendicant orders of the Roman Catholic Church, was founded by St. in 1215. Dominic, a priest of the Spanish diocese of Osma, accompanied his bishop on a mission among the Albigensian heretics of southern France, where he founded a nunnery at Prouille in 1206, partly for his converts, which was served by a community of preachers. From this developed the conception of an institute of preachers to convert the Albigensians, which received provisional approval from Pope in 1215. Dominic gave his followers a rule of life based on that of St. and made his first settlement at Toulouse; on Dec. 22, 1216, Pope gave formal sanction. The novelty of the institute was the commission to preach Christian doctrine, a task previously regarded as the prerogative and monopoly of bishops and their delegates; a corollary was the obligation of theological study, and, as early as 1218, Dominic sent seven of his followers to the University of Paris. The Dominican order has continued to be noted for an unswerving orthodoxy, based upon the philosophical and theological teaching of Aquinas, and has steadfastly opposed novelty or accommodation in theology.

[188] Albertus Magnus is the first scholastic who reproduced the whole philosophy of Aristotle in systematic order, with constant reference to the Arabic commentators, and who remodeled it to meet the requirement of ecclesiastical dogma. Albert was acquainted with a number of Platonic and Neo-Platonic writings; all of the works of Aristotle were accessible to him in Latin translations from the Arabic, and few of them in translation from the Greek. See Friedrich Ueberweg, History of Philosophy, from Thales to Present Time (New York: Charles Scribner's Sons, 1887), 436.

[189] Richard Woods, *Eckhart's Way*, 24.

the year in which it was the main textbook of the Middle Ages that formed the basis of intermediate theological studies.[190]

Eckhart left Paris to serve as prior of the Dominican convent in Erfurt. He served there for some years and was a provincial vicar for Thuringia at the same time. From that period a large number of spiritual instructions have been kept, which, as father superior, he gave to his younger fellow brethren. They were collectively entitled the *Reden der Unterscheidung*. These were informal lectures from a conversation on religious questions with his younger Dominican confreres given in Erfurt by the young prior who had just completed his studies in Paris.[191] Unlike his later sermons which were more difficult, these talks are readily comprehensible and practical in their spiritual advice.

According to Woods, although he was a devoted Thomist, Eckhart enthusiastically absorbed the ancient mystical tradition of Christian Neoplatonism.[192] Thus, while in some respects, he was very faithful to the intellectual legacy of his Dominican brothers, Albertus Magnus and Thomas Aquinas, his dominant philosophical framework was not that of the Schoolmen's Aristotelianism, but rather that of the Neoplatonism preserved in the mystics of the Greek Church.[193]

Eckhart was forty years old when he was invited to the non-French professional chair at the theological faculty in Paris. Thus, in 1302 Eckhart left Erfurt to return to Paris, in order to take up this position,[194] an honor that his predecessor, Thomas Aquinas held. It is possible that during this period, Eckhart wrote some scriptural commentaries in Latin.[195] In Paris, Eckhart was obliged to participate in academic disputes and to elucidate the Bible. Here he was involved in

---

[190] Meister Eckhart, *Selected Writings*, ed. by Oliver Davies (Penguin Book, 1994), xi; Davies, *Mystical Theologian*, 22.

[191] Dietmar Mieth, "Meister Eckhart, The Power of Inner Liberation," *Toward a New Heaven and a New Earth*, ed. Fernando F. Segovia (New York: Maryknoll, Orbis Books, 2003), 316.

[192] Woods, "In the Catholic Tradition," 435.

[193] Thomas O'Meara, O.P., "The Presence of Meister Eckhart," in *The Thomist*, 42, number 2 (1978), 171.

[194] Davies, *Mystical Theologian*, 24.

[195] Davies, *Selected Writing*, xi

debates with the Franciscan Master Gonzalvo of Spain, who later became the General of the Franciscans.[196] Blakney asserts that "the enmity of the Franciscans for Meister Eckhart probably dates from the Paris debate."[197] In this case Eckhart says, "When I preached at Paris, I said—and I regard it well said—that with all their science, those people at Paris are not able to discern what God is in the least of creatures—not even in a fly!"[198] His so called *Quaestiones Parisienses* or *Parisian Questions* were prepared for such disputes.[199] The main thesis of this treatise is that "God's being is his understanding" (*Deus est intelligere*).[200] Even though Eckhart does not deny that understanding is a form of existence, he claims that understanding is superior to existence and belongs to a different order.[201] Creatures, according to *Parisian Questions,* receive their being from God, who himself is beyond being. For Eckhart, insofar as creatures have being, God is not, or insofar as God is, creatures are nothing. (This last statement was eventually condemned by the papal bull of John XXII entitled *In agro dominico.*

In Paris, Eckhart's position was one of theologian and philosopher (*lesemeister*), a scholar who, much in the tradition of his predecessor, Thomas Aquinas, produced both the *Quaestiones Parisienses* and the *Opus Tripartitum.* In contradistinction to both his role and constituency in Paris, in Cologne he functioned primarily as preacher and spiritual advisor (*lebemeister*), speaking primarily to the laity, religious, and semi- religious communities, and addressing all the very concrete pastoral challenges set before a spiritual guide for people in religious life.[202] While in Paris, Eckhart channeled most of his energies into constructing systematic theology, he put his trust in quite a different medium in Cologne.

---

[196] Woods, *Eckhart's Way,* 30.

[197] Blackney, *Meister Eckhart, A Modern Translation* (New York, London, Harper & Brothers, c1941), xviii.

[198] Blackney, *Meister Eckhart*, xviii.

[199] Davies, *Mystical Theologian,* 24.

[200] Mieth, "Meister Eckhart," 317.

[201] A Maurer, *Meister Eckhart, Parisian Questions and Prologues* (Toronto: Pontifical Institute of Medieval Studies, 1974), 46.

[202] Maria R. Lichtmann, "The Way of Meister Eckhart," in *Mysticism, Medieval and Modern*, ed. Valerie M. Lagorio (Lewiston: Edwin Melen Press), nd, 89-90.

Here he embraced the genre of the vernacular sermon which he had mastered in his youth (and continued to perfect in Latin in Paris). Unlike the theological treatise, the sermon maintains the original pastoral situation of a discourse between preacher and audience, thus maintaining a certain tone of intimacy which the treatise lacks.[203]

Eckhart's career also found him in administrative positions in the Dominican order. It was really an honor when, in 1303, he was elected as the first "Provincial" of the Saxony province.[204] In the intervening period (1303-11) Meister Eckhart was provincial of the extensive German Dominican province of Teutonia. Thus, it seems that Eckhart here is successful with his administrative and regular duties. But his visits to the numerous monasteries, negotiation about the material situation of communities, conflicts with clerical and secular authorities with respect to the founding of new monasteries, and the many long journeys ensuing from this kind of work, all made it nearly impossible for Eckhart to write books during this period of time. A few sermons though have been preserved.

In 1307 Eckhart became the vicar general of the Bohemian province. Around this time he composed the *Book of Divine Comfort* for the widowed Queen Agnes of Hungary. It was this work from which his accusers would later draw heavily in their accusations of heresy. In 1310, the master was elected to Provincial of Teutonia, but the election was not confirmed, and he was sent again to Paris, where he had a chance to organize his scholarly writings.[205]

In 1313 Meister Eckhart was sent to Strassbourg, a center of great religious activity and mystical ideas, as vicar for the Dominican Master general, and to him was entrusted the spiritual care of the South-German sister convents along the Rhine, from Cologne to as far as Switzerland. Eckhart did this work for ten years[206] The majority of his German sermons came into existence in this period, as well as the influential writing '*Liber benedictus*', consisting of two parts which were dedi-

---

[203] Maria R. Lichtmann, "The Way of Meister Eckhart," 93.

[204] Woods, *Eckhart's Way*, 36.

[205] Mieth, "Meister Eckhart," 317.

[206] Mieth, "Meister Eckhart," 317.

cated to Agnes, Queen of Hungary.[207] This work came in two major sections: the very speculative brochure *Das Buch der Gottlichen Trostung'* (*The Book of Divine Consolation*) and the sermon *Von Edlen Menschen* (*On the Noble Man*). It is very possible that the so-called *Opus Tripartitum* dates back to this period as well. In the *Opus*, at the explicit request of his fellow brethren, Eckhart wishes to expound his spiritual teaching in a systematic way. According to O'Meara, it was in Eckhart and his work at Strassbourg that "German mysticism reached the culminating point of its development."[208]

Eckhart's sermons had an enormously liberating impact on his audience. According to Mieth, Eckhart had "an excellent reputation among the women during this time," and was "as modest as well as capable of listening and learning."[209] In fact it is his involvement with the pastoral problems that eventually led to his condemnation and accusations of heresy.

Meister Eckhart was charged by the pope with the task of preaching to the religious orders of women in the thirteenth century who did not receive formal theological training like their fellow men and could not read Latin. In doing his job, Eckhart combined the knowledge he received in his formal education with the elements of experiences in daily life among the Beguines to whom he preached. Eckhart transformed himself from the old reserved professor of the chair at that university where he used to teach, into the preacher of the pulpit and altar, thus becoming exposed to the living word of the people's language. According Meith, Eckhart's "innovative use of German language together with his thoughts, is an exceptionally challenging and profound topic."[210] In fact, Soudek asserts, "his extant sermons in Middle

---

[207] Davies, *Mystical Theologian*, 26.

[208] Thomas F. O'Meara, "The Presence of Meister Eckhart," 175.

[209] Mieth, "Meister Eckhart," 319.

[210] Mieth, "Meister Eckhart," 320. Cf. Gerald Hanratty, *Studies in Gnosticism and in the Philosophy of Religion* (Ireland and Oregon: Four Courts Press, 1997), 54.

High German are powerful monuments to a high flying poetic spirit and linguistic genius."[211]

Around the age of sixty, Eckhart was called back to the college at Cologne to the post of a professorship, a position once held by Albertus Magnus. In 1323-1326 he was in charge of the Dominican *Studium Generale* at Cologne. Thus, again a shift to academic activity."[212] During this time, the campaigns against him began that led, in 1326, to the opening of an inquisitional proceeding. His assistant was Nicholas of Strasburg, who was a papal visitor for the province of Teutonia in 1325. Thus Nicholas was Eckhart's superior and yet as assistant was his inferior. In this odd dual capacity, Nicholas initiated an investigation into the orthodoxy of his colleague's writings, and he concluded these legal proceedings with an acquittal.[213]

On January fourteenth 1327, Eckhart was required to answer the charges in Cologne. In fact, the archbishop was not appeased by this preliminary action of Nicholas, and the process went slowly without result. Eckhart, then, appealed personally to the pope in Rome. On February 13th 1327, he issued a statement to the effect that if erroneous statements were found in his writings or sermons, he would retract them.[214]

> He denied that he had ever taught that his little finger had created all things, saying that he had meant by this the little finger of the child of Jesus. He denied that he had taught that there was an 'uncreated something' in the soul, but stressed that if the human soul were all intellect according to its essence, then it could be said of it that it is uncreated.[215]

On February twenty second he was officially notified that his appeal to Rome had been denied, thus, as Mieth writes, "the resolution of this conflict, a compromise, was not found."[216] In 1328 the Archbishop

---

[211] Ernst H. Soudek, "Meister Eckhart," *Dictionary of the Middle Ages*, Joseph R. Strayer, ed. in chief, Vol. 4 (New York: Charles Scribner's Sons, 1982-89), 380.

[212] Mieth, "Meister Eckhart," 319; cf. Davies, *Mystical Theologian*, 26.

[213] Mieth, "Meister Eckhart," 322.

[214] Cf. Mieth, "Meister Eckhart," 323.

[215] Davies, *Mystical Theologian*, 28-9.

[216] Mieth, "Meister Eckhart," 323.

urged the Pope to decide Eckhart's case. Finally the bull *In agro domini-co* was issued on March twenty-seventh 1329, sometime shortly after Eckhart's death, and was promulgated in the region of Cologne, in which twenty-eight of Eckhart's articles were listed. The first fifteen were declared "heretical" and the remaining eleven termed "evil sounding and suspect of heresy."[217] A further two articles he was said to have preached were condemned.

Eckhart was not declared a heretic[218] but a man who "wished to know more than he should,"[219] as the bull said, and who for this reason, was "led astray by that Father of Lies" (i.e., Satan) and "sowed thorns and obstacle" in the field of the church.[220] According to the bull he was said to have "revoked" everything "insofar they could generate in the minds of faithful a heretical opinion, or one erroneous and hostile to the true faith."[221] Thus, not long after his death in the late 1320s, the master was both censured for potentially scandalous teachings and yet at the same time exonerated as a faithful son of the church.

3. Legacy

"[As] in his own day," says McGinn, "so too in ours, Eckhart remains difficult and controversial."[222] The nature of Eckhart's subjects and his daring language were calculated to cause him to be misunderstood. In fact, Eckhart was accused as a pantheist for his teaching on mystical union, where he says that the true union "must go beyond the mere uniting of two substances that remain potentially separable in order to attain total indistinction and substantial, or essential, identity."[223] Eck-

---

[217] The Bull "In agro dominico," *Meister Eckhart: The Essential Sermons, Commentaries, Treatises and Defense* (hereafter abbreviated as ESC), eds., Edmund Colledge and Bernard McGinn (New York: Paulist Press, 1981), 80.

[218] He said in his defense, ". . . I am not accused of heresy." See "Selection from Eckhart's Defense," *ESC*, 71.

[219] The Bull "In agro dominico," *ESC*, 77.

[220] The Bull "In agro dominico," *ESC*, 77.

[221] The Bull "In agro dominico," *ESC*, 81.

[222] *ESC*, xvii.

[223] Bernard McGinn, *The Mystical Thought of Meister Eckhart, The Man from Whom God Hid Nothing* (New York: The Crossroad Publishing Company, 2001), 148.

hart says, "God is indistinct and the soul loves to be indistinguished, that is, to be and become one with God."[224] But the general theme of his teaching and the broader context of his life as a faithful Dominican show that he was not a pantheist. Indeed, for anyone familiar with Eckhart's worldview as a whole, it is inconceivable to regard him as having held pantheistic beliefs. When such charges are leveled at the master, they usually proceed by taking certain passages entirely out of the context of his broader theological framework.

Eckhart expressed himself both in learned Latin for the clergy in his tractates, and more famously in the German vernacular in many of his sermons. Because, as he said in the defense he gave at his trial, that his sermons were meant to inspire in listeners (and also his readers) the desire above all to do some good, he frequently used exaggerated language or seemed to stray from a literal expression of orthodoxy. His unusual and new teachings made him suspicious in the eyes of some church intellectuals and hierarchs who took advantage of the novel character of his teachings and used them as a basis for a heresy trial in the final years of his life. The master died before a verdict was reached, but according to *In agro dominico*, he did not actually recant his teachings in any absolute sense, but rather only insofar as they may be misunderstood and lead the faithful astray. The bull closes by emphasizing that Eckhart "professed the Catholic faith at the end of his life."[225]

During the Middle Ages, Meister Eckhart's trial and conviction was "the most powerful"[226] and the only one involving such a respected theologian, who was at the center of Dominican intellectual and spiritual life. Many historians have speculated as to the origins of the process that resulted in *In agro dominico*. Some people suggest that the scholarly controversy between Thomism and Scotism, and thus between Dominicans and Franciscans respectively might have played a part. According to Koch, "Eckhart was 'sacrificed' in order to placate the Franciscans and to compensate them for the canonization of

---

[224] McGinn, *The Mystical Thought*, 146.

[225] Meister Eckhart, *ESC*, 81.

[226] McGinn, The Mystical Thought, 20.

Thomas Aquinas."[227] They point out that the committee of inquisitors
in Cologne predominantly consisted of Franciscans, and that prominent Franciscans like Willem Ockham and Michael of Cesena had
urgently pressed for Eckhart's conviction.[228] They also testified that
the Beghards and the Brethren of the Free Spirit quoted Meister Eckhart's doctrine as authoritative.[229] Others, like Kurt Ruh have "suggested that it was a result of the fact that much of Eckhart's teaching
was in vernacular, and thus might potentially exercise far greater influence among the masses."[230] It was possible that his daring language
and uncompromising views caused confusion here and there or con-
solidated already existing bewilderment. Tauler, Eckhart's student
says, "He spoke of eternity, but you understood him in a temporary
sense."[231] Thus, as Fox asserts, "his inquisitors, the literalists of yester-
day as well as the rationalists of today, will not be able to hear his
music, eager as they are to judge and not to listen."[232]

Other speculation on the church's harsh response to Eckhart was
his affinity for the Beguines and their spirituality. The accusation
against the Beguines and Beghards for their assertion that the annihilated soul is "no longer under an obligation to the virtues," was also "a
topos of contemplative experience which can also be found in Meister
Eckhart who also asserted that the perfect soul or the just person has

---

[227] J. Koch, *Kleine Schriften* I, Rome, 1973, p. 321, n. 195, quoted by Davies, *Mystical Theologian*, p. 44. Although according to Davies, this opinion is difficult to sustain. Cf. O. Karrer and H. Piesch, *Meister Eckharts Rechfertigungsschrift vom Jahre 1326, Einleitung, Uebersetzung und Anmerkungen, Ehrfurt*, 1927; also J. Ancelet-Hustache, Maitre Eckhart et la Mystique rhenane, Paris, 1956, translated: Eckhart en de Mystiek van zijn tijd, Untrech –Antwerprn, 1961.

[228] See, Davies, *Mystical Theologian*, 45.

[229] Wolfgang Wackernagel, "Two Thousand Years of Heresy: An Essay," *Diogenes* (International Council for Philosophy and Humanistic Studies, 1999), no. 187, 138-48.

[230] K. Ruh, *Meister Eckhart: Theologe, Prediger, Mystiker* (Munich, 1985), 173, cited by Davies, *Mystical Theologian*, 44.

[231] Johannes Tauler, *Predigten* Bd. I., Uebertragen und herausgegeben von Georg Hofmann, Einfuehrung von Alois M. Haas (Einsideln, 1979), 103.

[232] Fox, *Breakthrough*, 15.

all virtues in its status of being."[233] Eckhart himself would have been "horrified" at the idea of himself as a heretic. Yet, Blakney mentions that Eckhart was a heretic, in so much as he was "one dangerous to the Church as an institution." It is "paradoxical" that for Eckhart, "... his own inner certainty was more sacred to him than any outward symbol of religion."[234] Nevertheless, and regardless of the many different ways in which he has since been interpreted, Eckhart remained a devout orthodox Dominican, even if many of his fellow Catholics were unable to admit to the truth of what he was saying. Most recently, the late Pope John Paul II has quoted the master approvingly, suggesting that his legacy should be viewed as orthodox.[235]

That Meister Eckhart was one of the greatest medieval mystics of Latin Christendom is nearly undisputed. In the words of one of the twentieth and twenty-first centuries foremost experts on Eckhart, Bernard McGinn, Eckhart was "the most profound and influential, as well as the most controversial late medieval mystic author."[236] The fact that he was a renowned Dominican theologian and popular preacher, whose order was primarily entrusted with guarding doctrinal orthodoxy, provides a reasonable basis for suspecting that the charges of heresy against him had as much to do with his order's centrality and his popularity as it did with his actual teachings. This is why there has been much debate over whether the trial was justified. Winfried Trusen has proposed that the trial was "invalid since the instigators had been shown to be wholly disreputable."[237] According to Trusen "it started because of the malice of the two petty-minded and vindictive Dominicans and went forward until the promulgation of *In agro dominico* because of the logic of the legalities and the dictates of eccle-

---

[233] Mieth, "Meister Eckhart," 324. Cf. K. Ruh, 168-187, especially 173.

[234] *Meister Eckhart, A Modern Translation*, xxiv.

[235] McGinn, *The Mystical Thought of Meister Eckhart*, 20.

[236] McGinn, "The God beyond God: Theology and Mysticism in the Thought of Meister Eckhart," *The Journal of Religion*, Vol. 61, No. I (January 1981), 2.

[237] *Der Prozess gegen Meister Eckhart, Paderborn* (Schoningh, 1988), cited by Oliver Davies, *Mystical Theologian*, 31.

siastical politics."[238] In fact, in the medieval spiritual tradition, the line between heresy and orthodoxy could be exceedingly fine.

Apparently there were many reasons why Eckhart's twenty-eight propositions were condemned – some of them political, some historical, some personal. Some believe that the origin of his condemnation was completely political, a patent conspiracy by rival Cologne Franciscans, who initiated the process against Eckhart in 1326. One view even holds, as mentioned, that Eckhart's condemnation was a papal effort to appease Franciscans angered by the canonization of Thomas Aquinas and other favors bestowed on the Dominicans.[239]

According to McGinn, though Archbishop Henry could have been an enemy of the Dominicans, "there is little direct evidence for this," [240] though it is certain that he had repugnance of heresy. Two Dominican figures, Hermann de Summo and William de Nidecke, did play an unpleasant role in Eckhart's Cologne trial. "Neither of these two colorful personalities," says Davies, "seems to have enjoyed the respect of their brethren." [241] Gerard of Podahns, The Dominican Procurator General, blamed them for attacking Eckhart in order to free themselves from order discipline.[242] In fact, Henry used those two men, even sent Hermann to Avignon in the position of his ambassador in the Eckhart matter, thus, it, says McGinn "does cast suspicion on the purity of his motives, but is not in itself proof of a cabal."[243] Nevertheless, a keynote of Henry's reign is his abhorrence of heresy, as mentioned, thus, Davies insists, as soon as he took office in 1306,

---

[238] Robert E. Lerner, "New Evidence for the Condemnation of Meister Eckhart," *Speculum*, 72 (1997), 362. See also, Oliver Davies, *Mystical Theologian*, 32-3.

[239] See Otto Karrer, *Meister Eckharts Rechfertingungsschrift vom Jahre 1326* (Erfurt, 1927), 19, cited by Stevent Ozment, *The Age of Reform 1250-1550, An Intellectual And Religious History of Late Medieval And Reformation Europe* (New Heaven and London: Yale University Press, 1980), 133.

[240] McGinn, "Eckhart's Condemnation Reconsidered," *The Thomist, A Speculative Quarterly Review*, Vol. 44 (Washington D. C: The Thomist Press, 1980), 392.

[241] Davies, *Mystical Theologian*, 28.

[242] J. Koch, *Kleine Schriften* I (Rome, 1973), 328f. , quoted by Davies, *Meister Eckhart, Mystical Theologian*, 28; see also, McGinn, "Eckhart's Condemnation Reconsidered," 392..

[243] McGinn, "Eckhart's Condemnation Reconsidered," 393.

he addresses himself vigorously to the question of the so called the Beguines and the Beghards, spiritual groups who lived a life according to Christian spirituality but did not stick to a formal religious rule.[244] In addition, according to McGinn, although the three inquisitors the Archbishop appointed consist of Franciscans (Peter of Estate and Albert of Milan), there is nothing obvious to prove that the process leading to Eckhart's condemnation springs from the hostility between Franciscans and Dominicans.[245] As mentioned, Henry of Virneburg was well known as a zealous hunter of heretics, and it is therefore reasonable to believe Joseph Koch who insists that the criticism and protest that emerge and that became so intense from many sides as calls to question Eckhart's orthodoxy which motivated Henry the Archbishop to begin his inquiry.[246]

Some believe that the reason Eckhart was put on trial was because of the ambiguous and incautious phrasing found in the master's vernacular sermons, which was not present in his scholarly Latin writings. Almost all of Eckhart's defenders, however, see him as a profound esoteric thinker who was taken too literally by contemporaries incapable of grasping his thought.

In addition, the time in which Eckhart lived played a major role in his condemnation. It was, as we discussed in the opening section of this chapter, a period of great change and tumult in which no one was immune to attack from either supposed "friends" or supposed "foes." Similar mystical themes, though in less sophisticated formulations, had been set forth earlier by Beguines, for example. They were condemned by the Council of Vienne. Pope John XXII, who would later censure Eckhart, condemned the Spiritual Franciscans, and on the eve of Eckhart's condemnation Pope John also condemned Marsilius of Padua.[247]

---

[244] Oliver Davies, *Mystical Theologian*, 35.

[245] McGinn, "Eckhart's Condemnation Reconsidered," 393.

[246] McGinn, "Eckhart's Condemnation Reconsidered," 393.

[247] Marsilius Padua was trained in medicine, not in theology. His fundamental notion was that all coercive power on earth lay with "the people"; the people, as "human legislator," were the source of all worldly authority. It was not the "head bishop" in Rome, but the people who were judge by none save God; the people were lower than God but greater than man. See Steven Ozment, *The Age of Reform* , 150-1.

What made matters worse for the master was the fact that he had a commitment to social justice, as well as a commitment to preach to the "uneducated"—a commitment that was used against him at his trial, and to which he responded: "[I]f one does not speak to the uneducated about learned things, no one would ever become educated."[248]

As we have seen, the Later Middle Ages was not a time of tolerance; there was even a great fear of antinomian heresy that was often unjustified by actual circumstances. Thus, when what the so called "heresy" was on the increase elsewhere, the medieval church preferred to respond to them by applying repressive actions, such as fire and sword, inquisition and condemnation. By doing so, in fact, the papacy seems to have acknowledged its incapacity to direct the new religious movement peacefully into channels that served the medieval church and society. And as we witnessed, the later thirteenth and fourteenth centuries were disturbed by a series of condemnations. Thus it is the "special failure of the later medieval church in the absence of a countervailing spirituality," Leff said.[249]

The foundation Eckhart made for his defense lies in the distinction between heresy and error. Thus Eckhart says, "the first mistake they make is that they think that everything they do not understand is an error and that every error is a heresy."[250] Furthermore, he claims that "I can be in error, but I cannot be a heretic, because the first belongs to the intellect, the second to the will,"[251] and "only obstinate adherence to error makes heresy and a heretic."[252] Eckhart continued to maintain that the trial against him as heretic were "unjustified" because he said that he is ready to relinquish publicly anything found erroneous in his writing or preaching. Thus, it can be said that Eckhart was only defending him-

---

[248] The conclusion of the defense.

[249] Leff, *Heresy in the Later Middle Ages*, I: 29-30; Leff, *The Dissolution of the Medieval Outlook: An Essay on Intellectual and Spiritual Change in the Fourteenth Century* (New York, 1976), 120.

[250] Eckhart's Defense, "Conclusion 1," *ESC*, 75.

[251] Eckhart's Defense, "Introduction," *ESC*, 72.

[252] Eckhart's Defense, "Conclusion 1," *ESC*, 75.

self against the possibility of theological error. This can be seen in the term he used, i. e., "*erronea vel falsa*" not "*heretica*."[253]

In defending himself against the accusation of heresy, Eckhart also mentioned that the envious attack on him was actually like the attack against Thomas Aquinas in the condemnation of 1277, but it is also Thomas's exoneration by the canonization of 1323 which encouraged Eckhart to defend himself. In fact, McGinn asserts that Eckhart "appeals explicitly to Thomas eight times, and there are a number of other points where he defends positions which may be described as broadly or narrowly Thomistic," and by citing the *auctoritates*, McGinn continues, "Eckhart wanted to show that he was going to teach the same doctrine that they had taught."[254]

As mentioned above, on March twenty-seventh, 1329, the papal bull *In agro dominico* condemned fifteen articles taken out from Eckhart's works as *haereticos*, and eleven of them as *male sonates, temerarious, et suspectas de haeresi* (evil sounding and suspect of heresy)[255] The bull states that Eckhart "presented many things as dogma that were designed to cloud the true faith in the hearts of many, things which he put forth especially before the uneducated crowd in his sermons and that he also admitted into his writings."[256] Although the pope absolved Eckhart of conscious heresy, nonetheless, as McGinn notes, the pope did engage "in a *damnatio memoriae* of the deceased Dominican in the bull's preface."[257]

Historically, Eckhart lived and preached at a time when popular religious movements and royal aggression had successfully challenged the authority of the papacy. It is true that the condemnation of several of his sermons was due in part to the similarities they bore to certain previously condemned spiritual teachings. It is no less true, however,

---

[253] McGinn, "Eckhart's Condemnation Reconsidered," 400.

[254] McGinn, "Eckhart's Condemnation Reconsidered," 405.

[255] See McGinn, "'Evil-Sounding, Rash, and Suspect of Heresy': Tensions between Mysticism and Magisterium in the History of the Church," *The Catholic Historical Review*, VOL. XC, No. 2 (April, 2004).

[256] *ESC*, 77.

[257] McGinn, "Evil-Sounding, " 193.

that in times when significant challenges to the authority of established doctrine are emerging, mysticism is often perceived as more a part of the "problem" than any solution. Bernard McGinn believes that such tensions between mysticism and magisterium are "not merely accidental, the result of the bad will of heretics or the mistakes and incomprehension of authority figures, but that they are also partly the result of inherent issues in the relation of mysticism and magisterium in the history of Christianity."[258]

Long before Eckhart, other mystics had been condemned for advocating heretical mysticism. Berengar of Landora, Eckhart's colleague at the Dominican convent at Paris, was one of the theologians given the responsibility of examining Marguerite Porete's *The Mirror of Simple Souls*[259] which was eventually condemned. In fact, there are many speculations as to the reasons behind the condemnation of many mystics including Meister Eckhart, or the clashes between mysticism and church teaching in general. Some opine that declaring that mysticism has a direct and personal experience of God free of the constraints of ecclesiastical structures and mediations is a potential reason for so much tension between the church and mystical piety.[260] Steven E. Ozment, for example says, "Medieval mysticism was a refined challenge, always in theory if not in daily practice, to the regular, normative way of religious salvation."[261] And Don Cupitt argues that "mysticism's fundamental attraction to the postmodern mentality is its subversive character. It has always been a protest against dogmatic theology and more often than not it also served as a female critique of

---

[258] McGinn, "Evil-Sounding," 194.

[259] She was not a trained theologian nor did she belong to an established, papally supported order. She was "burned at stake in the Place de Greve in Paris as relapsed heretic," see Bernard McGinn, "Evil-Sounding," 195, see also McGinn, *The Flowering of Mysticism, Men and Women in New Mysticism (1200-1350)* (New York: 1998), 244-265.

[260] McGinn, "Evil-Sounding," 200.

[261] Steven E. Ozment *Mysticism and Dissent: Religious Ideology and Social Protest in the Sixteenth Century* (New Haven, 1973), 1, cited by McGinn, "Evil-Sounding," 200.

male dominated religion." [262] According to Cupitt, in other words, "mysticism is what saves us from religion." [263]

In light of the many condemnations mentioned above as indicative of the almost inherently "heretical" nature of mysticism, what Ozment, Don Cupitt, and others said could be true. But according to McGinn, while there are indeed certain built-in tensions between mysticism and magisterium, the theory that there will be an *inevitable* conflict between mysticism and organized religion cannot be supported by the historical record. McGinn points out that in the history of Christian spirituality there are abundant examples of mystical figures who were relatively non-controversial and who were, in their own day and long after their deaths understood to be champions of orthodoxy. Here McGinn is referring to the likes of Ambrose, Augustine, Gregory of Nyssa, Gregory the Great, Bernard, Bonaventure, Catherine of Siena, Gerson, Nicholas of Cusa, Ignatius Loyola, Theresa of Avila, and Theresa of Lisieux. [264] For him, the root of the conflict between mysticism and institution lies in "the mechanisms of control" in any given socio-historical context. In other words, one of the things that made Eckhart's mysticism controversial was the fact that there were significant tectonic shifts in the mechanisms of social control of his day and that—whether Eckhart liked it or not—he was at the epicenter of some of the tremors and quakes occurring as a part of this process.

Another highly contextual reason why Eckhart's teachings were controversial was because of the "social aspects of the new mysticism that emerged around 1200." [265] On the social aspect of new mysticism, some modern scholars refer to a "democratization" and "laicization" of mystical experience in the Middle Ages as a result of the pervasive lay interest in religious life and the egalitarianism that pervaded both orthodox and heterodox movements. Nevertheless, according to

---

[262] Don Cupitt, *Mysticism after Modernity* (Oxford, 1998), especially chapters 9 and 10, cited by McGinn, Evil Sounding, 200.

[263] Don Cupitt, *Mysticism*, cited by McGinn, "Evil Sounding," 200.

[264] McGinn, "Evil Sounding," 200.

[265] McGinn, "Evil Sounding," 209, on the new mysticism, see McGinn, *The Flowering of Mysticism*, 12-30.

McGinn, "although these aspects of the new mysticism would seem to counteract the suspicion of esotericism inherent in earlier magisterial attitudes toward mysticism, they actually fomented these fears because they were seen as allowing dangerous ideas wider dissemination among strata of society that, unlike enclosed religious, were less subject to everyday supervision."[266] It can be said then, that as far as mysticism remains only among monastic elites, it never makes trouble, but as soon as it went outside into and motivated the "uneducated crowd," the trouble begins as "it became automatically more dangerous to the guardians of orthodoxy."[267]

As important as these contextual issues are for understanding Eckhart's condemnation and legacy, let us now turn for a moment to the content of his teaching that was considered most suspect and objectionable.

One of the areas that led to Eckhart's condemnation was his concept of God's being, which his detractors took as a declaration that the world is coeternal with God. Eckhart says, "[I]n the one and the same time in which he was God and in which he begot his coeternal Son as God equal to himself in all things, he also created the world."[268] Here he was accused of saying that "the world has existed from eternity," which is contained in the second of Eckhart's condemned propositions.[269] In defending his statement, Eckhart mentions that it is the height of ignorance and stupidity that his accusers could not grasp this simple point. He says, "[I]f God exists in the eternal now and yet does not create in that eternal now, then there must be a second eternal now in which he creates."[270]

In his *Commentary on Genesis 7* Eckhart states: "So, when someone once asked me why God had not created the world earlier, I answered that he could not because he did not exist."[271] In fact, Eckhart seems

---

[266] McGinn, "Evil-Sounding," 209.

[267] McGinn, "Evil-Sounding," 209.

[268] "Commentary on Genesis 7," *ESC*, 85.

[269] "In agro dominico," *ESC*, 78.

[270] Eckhart's Defense, "Conclusion 5," *ESC*, 75.

[271] *ESC*, 85.

to place the creation of the world and the generation of the Second Person of the Trinity in the same time when he says: "In the one and the same time in which he was God and in which he begot his coeternal Son as God equal to himself in all things, he also created the world."[272] Thus Eckhart's detractors conclude that he is arguing that the "world has existed from eternity." To this, Eckhart responds with the following clarification: "How could he have created earlier when he had already created the world in the very now in which he was God? It is false to picture God as if he were waiting around for some future moment in which to create the world."[273] So, for Eckhart, God exists in the eternal now, there is no time, nor is there before or after. All that God does, he does in this eternal moment. Eckhart states that God "gives and works only from eternity" and adds "it must be said that he who denies this knows little."[274]

Thus, for Eckhart the world was created and exists within God's eternity. For him if God exists in the eternal now, yet does not create in that eternal now, then there must be a second eternal now in which he creates. Furthermore, Eckhart says that, "It does not follow from this that if God created the word from eternity, the world *is* therefore from eternity, as the uneducated think. For creation is not an eternal state, just as the thing created is not eternal."[275] Thus the world is finite, but its finitude is rooted in the infinity of God.

Along these lines, Eckhart and those influenced by the master have been accused of identifying themselves with God to the extent that they believed, as part of their interpretation of *unio mystica*, that their actions were really God's action. Here, the differences between Eckhart's understanding of *unio mystica* and traditional understandings of the concept come to the fore. For Eckhart, *unio mystica* is something more than simply becoming like God by conforming one's mind and will to His. *Unio mystica*, according to Eckhart, is a matter of becoming God again, of returning to the undifferentiated Godhead. Eckhart writes: "I am so

---

[272] *ESC*, 85.

[273] *ESC*, 85.

[274] From His Defense, *ESC*, 75.

[275] *ESC*, 75.

changed into him that he produces his being in me as one, not just similar."[276] It is important to note that Eckhart always refers to the pre-existent oneness of the Godhead as the paradigm for his understanding of the essence of the divine-human relationship. In this regard, Eckhart's conception of man's eternal birth and preexistence in God plays a defining role in his mystical teaching. Eckhart says, "Since the Father gives birth to the Son in eternity, and since there can be no temporal dimension in God, He is always giving birth to the Son."[277] In one of his sermons, Eckhart more explicitly relates *unio mystica* to preexistence in eternity. He writes:

> A great authority says that his breakthrough [*durchbrechen*] to God is nobler than his flowing out. When I flowed from God, all things said: "God is." And this cannot make me blessed, for with this I acknowledge that I am a creature. But in the breakthrough, when I come to be free of will of myself and of God's will and of all his works and of God himself, then I am above all created things, and I am neither God nor creature, but I am what I was and what I shall remain, now and eternally. . . , for in this breaking-through I receive that God and I are one.[278]

It is a matter of historical fact that the master did not live to read the final bull issued with respect to his case. It is also a matter of historical record that the bull never completely eliminated the impact of his teaching. In fact, Eckhart is credited with being one of the fathers of German theological language—a legacy to which Pope Benedict XVI is obviously beholden. He preached and wrote in the midst of a society that was undergoing a remarkable outpouring of interest in new forms of religious life and new styles of religious experience. As mentioned above, during this period, the Dominican order to which

---

[276] *ESC*, 188.

[277] *ESC*, 51, cf. DW 1: 32. 6-9, Meister Eckhart, Meister Eckhart, *Sermons and Treatises*, (hereafter abbreviated as ST), Vol. III, translated and edited by M.O'C. Walshe (Shaftesbury, Dorset: Element Books, 1987), 187, also McGinn, *The Mystical Thought*, 141.

[278] *ESC*, 203, *Deutsche Mystiker des 14 Jahrhunderts: Meister Eckhart*, ed. Franz Pfeiffer (Leipzig, 1857), 2: 184, I: 11-22, DW 2: 504. 6-505.1, also (with rather different formulation) DW 2: 31-32, McGinn, *Mystical Thought*, 143.

Eckhart belonged had experienced a remarkable period of growth (especially in its houses of religious women) which laid the foundation for the vitality of the order well into the future.

In the context of this vitality, a movement emerged to request an official reconsideration of the 1329 condemnation of excerpts from Meister Eckhart's writings. As recently as 1992, for example, there was a report at the General Chapter of the Dominican Order held in Mexico City, of a panel of "expert scholars commissioned twelve years before by the Chapter of Walberberg to review the papal condemnation with an eye to exonerating Eckhart."[279] Later, the Eckhart Society led by Ursula King, requested that the then Cardinal Joseph Ratzinger who was in charge of the Congregation for the Doctrine of the Faith reconsider the bull of condemnation and declare Eckhart's doctrine as authentically orthodox Christian. But for Woods, "whether or not Vatican authorities 'rehabilitate' him, as happened recently in the case of Galileo Galilei, Eckhart remains the Master."[280] The same is true for McGinn and some other of Eckhart's readers, that the proposed request is not essential. Of course such a recognition would have little impact on the very important question of whether Protestant churches can or might find value in looking upon Eckhart as an authentic expositor of Christian mystical experience and teaching.

The effect of the condemnation is that there are still those who may object to a consideration of Eckhart's teaching as perfectly consonant with mainstream Christianity. Such objections, however, do not change the fact that Eckhart's legacy is a strong one. We can still find Eckhart's influence on both his students Henry Suso and John Tauler, and other mystics, such as Nicholas of Cusa, Jacob Bohme, Thomas Müntzer, the anonymous author of *The Cloud of Unknowing*, Julian Norwich, and one of the leader of the Reformation, Martin Luther himself. There is also no denying that he has influenced and been appropriated by secular thinkers such as Marx, Jung, Heidegger, Fromm, Hegel, and Fichte, among others. Jung for example writes,

---

[279] Woods, "In the Catholic Tradition," 433.
[280] Woods, "In the Catholic Tradition," 433.

> The art of letting things happen, action through non action, letting
> go of oneself, as taught by Meister Eckhart, became for me the key
> opening the door to the way. We must be able to let things happen
> in the psyche. For us, this actually is an art of which few people
> know anything. Consciousness is forever interfering. . . [281]

The papal condemnation of Eckhart's teaching may cast a shadow
on Eckhart's reputation, but the depth and breadth of Eckhart's teaching has drawn seekers of truth, Christian and non-Christian alike, in
their journeys. Eckhart's thorough and insightful ideas makes him a
natural point of reference for a genuinely interfaith and intra-faith
understanding, as this book is trying to expose. Six hundred years after
his death Eckhart's legacy was so strong that it was perverted to support Nazi propaganda, which twisted his image into that of a founder
of its absurd Aryan supremacist ethos. However, for many of his contemporaries he was above all a great spiritual guide, and a growing
number of people today are discovering that he can be a spiritual guide
for them too. D. T. Suzuki and S. Ueda, for example, found deep
similarities between Eckhart's and Zen Buddhism.[282] Today, one may
say that Eckhart is one of the most powerful influences on the cutting
edge of Christian mysticism and one of the key links between Eastern
and Western insights on the subject of human consciousness.

One of the most powerful dimensions of the master's legacy is his
attempt to make his theology and his mystical understanding of God
available to the masses, and in particular to specific groups of women
such as the Beguines. Here it seems that Eckhart's significant concern
is to democratize mysticism. This can be seen also in his preaching

---

[281] C. G. Jung, Commentary to Richard Wilhelm's translation and explanation of The
Secret of the Golden Flower (New York: Harcout Brace Jovanovic, 1962), 93, cited by
Fox, *Breakthrough*, 3.

[282] See D. T. Suzuki, Mysticism, Christian and Buddhist (New York: Harper, 1957),
Ueda Shizuteru, Die Gottesgeburt in der Seele und der Durchbruch zur Gott: Die
mystische Anthropologie Meister Eckharts und ihre Konfrontation mit der Mystik
der Zen-Buddhismus, Gutersloh: Mohn, 1965; also Ueda Shizuteru, "'Nothingness'
in Meister Eckhart and Zen Buddhism," in The Buddha Eye, an anthology of the
Kyoto School, edited by Frederick Franck (New York: Crossroad, 1982).

where he used the vernacular language, in addition to Latin, then communicating with his lay women/men audiences. McGinn explains:

> Eckhart preached the possibility of a radical new awareness of God, in rich and often difficult terms, not to the clerical elite of the schools, but to women and men of every walk of life. Finding one's ground in the depth of the Godhead did not require adopting traditional religious ways of life, especially not one that involved fleeing from the world.[283]

One might say that Eckhart's use of the vernacular was a subversive act.[284] This would certainly be a dominant perspective within the Roman church after the great Reformation whose leaders (such as Luther and Calvin—to name but a few) saw the use of the vernacular to be critical to authentic evangelization. Since the time of the Second Vatican Council and its "call to universal holiness,"[285] however, Eckhart's spiritually "democratic" impulse has become a cornerstone of Roman Catholic teaching on spirituality.

In concluding this summary of Eckhart's historical context, life, and legacy, I must object to the contention of Woods and McGinn that an official Vatican exoneration of Eckhart is neither relevant (Woods) nor necessary (McGinn). Such a move would be very relevant, and at the very least extremely helpful in any attempt to what this book proposes: to place the teachings of Meister Eckhart in conversation with those of Ibn al-'Arabi in order to develop new resources for contemporary Christians and Muslims seeking to mine their authentic traditions in order to address some of the burning theological issues of our own day, specifically those related to religious diversity and interfaith dialogue.

---

[283] *Meister Eckhart and the Beguines: Hadewijch of Brabant, Mechthild of Magdeburg, and Marguerite Porete*, edited by Bernard McGinn (New York: Continuum, 1994), 8-9.

[284] Matthew Fox and Soelle may have shared this feeling.

[285] See *Lumen Gentium*, ch. 5, secs. 39-42.

Chapter III

IBN AL-'ARABI ON THE SELF-DISCLOSURE OF GOD

IBN AL-ʿARABI ON THE SELF-DISCLOSURE OF GOD

The purpose of this chapter is not to present a comprehensive review of Ibn al-ʿArabi's teachings, but rather to identify a central teaching around which we can group those aspects of his thought that have the greatest relevance to questions of religious diversity and interfaith dialogue. The central teaching I have selected is that of the Self-disclosure of God.[286] I have identified five concepts—all having to do with the teaching of the Self-disclosure of God—which are critical for understanding Ibn al-ʿArabi's perspective on religious diversity and, by implication, interfaith dialogue. These closely related and often overlapping concepts are: the so-called "Hidden Treasure" (kanz makhfi) motif; the metaphor of the "Breath of All-Merciful" (nafas al-rahman); the concept of perpetual creation; the human being and the "Perfect Man" (al-insan al-kamil); and the diversity of religions.

1. The Hidden Treasure Motif

Divine Self-disclosure or Self-manifestation is one of the most central teachings of Ibn al-ʿArabi's ontology. It is rooted in Ibn al-ʿArabi's reflection on a well-known hadith qudsi[287]: "I was a Hidden Treasure [lit., "a treasure which was not recognized"] and desired [out of love] to

---

[286] In the use of the term "Self-disclosure of God," I am indebted to William Chittick who, I believe, first coined the term with respect to the thought of Ibn al-ʿArabi and uses it as a title for his book focusing on Ibn al-ʿArabi's cosmology entitled, The Self-Disclosure of God: Principles of Ibn al-ʿArabi's Cosmology (hereafter abbreviated as SDG) (Albany: SUNY, 1998)

[287] A hadith qudsi (lit., "divine report" or "saying") in which God is depicted as speaking in the first person, but which is not found in the Qurʾan and which is generally understood to be divine logia in the spoken idiom of the Prophet Muhammad.

be recognized, so I created the creatures and introduced Myself to them, and thus they recognized me."[288] According to this concept, creation is God's Self-disclosure to Godself through the veils and signs of the creatures. For Ibn al-'Arabi, everything that exists in the world is, after all, nothing but the self-manifestation of the Absolute. In this case, Ibn al-'Arabi uses the term "hidden treasure" to refer to God's Being before it manifests itself and comes to be known by means of creation. Ibn al-'Arabi insists that "through the universe [which means by the creation of universe] God comes to be known."[289] But why does God want to be known, or why does God want to be manifested, or why does God create creatures? Some answers to these questions can be found in Ibn al-'Arabi's teaching in the chapter devoted to "Adam" in his *Fusus al-hikam*, where he refers to the purpose of creation by saying that God's intent in creating human beings and the cosmos which they inhabit was to "see the essence of [God's own] Most Beautiful Names, . . to see [God's] own Essence, in an all-inclusive object encompassing the whole [divine] Command, which, qualified by existence, would reveal to [God God's] own mystery."[290] This image of the divine Self-disclosure in creation can be found in Ibn al-'Arabi's own gloss on the creation story:

> when the real willed from the standpoint of its most beautiful names
> ... to reveal to it(self) through it(self) its mystery...
> and when the real had brought into being
> the world entire as a shaped form without spirit
> the world was like unpolished mirror
> for divine providence never shapes a form
> unless it receives divine spirit
> which is called the "inspiriting"
> which is the activation of the potential of that shaped image
> to receive the overflowing,
> the eternal manifestation

---

[288] *Fut.* II, 322. 29; II, 310. 20; II, 232. 11; II, 399. 29; *SPK*, 66, 126, 131, 204, 250.

[289] Sachico Murata, *The Tao of Islam* (New York: State University of New York Press, 1992), 11.

[290] *BW*, 50.

that always was and always will be
outside of which there is only vessel.... [291]

From these poetic passages, it is clear that the divine revealed
Itself, or was actualized, through the phenomenal world which is Its
mirror, and through human beings who are the polishers of that mirror.[292] In the words of Michael Sells, "The real creates the world as its
mirror and reveals to itself through the polished mirror its mystery."[293]
Thus, the universe is the mirror of God, and by this mirror God knows
and introduces God's face to both Godself and the world. Ibn al-'Arabi
says, "The whole cosmos is the locus within which God's Names
become manifest."[294] He concludes that, in the last analysis, "there is
nothing in existence but God's Names."[295] For Ibn al-'Arabi, the purpose of creation is also for the creatures, especially human beings, to
be able to "perceive the Inner [*al-batin*, one of the divine Names]
through our unseen and the Outer [*al-zahir*, another of the divine
Names] through our sensory aspect."[296]

Ibn al-'Arabi wants to show that God's love plays an essential role
in the origin and the structure of the world. In the version of the
hadith of the "Hidden Treasure" (mentioned above) that Ibn al-'Arabi
most often quotes, the main verb of the phrase sometimes rendered,
"and I desired to be recognized" is *ahbabtu* which literally means "I
loved." The emphasis on "love" here is critical to Ibn al-'Arabi's interpretation of this hadith. For Ibn al-'Arabi the primary motivation for
creation is none other than the loving desire of God to be in relation-

---

[291] Ibn al-'Arabi, *Fusus al-Hikam,* ed. Abu al-'Ila Afifi (Beirut: Dar al-Kutub al-'Arabi,
1946), I: 50-51, M ichaelAnthony Sells, *Mystical languages of Unsaying* (Chicago:
University of Chicago Press, 1994). 72-3.

[292] On Ibn al-'Arabi's teaching of the polished mirror, see, Michael A Sells, "Ibn 'Arabi's
"Polished Mirror": Perspective Shift and Meaning Event," *Studia Islamica,* 67
(1988), 121-149; Mustafa Tahrali, "The Polarity of Expression in *Fusus al-Hikam,*"
in *Muhyiddin Ibn 'Arabi: A Commemorative Volume,* eds. Hirtenstein and Tiernan
(Shaftesbury: Element, 1993).

[293] M ichaelAnthony Sells, *Mystical languages of Unsaying,* 73.

[294] *Fut.* II, 34. 3.

[295] *Fut.* II, 303.13.

[296] *BW,* 55.

ship with others. Ibn al-'Arabi insists that it was owing to God's love for the "Hidden Treasure" that God willed to speak the word "Be" (*kun*)[297] and exhale the Breath of the All-Merciful, thus creating the universe. For Ibn al-'Arabi, this divine hadith—verified on the basis of mystical intuition and "unveiling" (*kashf*) rather than transmission (*naql*)[298]—indicates that love is the source and motivating energy of the cosmos. God loves to be known, so God loves the creature through whom God comes to be known. In Godself, God is the non-manifest, the Hidden Treasure. However, it is precisely through and in divine love that the universe comes to be and has its purpose.

The "Hidden Treasure" that is the Divine Being (*wujud*) would have remained unmanifest if God had not brought the world into existence. Hence, as Chittick asserts, "the universe as a totality, in its full spatial and temporal extension, displays the properties of the whole array of Divine Names and Attributes in an infinite deployment."[299] It is in this sense that the existence of the universe is both identical to and the medium of the Self-disclosure of God. At one point, Ibn al-'Arabi actually describes the role of the creature in this process of divine Self-disclosure:

> The Cosmos can have no existence without Speech on God's part and listening on the part of the cosmos. Hence the existence of the paths of felicity only becomes manifest, and the differences between them and the paths of wretchedness only become known, through the Divine Speech and the engendered listening. Therefore all the messengers came with Speech, such as the Koran, the Gospel, the Psalm, and the Scriptures. There is nothing but speech and listening. There can be nothing else. Were it not for Speech, we would not know what the Desirer desires from us. Were it not for hearing (sam'), we would not reach the point of gaining what is said to us. Through Speech we move about, and as a result of Speech, we

---

[297] This is a reference to an expression—one variant of which is "And when He has decreed a matter, He but says to it, 'Be' and it is" (Q 2:117, 3:47, 19:35 and 40:68)—which occurs a total of eight times in the Qur'an.

[298] *Fut.* II, 399.28 in *SPK*, 391, n. 14.

[299] See William C. Chittick, "Islamic Mysticism," in Donald H. Bishop, ed., *Mysticism and the Mystical Experience, East and West* (Susquehanna University Press, London and Toronto, 1995), 303.

move about in listening. Hence Speech and listening are interrelated. Neither can be independent from the other, since they are two terms of a relationship. Through Speech and listening, we come to know what is in the Self of the Real, since we have no knowledge of Him except through the knowledge that He gives to us, and His giving of knowledge takes place through His Speech.[300]

It is important to note here that the object of God's love is, for Ibn al-'Arabi, always nonexistent. At one point, Ibn al-'Arabi maintains that "The created thing is nonexistent, so it is the object of God's love constantly and forever. As long as there is love, one cannot conceive of the existence of the created thing along with it, so the created thing never comes into existence."[301] A corollary to this is the realization that, because God never ceases in God's "love to be recognized," the medium of God's love—the created order—is in a constant state of becoming and unbecoming, coming into existence and passing out of existence.

The hadith of the "Hidden Treasure," above also implies that God desires and loves to be known, and for this reason God creates the universe. Thus, again, creation is the way for God to be known, or it can be said that creation is God's *tajalli*, God's Self-manifestation, God's revelation, or we might even say, God's form or face. In other words, God's love brings the universe into existence, thereby opening up the gap between God's uncreated Self and the created world. "God's love for creation," says Chittick, "gives rise to creation's love for him, and that love does not remain unfulfilled."[302]

Thus, again, the hadith of the "Hidden Treasure" is the key to explaining the reason behind God's bringing the cosmos into existence. God created the cosmos out of God's desire or "love" to be known. The cosmos is necessary since, according to Ibn al-'Arabi, although the existence of the servant . . . becomes manifest only through the existence of the Real and Its existence-giving, no knowledge of the Real would be manifest except through the knowledge of

---

[300] *Fut.* II, 366. 32-367. 2, *SPK*, 213.

[301] *Fut.* II, 113. 29. Cf. *Fut.* II, 399. 28; *SPK*, 131.

[302] William C. Chittick, *Ibn 'Arabi: Heir to the prophets* (Oxford: Oneworld, 2005), 31.

the cosmos.[303] Ibn al-'Arabi also says that in supporting our existence God indicates God's dependence on us and also God's independence from us.[304] God is dependent on us since God can be known only through our knowledge of God. According to Ibn al-'Arabi, the phrase "love to be known" in the hadith points to God's dependence on creatures through which the object of God's love is obtained. In the words of the great twentieth-century South Asian poet, the God of the hadith of the "Hidden Treasure" is "like us, a prisoner of Desire."[305]

However, for Ibn al-'Arabi, "God's love to be known is an indication that God is not known . . . since if God were to be known, God would be manifest, but God is the nonmanifest that does not become [fully] manifest."[306] Thus, the "Hidden Treasure" hadith also suggests that, though it is hidden, the treasure is pressed from inside by the "desire to be known." It means that there is something infinite in the Real in its state of being *in potentia* which eagerly tries to find an outlet or a vessel. This being *in potentia* then creates "an ontological tension within the Absolute, which finally relieves itself by bursting forth."[307]

For Ibn al-'Arabi, the "Hidden Treasure" is *al-Butun*, the Essence, the Godhead, which is beyond all dualism, all names, and all quiddity. In Ibn al-'Arabi's teaching, *al-Haqq*, the Real is always the Hidden Treasure, and will never be known. Only Its names and Its attributes that are disclosed to the universe can be known. Thus, the Real, on the level of Hidden Treasure, is totally transcendent. Here the hiddenness, which can be translated as the "mystery" of the Godhead which is the source of divine loneliness, makes the Real desire and love (*ahbabtu*) to be known in order not to be hidden anymore, by creating the universe, as mentioned. According to Izutsu, in this case the Hidden Treasure "refers to the stage of *ahadiyah* (in this sense,

---

[303] *Fut.* IV, 301. 16.

[304] *Fut.* IV, 301. 16.

[305] Muhammad Iqbal, *Zabur-i 'ajam* (Lahore, 1927), part 2, no. 29; trans. A.J. Arberry as *Persian Psalms* (Lahore, 1948), part 2, no. 29 in Schimmel, *Mystical Dimensions of Islam* (Chapel Hill, NC: University of North Carolina Press, 1975), 139.

[306] *Fut.* IV, 301. 16.

[307] Izutsu, *Sufism*, 488; Cf. *Fut.* II, 437. 20, *SPK*, 131.

"solitude" or "loneliness"), particularly in reference to the 'exterior' aspect of the *ahadiyah*; namely, that aspect in which the *ahadiyah* is turned toward the phenomenal world."[308] It is the essential source of all things that will come out in a phenomenal and concrete form. "The *ahadiyah*," Izutsu insists, "is nothing but pure Oneness."[309]

In fact, the "Hidden Treasure" mentioned in the hadith is for Ibn al-'Arabi the "storehouses" (*khaza'in*)[310] in which God keeps God's creatures before God creates them. He refers to the quranic teaching "there is nothing whose storehouses are not with Us, but We send it down only in a known measure" (Q 15:21). These are the possibilities of existence that are *in potentia* the divine names to be disclosed. These storehouses, however, are "still one and immovable," says, Izutsu, "but it somehow contains in itself a moving drive which, once activated, pushes the Absolute towards phenomenal evolvement."[311] This quranic metaphor of the "storehouses," therefore, is another expression of Ibn al-'Arabi's contention that God, who is Being (*wujud*), reveals God's own nature by uttering God's most beautiful Names, as God does in the revelation of the Qur'an. It also means that creatures never have their own being, but that their being belongs only to God, who creates by disclosing the divine Names which represent the various dimensions of the relationship between God and the creatures as existent entities. Ibn al-'Arabi calls these entities the "loci of manifestation" (*mazhar*), for they display Being (*wujud*) in specific and delimited phenomena.

Every phenomenon in creation thus constitutes a locus of manifestation, a *mazhar* for the *zuhur* or *tajalli* of the Real. This idea of the self-disclosure of God, which implies the relativity of creaturely being to the divine Being, is the very heart of Ibn al-'Arabi's metaphysics.[312] Ibn al-'Arabi says, "There is nothing in existence but God.

---

[308] Toshihiku Izutsu, *Creation and the Timeless Order of Things, Essays in Islamic Mystical Philosophy* (Ashland, Oregon: White Cloud Press, 1994), 91.

[309] Izutsu, *Creation*, 91.

[310] It is the term also used in Buddhist concept of *tathagata-garbha*, the "Storehouse of the Absolute." See Izutsu, *Creation*, 91.

[311] Izutsu, *Creation*, 91.

[312] "The term *self-disclosure* (*tajalli*)—often translated as 'theophany'—plays such a central role in Ibn al-Arabi's teachings that, before he was known as the great spokes-

Though we also exist, our existence is through God. But he who exists through something other than Godself is, in fact, nonexistent."[313]

Like Meister Eckhart, whose metaphysics I will elaborate in the next chapter, Ibn al-'Arabi is saying that creatures somehow "borrow" existence (*wujud*) and attributes from God, because in themselves they are "nonexistent." In other words, the phenomenal world of multiplicity is essentially "non *wujud*" (*'adam*). But it does not mean that this phenomenal world of multiplicity is an illusion. Rather, the ontological status of the phenomenal world is relational, that is, as Izutsu calls it, "the various and variegated relational forms of the Absolute itself."[314] It should be noted, however, that the multiplicity of phenomenal existence by no means hinders the pure unity of the Absolute, but rather "the two complement each other in disclosing the pure structure of Reality."[315]

The ontological relationship between the Absolute and the phenomenal things in Ibn al-'Arabi's teaching can be compared to the inseparable relationship between the "shadow" and its source. The world is a shadow (*zill*) of the Absolute, which manifests in three different modalities. One of these modalities is as the shadow of *al-a'yan al-thabita*, "the immutable essences" or "entities"[316]—the nonexistent "archetypes" of which every element of the phenomenal world is an existent manifestation. Izutsu interprets this by concluding that "every single part of the world is a *particular aspect* of the Absolute, and is the Absolute in a delimited form."[317] The problem with this interpretation is the language of "particular aspect" which can be taken to imply that, in Ibn al-'Arabi's thinking, there is an essential or substantive connection between the Absolute and the phenomenal—that the phenomenal "shares" or "participates" in the Being (*wujud*) of God. Unfortunately, this is not quite accurate. When speaking of the relationship

---

man for *wahdat al-wujud*, he had been called one of the Companions of Self-Disclosure (*ashab al-tajalli*)." See *SDG*, 52.

[313] *Fut.* I, 279.6.

[314] Izutsu, *Creation*, 27.

[315] Izutsu, *Creation*, 26.

[316] *Fut.* III, 46. 33, see *SPK*, 7, 12, and 83-84.

[317] Izutsu, *Sufism and Taoism*, 94, 492.; italics mine

between God and creation, Ibn al-'Arabi is very careful to choose the metaphor of the "shadow" (*zill*). As everyone knows, while the shadow simply would not exist without the combination of the light and the object casting the shadow, the shadow is by no means intrinsic to the object which casts it. In this respect, every constituent element of the phenomenal world is a "shadow" of the "immutable essences" (*al-a'yan al-thabita*)—not in the sense that they are "aspects" of the Absolute, but rather in the sense that they are *effects* of the Absolute. Before leaving this metaphor of the "shadow," however, one important point needs to be repeated. Insofar as the English word "shadow" connotes something which lacks substance and is illusory, the implications of Ibn al-'Arabi's use of this metaphor cease. As we stressed above, for Ibn al-'Arabi to speak of the existent realm as a "shadow" of the Absolute is not to suggest (as it would in the case of the Platonic allegory of the cave) that this realm is at all "illusory" or "unsubstantial."

In sum, the "Hidden Treasure" motif and its implications help articulate Ibn al-'Arabi's central doctrine of the "oneness of Being or *wujud*." For Ibn al-'Arabi, there is only one *wujud* (being) and this *wujud* is none other than God in God's most transcendental state. Everything else depends for its existence on this *wujud*, who is externalized in many different manifestations. God, then, is both the outer and the inner reality of all beings. This can be inferred from many quranic verses, like "wherever you turn, there is the Face of God" (Q 2: 115); "We are nearer to him than his jugular vein" (Q 50: 16); "We are nearer to him than you, and yet you see not?" (Q 56: 85); and "God is with you wheresoever you may be" (Q 57: 4).

2. The Breath of the Merciful

Besides that of the "shadow," Ibn al-'Arabi uses many other metaphors to convey his central teaching about the Self-disclosure of God. Among the most central of these is the metaphor of the "Breath of the Merciful" (*nafas al-rahman*).[318] Like almost all his metaphors, this

---

[318] The canonical version of this hadith found in the *Musnad* of Ahmad b. Hanbal (vol. 2, no. 541) in which the Prophet Muhammad is depicted as exclaiming, "I find the

one is rooted in scripture (in this case another hadith) and is employed by Ibn al-'Arabi to evoke an experiential understanding of the sense in which the existence of the cosmos—an existence which takes shape in the unceasing dynamic of flux and change—is an effect of the "inhalation" and "exhalation" of the divine Being. The metaphor of the "Breath of the Merciful" is linked with the hadith of the "Hidden Treasure" in the sense that the next step after God's "loving to be recognized" is the "exhalation" of the Creator (i.e., the breath carrying the command, "Be!") which results in the existence of phenomenal creation. God's loving desire, then, is the cause of the creative "exhalation"—the first journey from God to the world. This "exhalation" of phenomena coming into existence is then followed by an "inhalation"—a desire of the creature for the Creator which entails a passing out of existence—the second journey from the world back to God. And then there is a third journey of "exhalation" in a dynamic of breathing—of becoming and un-becoming—*ad infinitum*. For Ibn al-'Arabi, the divine command "Be"—carried on the Breath of the Merciful—engenders substance in a "Cloud" (*'ama'*) out of which the cosmos is fashioned:

> One of the characteristics of the Lover...is to breathe, since in that breathing is found the enjoyment of what is sought. The Breath emerges from a root, which is Love for the creatures, to whom He desired to make Himself known, so that they might know Him. Hence the Cloud [*al-'ama'*] comes to be; it is called the Real Through Whom Creation Takes Place. The Cloud is the substance of the cosmos, so it receives all the forms, spirits, and natures of the cosmos; it is a receptacle *ad infinitum*. This is the origin of His love for us. ...We became forms within the substance of the Cloud. Through our manifestation within the Cloud, He gave us an existence belonging to the Cloud. A thing whose existence had been intelligible gained entified existence. This is the cause of the origin of our love for Him.[319]

---

breath of your Lord coming from the direction of Yemen." The slightly different, non-canonical version which Ibn al-'Arabi uses and which is popular among Sufis is: "I find the breath of the All-merciful coming to me from the direction of Yemen." See *SPK*, 27 and his explanatory note, no. 8 on 398.

[319] *Fut.*II, 331.23 in *SPK*, 28.

Speaking about God's creation of the universe as the "Breath of all the Merciful," Ibn al-'Arabi maintains that the All-Merciful's exhalation of His Breath is equivalent to the bestowal of the gift of existence *(ijad)* on creation. He refers to the quranic teaching which mentions that it is God as the All-Merciful who sits on the Throne, who embraces the whole universe. God sits on God's Throne as All-Merciful because the determinative principle of all creation must be that very "love" to creation owes its existence. To underscore this point, the master makes reference to the famous hadith qudsi: "My mercy takes precedence over My wrath."[320] In this respect, Ibn al-'Arabi also references Qur'an 7:156, "My Mercy covers everything" *(wa rahmati wasi'at kulla shay')*. One could also point to the famous quranic verse declaring mercy to be the most essential and defining attribute of God, "God has prescribed for himself mercy" *(kataba 'ala nafsihi al-rahma),*[321] as well as the verse declaring mercy to be the essence of the mission of the Prophet Muhammad *(wa ma arsalnaka illa rahmatan li l-'alamin)*[322]

Describing further the symbolism of the "Breath of the Merciful," Ibn al-'Arabi maintains that by being unmanifest and nonexistent, the "immutable essences" *(al-a'yan al-thabita)* are in "distress" *(karb* or *kurba)* because their essence is one of radical potentiality. In compassionate response to this distress, the creative "exhalation" of the Merciful brings relief and healing to the immutable essences which, by their very nature, hunger to exist. Of this process, Ibn al-'Arabi writes:

> Were it not for straitness *(haraj)* and constriction *(diq)*, the All-merciful Breath would have no property. "Giving relief" is to eliminate straitness and constriction, and nonexistence is identical with straitness and constriction, since the nonexistent thing possesses the possibility of coming into existence. Hence, when the possible thing knows its possibility while in the state of nonexistence, it is distressed, since it yearns for the existence allowed by its reality in order to take its share of good *(khayr)*. The All-merciful relieves this straitness through His Breath, since He brings the pos-

---

[320] *Ghalabat* [or *sabaqat*] *rahmati ghadabi* is a well-known hadith qudsi found in the canonical collections of Bukhari, Ibn Majah, and Ahmad b. Hanbal.

[321] Q 6:12.

[322] Q 21:107.

sible things into existence. Hence His "giving relief" is His elimination of the property of nonexistence within the possible things.[323]

3. Perpetual Creation

One of the most significant implications of the metaphor of the "Breath of the Merciful" is that the act of creation never ceases. According to this metaphor, creation is perpetual process of constant renewal.[324] In Ibn al-'Arabi's own words, "Creation never ceases, while the entities are receivers which take off and put on [existence]. So in every instance [*nafas*] the cosmos in respect of its form undergoes a new creation in which there is no repetition."[325] Elsewhere he asserts:

> ...God creates perpetually at each instant (*ma'a l-anfas*). So among the things, some remain for the length of the moment of their existence and reach their term in the second moment of the time of their existence. This is the smallest duration (*mudda*) in the cosmos. God does this so that the entities will be poor and needy toward God at each instant. For if they were to remain [in existence] for two moments or more, they would be qualified by independent (*ghina*) from God in that duration. [326]

For Ibn al-'Arabi, to posit any alternative understanding of creation which suggests that stasis is ever achieved—even for one moment—is to commit the sin of *shirk* (i.e., ascribing a partner to God, and thus detracting from God's utter and absolute unicity and uniqueness.

As always, it is in deep reflection on scripture that Ibn al-'Arabi "receives" his understanding of the nature of reality. One of the quranic passages from which Ibn al-'Arabi receives the inspiration for this teaching on "perpetual creation" is: "No indeed, but they are in confusion as to a new creation" (Q 50:15).[327] Another scriptural source of inspiration for the teaching on perpetual creation can be found in the

---

[323] *Fut.* II, 459. 1 in *SPK*, 131.

[324] Chittick refers to this concept in Ibn al-'Arabi's teaching as "perpetual renewal." See *SPK*, 97.

[325] *Fut.* II, 677. 30 in *SPK*, 97.

[326] *Fut.* II, 639. 12 in *SPK*, 98.

[327] *bal hum fi labsin min khalqin jadid.*

passage: "Each day He is upon some task" (Q 55:29).[328] Based on this verse, Ibn al-'Arabi maintains that God has new tasks each day which constantly cause new changes within the cosmos. At another point the master writes, "God has effects manifest within the cosmos, they are the states within which the cosmos undergoes constant fluctuation (*taqallub*)."[329] And in *Fusus*, Ibn al-'Arabi articulates his principle of the "renewal of creation by similars"[330] by arguing that, "God is manifest in every Breath and that no [particular] Self-manifestation is repeated. . . every Self-manifestation at once provides a [new] creation and annihilates another. Its annihilation is extinction at the [new] Self-manifestation, subsistence being what is given by the following [other] Self-manifestation; so understand[!]"[331] In other words, the apparent continuity one witnesses in the existence of a certain thing is a continuity which results from the fact that when God annihilates a thing and then recreates it, what he recreates is very similar (although not identical) to that which He has annihilated.

As we can see, in order to articulate his vision in more depth, the master places verses such as Q 50:15 and Q 55:29 into conversation with important Sufi concepts such as *fana'* (annihilation), which itself is also a quranic concept.[332] In one of the many poems embedded in the discourse of the *Futuhat*, Ibn al-'Arabi intones: "Say not, My servants, / 'Surely you, surely I,' / for I subsist, / but you are annihilated and disappear. / At every moment / you are a new creation-- / that is why to you belong / annihilation (*fana'*) and upstirring (*nashr*[333])."[334]

In keeping with his signature methodology of rooting his perceptions of the nature of reality in sacred scripture, Ibn al-'Arabi selects a

---

[328] *kulla yawmin huwa fi sha'n.*

[329] *Fut.* III, 315. 11, 16 in *SPK*, 100; *SDG*, 31.

[330] *BW*, 194.

[331] *BW*, 155.

[332] See Q 55:26—"All that is on [earth] will be annihilated, but the Face of your Lord, full of majesty and honor will abide [forever]." (*kullu man 'alayha fan wa yabqa wajhu rabbika dhu l-jalal wa l-ikram*)

[333] *Nashr* may be less ambiguously translated as a quranic synonym for "resurrection." E.g., see Q 35:9.

[334] *Fut.* IV, 8. 32 in *SDG*, 41.

fascinating quranic example to support his insights into perpetual creation as a ceaseless dynamic of annihilation and upstirring. In the chapter of *Fusus* dedicated to Solomon, Ibn al-ʿArabi calls to the attention of the reader the incident of the Ifrit's apparently magical "transportation" of the throne of Bilqis from her throne room to that of Solomon (Q 27:38-42). The point Ibn al-ʿArabi wishes to emphasize is that there is no extraordinary occurrence involved in the apparent "transportation" of this throne over great distances. In fact, for Ibn al-ʿArabi, this was a not a matter of "transportation" at all, but simply of the ceaseless dynamic of annihilation and upstirring. He writes:

> The matter of the obtaining of the throne of Bilqis is no different from most other [theological] questions, except for those who have inner knowledge of what we have said about it. Asaf's [the ʿIfrit's] only merit in the matter was that he effected the renewal in the court of Solomon. One who truly understands what we have said will realize that the throne covered no distance, that no land was folded up for it, nor was it penetrated. . .When Bilqis saw her throne, knowing the great distance involved and the impossibility, in her view, of its being moved in such a short time, she said, *It is as if it were it* [Q 27: 42], so confirming what we have said concerning the renewal of creation by similars. It is it, and so confirms the [divine] command, since you are, in the moment of recreation, [essentially] the same as you were before it.[335]

4. Human Being and the Perfect Man

For Ibn al-ʿArabi, among the creatures, only the human being represents the full Self-disclosure of the Absolute in its determinate being. It is for this reason that Ibn al-ʿArabi identifies the human being as the receptacle and the mirror of the Divine qualities, to whom and through whom these qualities are disclosed. Thus, the human being is the place to make possible a particular mode of self-knowledge of God. Human being, according to a well-known prophetic hadith, was created in God's form or, as the text reads, "upon His form," (*ʿala suratih*).[336] For

---

[335] *BW*, 193-4.

[336] There is a tradition of interpreting this hadith to say that "God created Adam in his [i.e., Adam's own] image."

Ibn al-'Arabi, "form" refers to "anything that becomes manifest, anything or any quality or attribute that can be distinguished or differentiated." [337] Thus, to say that the "human being was created in God's form means that the human being is God's "locus of disclosure"[338]—a place of a very significant event, that is a place within which all the Names of God are displayed in their "full splendor."[339] It is for this reason that the human being is the "'epitome' (*mukhtasar*) of God's manifestation."[340] According to Ibn al-'Arabi, the difference between the human being and any other individual creature is that, because the human being is made "upon the form of God, she or he has *at least the potential* to display the effects and properties of all God's Names, while other creatures manifest only some of God's names, and not all of them. It is important to note that for Ibn al-'Arabi, only when the human being has actualized God's divine form is she or he able to understand the true significance of the concept of "All are He," meaning that the whole cosmos is the locus within which God's Names become manifest. Ibn al-'Arabi explains these points by referring to the quranic verse, "He [God] is with you where you are" (57: 4), and maintains, God accompanies us in our every state, but we do not accompany Him unless we stand within His limits (as prescribed by the Divine Law). So in reality we do not accompany His statutes: He is with us, but we are not with Him.[341] In more philosophical terms, Ibn al-'Arabi makes the same points:

> God is identical with what becomes manifest (in the cosmos), but what becomes manifest is not identical with Him. For He is the Nonmanifest just as He is the Manifest (Q 57: 3)[342] in the state of His manifestation. Hence we say, "He is like the things, but the

---

[337] *SDG*, 27.

[338] *Fut.* II, 345. 22 in *SDG*, 28.

[339] *SDG*, 27.

[340] *Fut.* II, 391. 1: *SPK*, 276.

[341] *Fut.* II, 278. 7.

[342] "He is the First, and the Last and the Manifest and the Nonmanifest and He knows all things" (*huwa l-awwal wa l-akhir wa l-zahir wa l-batin wa huwa bi-kulli shay'in 'alim*).

things are not like Him," since He is identical with the things, but they are not identical with Him.[343]

Thus, for Ibn al-'Arabi, when God mentioned in the Qur'an that He created Adam as his vicegerent (*khalifa*), God, in fact, made him a Perfect Man (*insan kamil*).[344] Indeed, there are two key quranic concepts which can be roughly translated as "human being." They are *bashar* and *insan*. If *bashar* always relates to the human being as a biological entity—a specie among the species—the word *insan* is related to the animating breath breathed into the human by God and therefore is indicative of the special relationship the human person has with God. The human being, who was created in "God's form" is a creature to assume the divine traits, and who is thus responsible for reflecting these attributes in his or her life. As mentioned in the Qur'an, the human being as *insan* is the only creature who volunteers to bear the *amana*, or divine "Trust" which God "offered to the heavens and the earth and the mountains," each of which, despite their majesty and strength, declined to bear it (Q 33: 72). It was the human being alone who opted to accept the *amana* to uphold divine law, thus holding himself or herself accountable for building just societies.[345] In fact, according to Ibn al-'Arabi, it is because of this "form" that the human being was not allowed to reject this trust (*amana*).[346] For Ibn al-'Arabi, God made the human being the "locus of manifestation" (*mazhar*)[347] for God's own "all-comprehensive" Name, i.e., Allah, the name that embraces all names and includes all of the ninety-nine Most Beautiful Names. For the Qur'an declares, "He taught Adam the

---

[343] *Fut.* II, 488. 25; cf. *Fut.* II, 21.35; *SPK*, 90.

[344] On perfect man see Takeshita, Masataka, *Ibn 'Arabi's Theory of the Perfect Man and Its Place in the History of Islamic Thought* (Tokyo, 1987); Chittick, "The Perfect Man as a Prototype of the Self in the Sufism of Jami," *Studia Islamica*, 49 (1979), 135-158: John T. Little, "al-Insan al-Kamil: The Perfect man according to Ibn al-'Arabi," *The Muslim World*, vol. vii (1987).

[345] Fazlur Rahman, "The Quranic Concept of God, the Universe, and Man," *Islamic Studies*, March (1967), VI, I, 9.

[346] *Fut.* II, 170. 6; *SPK*, 276.

[347] Throughout his book, Chittick discusses this concept of "locus of manifestation," (see *SDG*).

Names, all of them" (Q 2: 31). "Adam," writes Ibn al-'Arabi, "entered creation upon the Form of the Name "Allah," since this Name embraces all the Divine Names."[348] Hence, Ibn al-'Arabi continues, "God's Names do not become manifest in their entirety except in the human being."[349] Furthermore, according to Ibn al-'Arabi, it is because the human being is created in God's "Form," that he is identical with God. "Whatever is given form by a form giver is identical with the form-giver, not other than him, since it is not outside him."[350]

To say that human being is created in God's form, also means that God "created them in the form of all the divine names,"[351] including All-Merciful, Forgiving, Just, Creator, Generous, Powerful, Exalter, Abaser, and so on. God placed within human beings every one of His own attributes. According to Chittick, one of the interpretations of the quranic verse "God taught Adam all Names" (2: 30), is that "human beings display an indefinite variety of divine aspects or "faces" (*wujuh*, sing. *wajh*):"[352]

> If Adam had been created not in the form of God, but in the form of the All-Compassionate, no human being could be angry or cruel. If he had been created in the form of Vengeful, no one would ever forgive his enemy. If he had been created in the form of the Almighty or the Inaccessible, no one would ever obey God or any or else. But since human beings were created in the form of all names, they can make manifest any conceivable attribute.[353]

Thus, the human being, in this sense, is a perfect man—the manifestation of the Name "Allah," the all-comprehensive Name which conveys both God's incomparability and similarity. On this relationship of the incomparability and similarity, Ibn al-'Arabi writes:

---

[348] *Fut.* II, 124. 5. CF. *Fut.* I, 216. 9; *SPK*, 276.

[349] *Fut.* I 216. 12.

[350] *Fut.* II, 123. 35, *SPK*, 276.

[351] William Chittick, *Imaginal Worlds: Ibn al-'Arabi and the Problem of Religious Diversity* (hereafter abbreviated as IW) (Albany: State University of New York Press, 1994), 32.

[352] *IW*, 32. Cf. *SPK*, 276 and *Fut.* I, 216. 9

[353] *IW*, 32.

When the servants of the real witness Him, they see Him as possessing two relationships, the relationship of incomparability, and that of descent to the imagination through a kind of similarity. The relationship of incomparability is His self-disclosure in the Prophet's words, "Worship God as if you see Him," and his words, "God is in the *kibla* of him who performs the prayer." It is also mentioned in God's words, "Whithersoever you turn, there is the Face of God" (2: 115)—"there" being an adverb of place, while the "Face" of God is His Essence and Reality.[354]

It is important to note, however, that not all human beings fulfill the potential inherent in the fact that they are created in God's "Form." "Perfection," Ibn al-'Arabi insists, "belongs to the Form."[355] According to Ibn al-'Arabi, there are two kinds of human being: the Perfect Man (*al-insan al-kamil*) and the animal man (*al-insan al-hayawan*). The perfect man is "the most perfect through bringing together all things (*majma'*)."[356] He is the locus wherein the divine Names become manifest. Here Ibn al-'Arabi bases his teaching on the hadith "My earth and My heaven embrace Me not, but the heart of My believing servant does embrace Me." He commented, "It is as if He is saying, all My Names become manifest only within the human configuration."[357] Conversely, as Chittick interprets the master's teaching, "'Animal man' is the opposite of perfect man. In perfect man the Divine Form is manifest, while in animal man it remains but a virtuality.[358]

In fact, among all the created things, the human being is the one to which is attached such great importance in the Qur'an that there is nearly as much discourse about the human being as there is about God. For Ibn al-'Arabi, there is a key teaching embedded in the very fact that the divine revelation of the Qur'an has so much to say about the human being. This teaching is unlocked by the prophetic hadith (very popular among Sufis), *"man 'arafa nafsahu faqad 'arafa rabbahu,"* meaning "One who knows oneself knows one's Lord." Thus, self-

---

[354] *Fut.* II, 3. 28, 4.3, 26; *SPK*, 277.

[355] *Fut.* I, 163. 21; *SPK*, 276.

[356] *Fut.* I, 163. 21; *SPK*, 276.

[357] *Fut.* I, 216. 9; *SPK*, 276.

[358] *SPK*, 276.

awareness is the critical station through which the human being must pass in order to get to the higher station of the knowledge of God. Ibn al-'Arabi also says that the human being "is called *insan* for it is by him that the Reality looks on His creation and bestows the Mercy [of existence] on them."[359] By this, Ibn al-'Arabi seems to be reflecting on the root from which we get the word *insan*, a root which has to do with being "friendly," "sociable," "familiar," "intimate," "happy," and even "tranquil" and "domesticated" (as opposed to "wild").[360]

Synthesizing all of these various insights into the nature of the human person, Ibn al-'Arabi writes:

> The Reality wanted to see the essence of His Most Beautiful Names or, put in another way, to see His own Essence, in an all-inclusive object encompassing the whole [divine] Command, which, qualified by existence, would reveal to Him his own mystery. . . . The Reality gave existence to the whole Cosmos [at first] as an undifferentiated thing without anything of the spirit in it, so that it was like an unpolished mirror. . . . Thus the [divine] Command required [by its very nature] the reflective characteristic of the mirror of the Cosmos, and Adam was the very principle of reflection for that mirror and the spirit of that form.[361]

He continues by emphasizing that, as the point of manifestation of all the Names, the human being is a microcosm of the entire created order:

> Creation has many levels, and the most perfect level is occupied by man. Each kind in the cosmos is a part with regard to man's perfection. Even animal man is part of Perfect Man . . . He created Perfect man in his form, and through the form He gave him the ability to have all of His names ascribed to him, one by one, or in groups, though all the names together are not ascribed to him in a single word—thereby the Lord is distinguished from the Perfect

[359] *BW*, 51.

[360] E.W. Lane, *Arabic-English Lexicon* (Cambridge: Islamic Texts Society, 1984), reprint of original in 1863, vol 1, 113.

[361] *BW*, 50-51. On Ibn al-'Arabi's concept of "polished mirror," see Michael A. Sells, "Ibn 'Arabi's 'Polished Mirror': Perspective Shift and Meaning Event," *Studia Islamica*, 67 (1988), 121-149.

Servant. Hence there is none of the most beautiful names—and all of God's names are most beautiful—by which the Perfect Servant is not called, just as he calls his Master by them.[362]

In Ibn al-ʿArabi's teaching, as the microcosm of creation, "human beings embrace all the hierarchy of all things within existence, from the most luminous to the darkest."[363] Thus, Chittick writes, "in some mysterious way, every human being contains everything in the cosmos."[364] They were created from God's Spirit breathed into the clay of this world,[365] thus, "they combine the most intense light of existence and awareness with the dullest and most inanimate dust of the universe."[366] This is, in fact, what is called the "Perfect Man," mentioned above, who is the *imago dei*, "a perfect epitome of the universe, the very spirit of the whole world of Being."[367]

Although it is true that the human being is made upon the form of all the Divine Names, for Ibn al-ʿArabi, there is a right way and a wrong way to assume the divine traits. In this case, the wrong way, is exemplified by the sin of Satan. According to the Qurʾan, when God finishes creating Adam, he commands the heavenly hosts to prostrate themselves before this marvelous new creation. All the angels comply, but Satan refuses to bow down. The verse indicates that the reason Satan refused was because he was 'arrogant' (*aba wa istakbara*).[368] Ibn al-ʿArabi explains the nature of this arrogance by claiming that Satan perceived that the light within himself was more intense than in Adam, so he declared, "I am better than he– You created me of fire and him of clay" (Q 7:12; 38: 76). By this declaration, according to Ibn al-ʿArabi, Satan claimed a greatness which did not in fact belong to him.[369] For this pride, Ibn al-ʿArabi says, Satan "came to manifest

[362] *Fut.* III, 409. 16.

[363] *SPK*, 17.

[364] *IW*, 31.

[365] Q15: 28-29, 32: 7-9, 38: 71-72.

[366] *SPK*, 17.

[367] Izutsu, *Sufism*, 218.

[368] Q 2:34.

[369] This false pride is practically what the Qurʾan terms equated to. It is also said that because of the hastiness of man, that he becomes so full of pride. See Q 21: 37; 17: 11.

the divine name [, "]Magnificent[,"] outside of its proper limits within the created world. He claimed incomparability for himself and as a result came face to face with the Divine Wrath."[370]

Related to the creation of the human being and the pride of Satan is the quranic verse that elaborates the special method God uses to create the human being, i.e., with His "two hands." After Satan's refusal to prostrate himself before Adam, God asks him, "What prevented you from prostrating yourself to him whom I created with My two hands?" (38: 75)[371] According to the Mu'tazila and their followers, the "two hands" is a simple metaphor for the "power" (*qudra*) of God. For others, one hand is the hand of blessing and the other is the hand of power. For Ibn al-'Arabi, neither interpretation is in accordance with the intent of God's words. According to Ibn al-'Arabi, when God says that God has created the human being with "My two hands," God's intention is to "point out [Adam's] eminence (*sharaf*)," as the creature with the potential to reflect all the divine attributes—both those of incomparability and those of similarity.[372] "The perfect servant," Ibn al-'Arabi writes, "stands between these two relationships [i.e., the relationship of incomparability and that of similarity], standing opposite each in his own essence."[373] Further elucidating what Ibn al-'Arabi teaches about the significance of God's having created Adam with His "two hands," Michael Sells writes:

> In his own interpretation of the "two hands," Ibn 'Arabi gives a sequence of polarities that characterize the human being. The complete human encompasses both the hidden and the manifest. It exists in simultaneous states of intimacy (*uns*) and awe (*hayba*) in its relation to the real. …The human thus reflects two modes of the divine, the manifest mode of witness (*shahada*) and the hidden pole of the unknowable (*al-ghayb*). … In a final summation Ibn 'Arabi returns to the theme of knowledge and attributes. The two hands "stretch out over the complete human being," who is both completely reflective of the divine attributes (as regent or *khalifa*) and yet, insofar as

---

[370] Cited in *SPK*, 24.

[371] *Ma mana'aka an tasjuda lima khalaqtu bi yadiyya.*

[372] *Fut.* II, 3. 28; *SPK*, 277.

[373] *Fut.* II, 4. 26 in *SPK*, 277; Cf. *Fut.* II, 3. 28.

it is of the originated world, can never know the real as the real knows itself, because "originated being has no way there." [Satan] did not understand the two handed creation of Adam.[374]

Like many Sufis before and after him, Ibn al-'Arabi also describes "stations" and "states" on the path to perfection, which is in fact the way of coming to know oneself as the microcosm of the Real. Also, like other Sufi masters, he differentiates between station and state. For him, "Every station [*maqam*] in the path of God is earned and fixed, while every state [*hal*] is a bestowal, neither earned nor fixed."[375] The stations of the path represent every positive human attribute that the travelers strive to achieve. Through this station the travelers are brought into the states by which they come to embody the divine realities embraced by the name of Allah. Although the human being is made in the form of all the Names of God, he does not actualize these names until they become an established and deeply rooted part of his character. It is in this state that the human being must "assume the traits" of the names of God (*takhalluq bi al-asma'*).[376] For Ibn al-'Arabi, assuming the traits of God's Names is precisely the way of the Sufi. In this case, human beings have to bring all these Names into actuality. In traveling to God, when the human being follows the spiritual path, he passes from station to station, and never loses an attribute after gaining it. One by one he assumes the traits of the divine attributes, and thus he manifests the names of Allah himself. For Ibn al-'Arabi this is the highest station, what, with a reference to Q 33:13,[377] he calls the station of "no station" (*la maqam*).[378] In this station, human beings recognize God in all things.

It is thus on the Sufi path—a path fundamentally defined by the dynamic of "assuming the traits of God's Names"—where the *desire* of God to be "recognized" and the *need* of the human to exist to his or

---

[374] Michael Sells, *Mystical Languages of Unsaying*, 85-86.

[375] *Fut.* II, 176. 10; *SPK*, 278.

[376] *Fut.* II, 126. 8, Cf. *SPK*, 275.

[377] *Wa idh qalat ta'ifatun minhum ya ahla Yathriba la muqam la-kum* ("Behold, when a group from among them said, 'O people of Yathrib, you have no station!")

[378] *Fut.* II, 646.27; *SPK*, 376.

her fullest potential, meet. It is important to note here that, for Ibn al-'Arabi, to assume the traits of God, human beings need the guidance of God's Law. This is just one of the ways in which the master ascribes to the central Sufi maxim: *la tariqa bi la shari'a* ("Without the Law, there can be no Path").[379] In the context of Ibn al-'Arabi's teaching, this maxim is an expression of the fact that because God in Godself is unknowable, the human being cannot manifest God's Names unless God Godself shows the human being the way in which this can be accomplished.[380] We should take careful note here of the fact that, in saying this, Ibn al'Arabi is declaring that the sine qua non of authentic human existence is the Shari'a. Without the Shari'a, not only can the human being not traverse the Sufi path. Without the Shari'a, the human being cannot be fully human. It will be important to keep this in mind when, in chapter six, we discuss the orthodoxy and orthopraxy of the Greatest Shaykh.

5. Diversity of Religions

One other key concept related to Ibn al-'Arabi's teaching about the Self-disclosure of God is his view of religious diversity. It is important that we conclude our review of his central teaching of divine Self-disclosure by turning to this concept, especially because, in chapters five and six, our specific task will be to see what Ibn al-'Arabi's teaching on Self-disclosure yields in terms of a new matrix for Christian-Muslim dialogue when put into conversation with the teachings of Meister Eckhart on "detachment."

For Ibn al-'Arabi, religious diversity is a natural consequence of the unlimitedness of God's Self-disclosure and the concomitant degree of "preparedness" of any element of the phenomenal world to be a *mahall* or "locus" of the Self-disclosure. Another way of articulating this point would be to say that diversity in the phenomenal world is a

---

[379] On Ibn al-'Arabi's teaching of the Shari'a, specifically on "fiqh," see Erick Winkel, *Islam and The Living Law, The Ibn al-Arabi Approach* (Oxford: Oxford University Press, 1997) and Eric Winkel, "Ibn al-Arabi's fiqh: Three Cases from the Futuhat," *Journal of the Muhyiddion Ibn 'Arabi Society*, 13 (1993), 54-74.

[380] *SPK*, 274.

direct function of the varying "preparedness" or capacity of creatures to receive the divine Self-disclosure. Like Eckhart, (whose teachings will be elaborated in chapter four), for Ibn al-'Arabi, God's Self-disclosure or his *tajalli* is very much connected with the "receptivity" (*qabul*) and "preparedness" *(isti'dad)* of the creatures or the vessels (*mahall*). Thus, when God discloses Godself, the degree to which a thing receives God's Self-disclosure is determined by its "preparedness" to bear it. In Ibn al-'Arabi's teaching, receptivity "must be taken into account not only on the cognitive level, but also on the existential level."[381] About preparedness, Ibn al-'Arabi writes:

> God says, "the giving of thy Lord can never be walled up" (Q 17:20). In other words, it can never be withheld. God is saying that He gives constantly, while the loci receive in the measure of the realities of their preparedness. In the same way we say that the sun spreads rays over the existence of things. It is not miserly with its light toward anything. The loci receive the light in the measure of their preparedness.[382]

According to the quotation above, the essence of God never manifests in the universe; rather, it is God's specific attributes and Names that manifest themselves. Ibn al-'Arabi refers to God in God's manifestation as the divine presence (*al-hadra al-ilahiyya*), and he distinguishes this from God as non-manifest which Ibn al-'Arabi refers to as the primordial presence (*al-hadra al-qadima*).[383] This distinction plays an important role in al-'Arabi's understanding of spiritual attainment. The master claims that no human being can go beyond the Realm of God's Self-disclosure because the Absolute in Its Essence is absolutely unknowable. The only and the highest possibility for the human being comes in seeking the Absolute within the parameters of a particular instance of divine Self-disclosure within the human self. Now the viability of any particular instance of divine Self-disclosure is ultimately determined by the receptivity or preparedness of the existent entity. It

---

[381] *SPK,* 91.

[382] *Fut.* I, 287. 10; *SPK,* 91-2.

[383] Samer Akkach, *Cosmology and Architecture in Premodern Islam, An Architectural Reading of Mystical Ideas* (Albany: State University of New York press, 2005), 67.

is for this reason that there is a distinction between God's prophets and "friends" (*awliya'* or *akhilla'*) on one hand, and ordinary people on the other. The prophets and friends of God are loci of the manifestation for all the divine Names, but other people are more limited in their receptivity and can only make certain Names manifest. It is important to note that, although God's Self-disclosure depends on the receptivity and preparedness of the locus or vessel (*mahall*), this does not mean that God's Self-disclosure, which is God's Mercy, is suspended.

For Ibn al-'Arabi, the concepts of receptivity and preparedness are closely connected to the question of the divine "measuring out" of human "destiny" (*qadar*). Before it comes into existence, God knows the qualities and characteristics of each entity, because its "treasuries are with Him." Then, in the process of creation, God measures out these qualities and characteristics—including one's destiny (which ultimately is identical to one's capacity to receive divine manifestation)—according to the creature's preparedness to receive. To illustrate this point, Ibn al-'Arabi has recourse to one of his favorite ontological metaphors, the metaphor of the mirror: "Try, when you look at yourself in a mirror, to see the mirror itself, and you will find that you cannot do so. So much is this the case that some have concluded that the image perceived is situated between the mirror and the eye of the beholder."[384] Thus, the recipient sees nothing other than his own form in the mirror of Reality. It also means that the existent entity, fixed forever in God's knowledge, can never receive anything beyond what it demands in itself and according to its own capacity. This is one of the foundational principles behind Ibn al'Arabi's approach to the diversity of destiny among human beings, but also his approach to the diversity of religions (as we will see below).

When God brings the cosmos into existence, God, the One, discloses itself in the diversity of modes, which means that the One, the unlimited, delimits itself in its delimited *wujud*. With regard to human beings, their diversity is an expression of the infinite potentiality of Being which is underscored by the unrepeatability of the human soul. For Ibn al-'Arabi, diversity of religions is essentially due to the nature

---

[384] *BW*, 65.

of the non-redundant diversity of human souls as they are brought into existence by the One. As constituent elements of the phenomenal world, each human being is by nature, as mentioned above, a *mahall* (lit. a "place") or *mazhar* (locus of manifestation) in which the One discloses Itself in and to the phenomenal realm. Because religious traditions realize themselves in the lives of the human individuals who constitute any religious community, the diversity of persons as distinct and particular manifestations of the One Being is reflected in the particular traditions as a whole. Speaking fairly directly to the issue of religious diversity, the master writes:

> You worship only what you set up in yourself. This is why doctrines and states differed concerning Allah. Thus one group says that He is like this and another group says that He is not like this, but like that. Another group says concerning knowledge (of Him) that the color of water is determined by the color of the cup. . . . So consider the bewilderment that permeates (*sariyya*) every belief.[385]

Ibn al-'Arabi is very fond of quoting the great ninth-century mystic master of Baghdad, Abu l-Qasim Muhammad al-Junayd (d. 910) who once used the metaphor of water colored by its container as a metaphor for unity or identity in diversity: "The color of the water is the color of its container."[386] Ibn al-'Arabi's fondness for this metaphor, however, by no means indicates that he considered all religions to be equally valuable, but simply that, like every other constituent element of the existing order, all religions have their origin in God. One might paraphrase Ibn al-'Arabi's interpretation of Junayd's water metaphor by asserting that if the water represents the divine Being, the differences between religions is represented by the color or colors of the container. The color or colors, therefore, are directly related to the "preparedness" of a given religion to receive its particular manifestation of the Real. There are some religions which may be monochromatic or whose colors are strictly limited or faded. Other religions may

---

[385] *Fut.* II, 212.1-7, also quoted by Bashier, *Ibn al-'Arabi's Barzakh, the Concept of the Limit and the Relationship between God and the World* (Albany: State University of New York Press, 2004), 123.

[386] *Fut.* II, 316.10; *SPK*, 149, 229, 341-344.

have more distinct colors, but all of the same basic hue. Still others may have distinct colors of different hues, etc. "He who discloses Himself," Ibn al-'Arabi writes, "in respect to what He is in himself, is One in entity, but the self-disclosures—I mean their forms [e.g. the various religions]—are diverse because of the preparedness of the loci of self-disclosure."[387] As always, Ibn al-'Arabi roots this idea in the Qur'an. In this respect he makes specific reference to Q 11:118-119: "If your Lord had willed [it], He would have fashioned humanity into one community, *but they will not cease to differ*, except those upon whom your Lord has been merciful."[388]

Just as God never ceases to love or desire to be "recognized," or to be manifest, God's Self-manifestation also takes an infinite multiplicity of loci or receptacles (*mahallat*). Thus, phenomenal multiplicity, which is rooted in divine infinity, in fact has only one ontological entity, but because God's self-manifestation never ends, the loci of manifestation (*mazahir*) are infinitely diverse. This logic quite straightforwardly carries over to the phenomenon of the diversity of religions. In more direct terms, Ibn al-'Arabi writes, "every observer of God is under the controlling property of one of God's Names. That Name discloses itself to him or her and gives to him or her a specific belief through its Self-disclosure."[389]

One might also note that, from a slightly different angle, Ibn al-'Arabi's teaching on the diversity of religions can be inferred from what he has to say about perpetual creation (discussed above). As part of his teaching on this subject, the master emphasizes that "the Real does not manifest Itself twice in one form, nor in a single form to two individuals."[390] Ibn al-'Arabi strongly asserts, not only that creation is a never ending process, but also that God never manifests in a single form twice. Thus, for the master, the belief of believers is the cognitive manner in which the Self-disclosure of the Real is understood or mis-

---

[387] *Fut.* I, 287. 19, also quoted by *IW*, 141.

[388] *Wa law sha'a rabbuka la-ja'ala al-nasa ummatan wahidatan wa la yazaluna mukhtalifin illa man rahhima rabbuka.*

[389] *Fut.* II, 85.14, also quoted by *IW*, 141.

[390] *Fut.* II, 657.13.

understood, cognitively conceived or misconceived.[391] In a similar vein, Jalal al-Din Rumi (d. 1273), who appears to have been highly influenced by the master, asks: "If you pour the ocean into a jug, how much will it hold?"[392] Thus, every believer worships God the Real according to the particular "Lord" (*rabb*) whom she or he recognizes in her or himself.[393] "Since there are as many cups as drinkers at the Pool which will be found in the abode of the hereafter," Ibn al-'Arabi himself writes, "and since the water in the cup takes the form of the cup in both shape and color, we know for certain that knowledge of God takes on the measure of your view, your preparedness, and what you are in yourself."[394] In many ways this statement is similar to the words of Thomas Aquinas: "Things known are in the knower according to the mode of the knower."[395] "Although the Real is One," Ibn al-'Arabi affirms,

> beliefs present Him in various guises. They take Him apart and put Him together, they give Him form and they fabricate Him. But in Himself, He does not change, and in Himself, He does not undergo transmutation. However, the organ of sight sees Him so. Hence location constricts Him, and fluctuation from entity to entity limits Him. Hence, none becomes bewildered by Him except him who combines the assertion of similarity with the declaration of incomparability.[396]

Ibn al-'Arabi's explanation above is based on the opinion that the "God of belief" is Being (*wujud*), which manifests itself to every believer. Because every one of God's Self-manifestations is single and never repeats, every belief is single and exclusive. And because the object of every belief is single—i.e., the "God of belief" or the "God worshipped by each believer" differs from the God of every other believer. In fact, Ibn al-'Arabi attempts to emphasize this point by talking about a multiplicity of "Lords" manifesting the one God:

---

[391] *SPK*, 340, see *Fut*. II, 509. 31.

[392] *IW,*163.

[393] From the hadith: "He who knows himself knows his Lord."

[394] *Fut*. IV, 443. 33, II, 597. 35; Cf *SPK*, 342.

[395] Thomas Aquinas, *Summa Theologia* 2.2ae.1.2, cited by John Hick, "Ineffability," *Religious Studies* 36 (United Kingdom: Cambridge University Press, 2000), 40.

[396] *Fut*. IV, 393. 6, also quoted by *IW*, 163.

Every believer has a Lord in his heart that he has brought into existence, so he believes in Him. Such are the People of the Mark on the day of resurrection. They worship nothing but what they themselves have carved.[397] That is why, when God discloses Himself in other than that mark, they are confounded. They know what they believe, but what they believe does not know them, for they have brought it into existence. The general rule here is that the artifact does not know the artisan, and the building does not know the builder.[398]

Ultimately, for Ibn al-'Arabi, it is crucial for the believer to transcend the "God created in belief,"[399] (a concept to be discussed in fuller detail below in chapter five). For the master, the path ultimately leads one to transcend the "color" conveyed by religious affiliation. This is not, however, a prescription for a relativistic approach to religion. We should remember, as stressed above, that in Ibn al-'Arabi's mind God's Law (i.e., the Shari'a) is crucial for the realization of the Real (*la haqiqa bi la shari'a*). Thus, the path to God must be facilitated by the purest and most correct beliefs and practices possible. For Ibn al-'Arabi, these are found in the proper interpretations and practices of the Sunna of Muhammad, the Seal of the Prophets—i.e., the religion commonly referred to as "Islam."

Most contemporary Muslims' understanding of diversity of religions is rooted in quranic verses which describe religious traditions other than Islam. Unlike many Muslims who believe that certain exclusive verses in the Qur'an abrogate (*naskh*) certain inclusive verses in the Qur'an—thereby concluding asserting that Islam abrogates previous religions—Ibn al-'Arabi does not draw such a conclusion. For Ibn al-'Arabi,

All the revealed religions (*shara'i'*) are lights. Among these religions, the revealed religion of Muhammad is like the light of the sun among the lights of the stars. When the sun appears, the lights of the stars are hidden, and their lights are included in the light of the sun. They being hidden is like the abrogation of the other

---

[397] According to Chittick, here Ibn al-'Arabi is alluding to the words of Abraham quoted in the Qur'an, "Do you worship what you yourselves carve, while God created you and what you do?" (Q 37: 95-96. see *IW*, 185. n. 7.

[398] *Fut.* IV, 391. 12, quoted by *IW*, 151.

[399] *BW*, 282.

revealed religions that takes place through Muhammad's revealed religion. Nevertheless, they do in fact exist, just as the existence of the lights of the stars is actualized. This explains why we have been required in our all-inclusive religion to have faith in the truth of all the messengers and all the revealed religions. They are not rendered null (*batil*) by abrogation—that is the opinion of the ignorant.[400]

What Ibn al-'Arabi is basically saying is that it is incumbent on Muslims to follow the path of their Prophet Muhammad and stick to the guidance of the Qur'an. At the same time, he also emphasizes that the nature of the Qur'an is inclusive; that it includes within itself the paths of all the prophets preceding Muhammad. He writes:

> Among the path is the path of blessing. It is referred to in God's words. "To every one of you We have appointed a right way and a revealed law"[401] (5: 48). The Muhammadan leader chooses the path of Muhammad and leaves aside the other paths, even though he acknowledges them and has faith in them. However, he does not make himself a servant except through the path of Muhammad, nor does he have his followers make themselves servants except through it. He traces the attributes of all paths back to it, because Muhammad's revealed religion is all-inclusive. Hence the property of all revealed religions has been transferred to his revealed religion. His revealed religion embraces them, but they do not embrace it.[402]

In the *Futuhat* Ibn al-'Arabi further explores the phenomenon of the diversity of religions. To summarize what we have already stated, for Ibn al-'Arabi, God Self-discloses in numerous ways, infinitely diverse and thus unique and different from one another. Although God in Godself is immeasurably greater than all God's manifestations, God also is somehow manifest in the form of every belief. But God does not constrain Godself within one particular belief. One belief may well be more accurate than another (e.g., "I believe there is only one God" versus "I believe there is no God"), but God is too glorious to delimit Godself to one form of belief rather than another.

---

[400] *Fut.* III, 153. 12, quoted by *IW*, 125.

[401] This translation should read: "a revealed law and a way (*shir'atan wa minhajan*)."

[402] *Fut.* III, 410. 21, quoted by *IW*, 145.

In fact, Ibn al-'Arabi plays with the root *'QL* in order to convey the inherent potential of discursive language and rationalist thought to delimit that which cannot be limited. The trouble with speculative thinking—especially when taken to the extreme—is that the *'aql* or "intellect" that is the human faculty enabling us to engage in such thought, acts like a "fetter" (*'iqal*—from the same root), which at times is very useful (i.e., helping us to develop categories with which to better understand ourselves and our world), but at other times can be very dangerous. The danger lies in the capacity of the intellect to attempt to "fetter" and pin down, that which is beyond fettering. Ibn al-'Arabi, then, criticizes speculative thinking and formulation when it acts to confine the infinite Essence of God. Ibn al-'Arabi goes on to strengthen this argument by reflecting on the root of the words for "creed" (*'aqida*) and "belief" (*i'tiqad*). The root is *'QD* which has to do with "binding" and "tying" a knot. He is not attacking "creeds" and "beliefs" because he thinks they have their place in the life of faith. What he is criticizing is the attempt to absolutize "creeds" and "statements" to the point at which one is involved in the futile (and perhaps even blasphemous) attempt to "tie a knot" around God. He writes:

> God is known through every knotting. Although the beliefs are totally diverse, their aim is one. He is a receptacle for everything that you tie Him to and every knotting you make concerning Him. And within that He will disclose Himself on the day of resurrection, for it is the mark which is between you and Him.[403]

For Ibn al-'Arabi, only the *'arif* (lit. "gnostic"), who has attained the station and state of the Perfect Human, can see God as manifested in every belief, and as unconstrained by any belief. The true *'arif* identifies the Truth in any belief and understands that any belief involves a Self-disclosure of the Real. He or she understands that, while some beliefs may be true and others false, all beliefs are delimitations of the non-delimited *wujud*, which according to Chittick, "embrace[s] all reality on whatever level it is envisaged."[404] As the "locus of manifesta-

---

[403] *Fut.* IV, 416. 29; *IW*, 164.
[404] *IW*, 139.

tion" of the all-comprehensive Name of God (i.e., Allah), and thus as one who stands in the "station of no station," the Perfect Human acknowledges any station and any belief insofar as it corresponds to one of the infinite multiplicities of the Self-disclosure of God.

Perhaps the quranic text which Ibn al-'Arabi quotes most frequently in support of his argument that all religions are manifestations of the Real is: "Wheresoever you turn, there is the face of God" (2: 115).[405] Commenting on this verse and a few others like it, Ibn al-'Arabi writes, "God has made it clear that He is in every direction turned to, each of which represents a particular doctrinal perspective regarding Him."[406] Indeed, for Ibn al-'Arabi, because God is the *wujud* or essential reality of all phenomenal multiplicity, no path is essentially distorted or warped; every path according to him essentially brings believers to God. Quoting the quranic verse "To Him all affairs shall be returned" (Q 11: 123), Ibn al-'Arabi writes, "certainly, all roads lead to Allah, since He is the end of every road."[407] Thus, every believer serves God on the basis of God's Self-disclosures and their preparedness, so all beliefs in fact are rooted in God the infinite. By saying this, it does not mean that all beliefs are similar and have the same effect on the transformation of human consciousness toward God.[408] It means that each belief manifests truth and, insofar as it does this, it is part of the path to human perfection in service to God.

One of the most touching and profound aspects of Ibn al-'Arabi's teaching on the diversity of religions can be found in the *Futuhat* where the master refers to God as "taking care of the needs of misbelievers" and "giving them to drink."[409] According to Ibn al-'Arabi, all those who are worshipping God, even though they may be doing so

---

[405] *Wa li-llah al-mashriq wa al-maghrib fa aynama tuwallu fa thamma waju Allah*; see for example Ibn al-'Arabi, *Fusus*, 113, and *IW*, 137.

[406] *IW*, 138.

[407] *Fut.* II, 148. 11; *SPK*, 303.

[408] On the transformation process in Ibn al-'Arabi's teaching, see William C. Chittick, "Belief and Transformation: Sufi Teaching of Ibn al-'Arabi," *The American Theosophist* 74 (1986).

[409] *Fut.* II, 661. 27; *SPK*, 381, also cited by Dom Sylvester Houedard, "Ibn 'Arabi's Contribution to the Wider Ecumenism," in *Muhyiddin Ibn 'Arabi, A Commemorative*

falsely by attaching the name "God" to their idols, are nonetheless the loci of God's Self-disclosure, and as such are de facto recipients of God's mercy. "God takes care of their need and gives them to drink," Ibn al-'Arabi writes, "He punishes them if they do not honor the Divine Side in this inanimate form."[410] Here Ibn al-'Arabi's phrase "giving them to drink" echoes his discussion of "the drinking places," a discussion in which he refers to many quranic verses:

> The drinking places have become variegated and the religions diverse. The levels have been distinguished, the divine names and the engendered effects have become manifest and the names the gods have become many in the cosmos. People worship angels, stars, Nature, the elements, animals, plants, minerals, human beings and jinn. So much is this the case that when the One presented them with His Oneness, they said, "Has He made the gods One God? This is indeed a marvelous thing." (23: 117). . . . [T]here is no effect in the cosmos which is not supported by a divine reality. So from whence do the gods become many? From the divine realities. Hence you should know that this derives from the names. God was expansive with the names: He said, "Worship Allah (4:36), Fear Allah, your Lord (65:1), Prostate yourself to the All-merciful (25: 6). And He said, "Call upon Allah or call upon the All-merciful; whichever, that is Allah or the All-Merciful, you call upon, to Him belong the most beautiful names" (17: 110). This made the situation more ambiguous for the people, since He did not say, "Call upon Allah or call upon the All-merciful; whichever you call upon, the Entity is One, and these two names belong to it." That would be the text which would remove the difficulty, God only left this difficulty as a mercy for those who associate others with Him, the people of rational consideration—those who associate others with Him on the basis of obfuscation. [411]

Volume, Stephen Hirtenstein and Michael Tiernan, eds. (Shaftesbury: Element, 1993), 295.

[410] *Fut.* II, 661. 27; *SPK*, 381, also cited by Dom Sylvester Houedard, "Ibn 'Arabi's Contribution to the Wider Ecumenism," 295.

[411] *Fut.* III, 94. 19; *SPK*, 363-364, also cited by Dom Sylvester Houedard with slightly different translation in "Ibn 'Arabi's Contribution," 295.

Chapter IV

MEISTER ECKHART ON DETACHMENT

MEISTER ECKHART ON DETACHMENT

A*begescheidenheit* or "detachment" is the constant theme of Eckhart's preaching. "No theme," Kelley writes, "is more pervasive throughout the commentaries, tractates, and sermons of Eckhart than that of detachment."[412] For Eckhart, the foundation of this concept of "detachment" (*abegescheidenheit*) is the biblical verse "and Jesus entered the temple and drove out all who were selling and buying in the temple, and he overturned the tables of the money-changers and the seats of those who sold doves" (Mat. 21:12).[413] In fact, Meister Eckhart's point of departure for all his sermons are scriptural texts, but his interpretation of passages is, as he says, "parabolical" and "mystical."[414] This chapter will elaborate Eckhart's concept of detachment, and will examine many other concepts and clusters of concepts which he employs that are deeply connected and even overlap with the concept of detachment. Specifically, these concepts and clusters of concepts are: the merchants and the virgin/wife; "detachment is not withdrawal"; "living without a 'why?'"; poverty, breakthrough, and union; "pray to God to be free of God"; and the pathless path.

1. The Merchants and the Virgin/Wife

This cluster of concepts is rooted in the Gospel motif of Jesus' driving out of the Temple those who were selling and buying within the sacred

---

[412] C. F. Kelley, *Meister Eckhart on Divine Knowledge* (New Haven: Yale University Press, 1977), 264, n. 23.

[413] Unless otherwise indicated, all biblical citations are taken from *The NRSV Catholic Edition* (Oxford: Oxford University Press, 1999). This does not include biblical citations quoted in the work of other authors.

[414] On Eckhart's hermeneutic, see Konrad Weiss, "Meister Eckharts Biblische Hermeneutik" in *La Mystique Rhenane* (Paris, 1963).

precincts—a group which Eckhart collectively identifies as "merchants."[415] According to Eckhart, Jesus drove out the merchants because he wanted the Temple to be empty. Seeking the deepest meaning of this verse, Eckhart concludes that the Temple symbolizes the human soul which God created so much like Godself[416] that nothing else in heaven or on earth resembles God as much. For Eckhart, the human soul's unique resemblance of God is concomitant with the unique capacity of the human soul to be, like the Temple of ancient Israel, the unique dwelling place of God. It is for this reason that Eckhart affirms God's wish that the Temple/soul be empty, so that there will be nothing in the Temple/soul but Godself.[417]

In his elaboration of the Matthean verse above, Eckhart uses Jesus' cleansing of the Temple as an image of detachment—the complete clearing and emptying of the soul for the purpose of maximum receptivity to the divine. For Eckhart, the strong emotions which Jesus displays in this verse are directly reflective of the ardent desire of Jesus that every human soul actualize its capacity to be truly empty[418] so that the divine in its nothingness could dwell in and fill this empty space. The Temple/soul should be empty "so that no one is in it but [God] alone."[419] The logic here is very straightforward. If the human soul is filled already with a myriad of things calling out to us for our undivided attention (i.e., those who were buying and selling), then God will not enter it and dwell

---

[415] The specific verse on which Meister Eckhart focuses is Mat. 21:12 which runs as follows: "Then Jesus entered the temple and drove out all who were selling and buying in the temple, and he overturned the tables of the money-changes and the seats of those who sold doves." A much abbreviated version occurs in Luke (19:45-46). The most detailed version of the story is found in John 2:13-22.

[416] Meister Eckhart refers to biblical passage "Let us make man according to our image and likeness" (Gn. 1: 26)." See Meister Eckhart, *Teacher and Preacher* (hereafter abbreviated as TP), ed. by Bernard McGinn, Classics of Western Spirituality (New York: Paulist Press, 1986), 239, *Meister Eckhart, A Modern Translation*, ed. by Raymond B. Blakney (New York: Harper & Brothers, 1941), 156.

[417] Blakney, *Meister Eckhart,* 451.

[418] *TP*, 239.

[419] Meister Eckhart, *Die deutschen und lateinischen Werke,* ed. by Joseph Quint (hereafter abbreviated as LW and DW), I (Stuttgart, 1936), sermon 1, "Intravit Jesus in templum," 6 in *TP*, 239.

therein. Thus, somewhat analogous to how Ibn al-'Arabi insists that although God always stands ready to disclose Godself in the human heart that is properly "prepared," for Eckhart, God stands ready to enter into a soul which has emptied itself, ridding itself of attachment to the objects of all its desires, passions, and worldly inclinations. "Empty yourself, so that you may be filled," Eckhart quotes Augustine of Hippo. Eckhart then continues: "[E]verything that is to receive and be capable of receiving should and must be empty."[420] In the words of one contemporary scholar of Eckhart, the master maintains that "if God is to enter, the creature must exit."[421]

As his interpretation delves more deeply into the meaning of this verse, Eckhart poses the question as to the precise identity of those who bought and sold and whom Jesus drove out of the Temple. To this question, in his sermon, Eckhart replies that they were "all [merchants] who guard against serious sin, would like to be good people, and perform their good works for God's glory, such as fasting, vigils, praying, and whatever other good works there are."[422] They do these things, however, so that God may do something dear for them; as people of commerce they are engaging in a cosmic *quid pro quo*. For their devotion, the merchants want and expect something in exchange. So, for Eckhart, all these people are merchants because they wish to give one thing in return for another.[423] In this way they wish to bargain with God.[424] "They are very foolish people," says Eckhart, those who wish to barter with God. [425] That is why they were driven out of the Temple. For Eckhart, "light and darkness cannot exist side by side."[426] Eckhart here also mentions the poignant example of Judas. He argues

---

[420] *ESC*, 220.

[421] Richard Kieckhefer, "Meister Eckhart's Conception of Union with God," *The Harvard Theological Review*, Vol. 71 (1970), 210.

[422] *TP*, 240.

[423] Blakney, *Meister Eckhart*, 157.

[424] Fox, *Breakthrough*, 451; Blakney, *Meister Eckhart*, 157, see also Frank Tobin, *Meister Eckhart, Thought and Language* (Philadelphia: University of Pennsylvania Press, 1986), 121.

[425] Blakney, *Meister Eckhart*, 157.

[426] *TP*, 240.

that we condemn Judas for having forsaken Jesus Christ for thirty silver coins, but most of us are busy selling God for much less than that on an everyday basis since we fear the loss of anything more than we fear the loss of God.[427] For Eckhart, the only way for the soul to open itself to the love of God is to forsake the way of the "merchants" and become detached.

It is important to note that, for Eckhart, to become detached is to "become like God,"[428] who *seeks* nothing just as God *is* no-thing. "If man is to become equal with God," says Eckhart, "insofar as a creature can have equality with God, that must happen through detachment."[429] In his sermon Eckhart describes how one can empty oneself in order to become detached like God, thus enabling God to be born within the depths of one's soul:

> And you should be as empty as that nothing [God] is empty which is neither here nor there [as creatures are]. [. . .] Look! The person who does not regard himself or anything else but God alone and God's honor is truly free and rid of all mercantilism in all his works and seeks nothing of his own, just as God is free and unencumbered in all his works and seeks nothing of his own.[430]

Eckhart says, "So detach yourselves from the image, and unite yourselves to the formless being, for God's spiritual consolation is delicate; therefore, he will not offer it to anyone except to he who disdains bodily consolation."[431] Indeed, in order to do God's beneficial work in the soul, there must be no obstacles God faces on God's way; the soul has to be entirely free and unconditioned. It is also because only the like can meet the like, so God, the Unconditioned One, must meet an unconditioned soul in order to unify and be one. In this case, the soul

---

[427] *LW* 4, Sermon XLVI, *Domine, descende, prius moriatur filius meus* (Lord come done before my son dies, Jn. 4: 49), n. 471, 389 .

[428] Note the limited but nonetheless intriguing similarity between Eckhart's language about "becoming like God" and Ibn al-'Arabi's teaching regarding 'taking on the traits of God' (*takhalluq bi-akhlaq Allah*). The latter is discussed above in chapter three.

[429] *ESC*, 220.

[430] *DW* 1, Sermon 1, *Intravit Jesus in templum*, 9-10 in *TP*, 240-1.

[431] *DW* V, 431 in *ESC*, 293.

can only be free and unconditioned if it is not enslaved by the senses and the outside world.

According to Eckhart, then, for the soul to grow in its spiritual capacity, it must become detached from all outward conditions. This does not mean that the soul should get rid of all external impressions and stimuli, but it does mean that the soul has to be unmoved and unshaken by them, like God who is unmoved and unshaken (detached). "True detachment," Eckhart writes, "is nothing else than for the spirit to stand as immovable against whatever may chance to it of joy and sorrow, honor, shame and disgrace, as a mountain of lead stands before a little breath of wind. This immovable detachment brings a man into the greatest equality with God, because God has it from his immovable detachment that he is God."[432]

Eckhart also refers to Avicenna on this teaching of detachment:

> an authority called Avicenna says: 'the excellence of the spirit which has achieved detachment is so great that whatever it contemplates is true, and whatever it desires is granted, and whatever it commands one must obey.' And you should know that this is really so; when the free spirit has attained true detachment, it compels God to its being; and if the spirit could attain formlessness, and be without all accidents, it would take on God's properties.[433]

According to Eckhart, detachment also takes a person closer to her/his image in her/his pre-condition, wherein there was no difference between her/him and God. This is because, Eckhart insists, all other virtues "have some regards to creatures, but detachment is free of all creatures."[434] According to him, God himself is pure detachment:

> For God is God because of His immovable detachment, and from detachment He has his purity and His simplicity and His unchangeability. If God himself is pure detachment then the way of the soul to God is the way of detachment. Consequently, should

[432] *ESC*, 288.

[433] *ESC*, 288.

[434] Meister Eckhart, *Sermons and Treatises* (hereafter abbreviated as ST), trans. and ed. by M. O. 'C. Walshe (Dorset, 1979), Vol. III, 117.

a man wish to be like God insofar as a creature can have likeness with God, then this can only come about through detachment.[435]

Eckhart uses the image of a "virgin/wife" to elaborate the idea of detachment. The master elaborates his teaching on detachment in his mystical reflections on the biblical text for his sermon 2, which says: "Jesus entered a little castle, where a woman named Martha welcomed him into her home" (Luke 10:38).[436] Eckhart interprets the verse freely: "I have spoken a little verse in Latin, which stands written in the Gospel and says this in German: 'our Lord Jesus Christ went up into a little castle and was received by a virgin, who was a wife" (*Unser herre Jesus Kristus der gienc uf in ein burgelin und wart enpfangen von einer juncvrouwen, diu ein wip was*). [437] Here Eckhart is employing a striking oxymoron to elucidate his central teaching on detachment. This is not entirely surprising, but what does it mean?

It is clear from his interpretation that he is identifying Martha as "a virgin who [is] a wife," and that this identification has something to do with the role she plays in the story which is about to unfold. In the very next verse (Lk. 10:39), Martha's sister, Mary is introduced to reader and described as sitting "at the Lord's feet" listening "to what he was saying." The story goes on to say that Martha, who is very busy serving her guests as the biblical virtue of hospitality so strictly demands, complains to Jesus, saying, "Lord, do you not care that my sister has left me to do all the work by myself? Tell her then to help me" (Lk. 10:40). In response to Martha's complaint, Jesus appears to be scolding her by saying, "Martha, Martha, you are worried and dis-

---

[435] Caputo, *The Mystical Element,* 13 and *ESC,* 288.

[436] The Latin text heading the sermon is, "Intravit Jesus in quoddam castellum et mulier quaedam, Martha nominee, except illum in domain suam," *DW* I, 24: 1-2 in *ESC,* 177.

[437] *DW* I, 26, "vri ist und megetlich" in *ESC,* 177. According to Amy Hollywood, Eckhart's teaching on this "virgin who is a wife" is rooted in Beguine spirituality, especially that of Mechthild of Magdeburg. See Hollywood's *The Soul as Virgin Wife: Mechthild of Madgeburg, Marguerite Porete, and Meister Eckhart* (Notre Dame: University of Notre Dame Press, 1995), 149.

tracted[438] by many things; there is need of only one thing. Mary has chosen the better part, which will not be taken away from her" (Lk. 10:41-42).

More conventional interpretations of this story, portray Martha as the spiritual ignoramus and Mary as the spiritual adept. Although service (*diakonia*) of others is normally an important duty, especially for those who wish to follow Christ, nothing can be more important than listening to God's word. In fact, most mainstream Christian theology would assert that true Christian "service" must be rooted in and stem from attentiveness to the word of God. Very much in line with the characteristic way in which mystical interpretation oftentimes contradicts the plain sense meaning or even the "tropological and moral" interpretation of scripture,[439] Eckhart offers a stark counterpoint to any interpretation which ranks Mary higher than Martha with respect to spiritual development.

According to Eckhart's mystical interpretation of this story, Martha is the one who is more spiritually advanced because, while Mary is a spiritual "virgin" only, Martha is a spiritual "virgin who [is] a wife." In his view of Mary as a spiritual virgin only, Eckhart sees her as spiritually immature. Although she eagerly embraces the life of contempla-

---

[438] The NRSV translation of the pericope found in Luke 10:38-42 describes Martha in two places as "distracted"—first in verse 40 ("but Martha was distracted by her many tasks") and second in verse 41 ("Martha, Martha, you are worried and distracted by many things"). The original Greek actually uses the verb *perispein* meaning "to be busy" or "to take diligent care of" in verse 40 and the verbs *merimnao* meaning "to be anxious about" and *thorubazo* "to be troubled by") in verse 41. While it is certainly understandable how one could read a sense of "distraction" into these verbs, it seems likely that the translators chose to translate these expressions this way because they interpret Jesus as scolding Martha for being "distracted" from "the better part" of hearing the word of God. Indeed, it is this interpretation that renders this pericope the locus classicus for exalting the spiritual state of the contemplative over that of the active. Given Meister Eckhart's mystical interpretation of this pericope and his rejection of this conventional interpretation, it is important to note that the original Greek need not be understood to be describing Martha as "distracted."

[439] For a detailed discussion of what he calls "the four-fold method of [medieval] scriptural interpretation, see Michael Fishbane, *Garments of Torah: Essays in Biblical Hermeneutics* (Bloomington, IN: Indiana University Press, 1989), 112-120.

tion—of quiet 'listening' to the word of God—she does so by utterly rejecting the world of activity and service, a world involvement in which Eckhart understands to be absolutely essential for the life of the Christian. Martha, on the other hand, not only has attended to the word of God, like her sister. She is also *acting* on this word by serving her guests. Thus, while Mary is only a spiritual virgin, her sister Martha is both virgin (one who undistractedly attends to God's word in prayer and contemplation) *and* wife (one who takes responsibility and commits oneself to the service of others).

Eckhart's counter-intuitive ranking of Martha above Mary does not mean that he attributes a negative status to Mary the way conventional interpretations attribute a negative status to Martha. She is merely a well-intentioned spiritual neophyte. "Three things," Eckhart asserts in his eighty-sixth sermon, "caused Mary to sit at the feet of Christ. The first was that God's goodness had embraced her soul. The second was ineffable longing: she longed for she knew not what and she wanted she knew not what. The third was the sweet consolation and delight she drew from the eternal words which flowed from the mouth of Christ."[440]

For Martha, however, Eckhart has even greater praise. He interprets Martha's critique of Mary's behavior not as a self-centered complaint, but rather as an act of compassionate concern for her younger and spiritually less experienced sister. According to Eckhart, Martha asks Jesus to intervene because "She realized that Mary had been overwhelmed by a desire for the complete fulfillment of her soul."[441] Eckhart then goes on to admit that he "harbor[s] the suspicion that dear Mary was sitting there more for enjoyment than for spiritual profit. Therefore Martha said, 'Lord, tell her to get up,' because [Martha] feared that [Mary] would remain stuck in this pleasant feeling and would progress no further."[442] As for what appears to be Jesus's chastisement of Martha ("Martha, Martha…"), Eckhart says: "Christ did

---

[440] Sermon 86: *Inravit Jesus in quoddam castellum, et mulier quaedam, Martha nominee, exepit illum in domum suam* in *TP*, 338.

[441] *TP*, 338.

[442] *TP*, 339.

not speak these words to chasten [Martha]. Rather, he responded by giving her the comforting message that it would turn out for Mary as she desired."[443] In fact, going even more deeply into mystical aspects of Martha's identity as a "virgin who [is] a wife," Eckhart says that the reason Jesus addresses Martha by repeating her name twice (verse 41) is as follows:

> Why did he name Martha twice? He wanted to indicate that Martha possessed completely everything of temporal and eternal value that a creature should have. When he said "Martha" the first time, he indicated her perfection in temporal works [i.e., her perfection as a spiritual wife]. With his second calling out, "Martha," he affirmed that she lacked nothing of all that is necessary for eternal happiness [i.e., that she lacks nothing as a spiritual "virgin"]. [444]

As intriguing as it may be in its own right, how is Eckhart's interpretation of the story of Jesus, Martha, and Mary in Luke 10:38-42 related to his teaching on detachment? For Eckhart, the soul of the spiritual "virgin/wife"—be the virgin male or female—is "free of all alien images." Basing his mystical exegesis on his own German translation of the Latin Vulgate version of verse 38 (*"excepit illum in domum suam"*[445]), Eckhart teaches that only a virginal soul (*juncvrouwen*) can *receive* the Son, since it is free of alien images just as it was "when [it] was not yet."[446] Here Eckhart is translating the Latin active verb *excepit* (i.e., "she received") into the German passive construction *Jesus Kristus… wart enpfangen (von einer juncvrouwen, diu ein wip was)*, where the participle *enpfangen* can carry the double meaning of both "received" and "conceived."[447] Thus the status of the spiritual virgin/wife, according to Eckhart, is a necessary precondition for "receiving" and "conceiving" (*enpfangen*) Jesus Christ.[448] It is only when the soul

---

[443] *TP*, 339.

[444] *TP*, 340.

[445] *NRSV* : "…welcomed him into her home."

[446] *DW* 1, Sermon 2, *Intravit Jesus in quoddam castellum*, 24 in *ESC*, 177.

[447] Michael A. Sells, *Mystical Languages of Unsaying* (Chicago: University of Chicago Press, 1994), 199; see also *MP*, 11.

[448] *ESC*, 177. Eckhart transforms Martha into a type of the Virgin Mary, first by describing her as "the virgin who was a wife" (*einer juncvrouwen, diu ein wip was*)

is both virgin *and* wife (when it attains the status of Martha, not Mary), that it attains true detachment—detachment from the world *coupled with* detachment from detachment. Thus, when the soul abstains from everything or when it "has nothing in common with anything, nor does anything created have anything in common with it,"[449] the virgin/wife, which is the truly detached soul, will gain her ability to "receive" and "conceive" Christ, the "Son." When the soul finally achieves true detachment, she is truly virgin (*juncvrouwen*) and truly wife (*wip*). In this condition, she becomes a perfectly "empty" vessel in which God gives birth to God's Son.[450] The soul as virgin/wife becomes "pregnant with nothing as a woman does with a child, and in this nothing God [is] born."[451] Concerning the virgin/wife, Eckhart writes:

> A virgin who is a wife is free and unpledged, without attachment, she is always equally close to God and to herself. She produces much fruit, and it is great, neither less nor more than is God [God] self. This virgin who is a wife brings this fruit and this birth about, and every day she produces fruit, a hundred or a thousand times, yes, more than can be counted, giving birth and becoming fruitful from the noblest ground of all—or, to put it better, from that same ground where the Father is bearing his eternal World, from that ground is she fruitfully bearing with him.[452]

The oxymoronic nature of the concept of the virgin/wife is one of many indications that Eckhart has no concept of duality in his teaching. For Eckhart, the divine is rarely, if ever, found in the "either...or" and usually found in the "both...and." It is important to

---

and second by using the word *enpfangen* ("excepit"), which means "conceived" as well as "received," a wife who gives birth. See Bruce Milem, *The Unspoken Word, Negative Theology in Meister Eckhart's German Sermons* (Washington, D. C: The Catholic University of America Press, 2002), 51, n 3, and also Sells, *Mystical Languages*, 199.

[449] *TP*, 269.

[450] On Eckhart's teaching of the birth of God in Soul, see Karl G. Kertz, "Meister Eckhart's Teaching on the Birth of the Divine World of the Soul," *Traditio* 15 (1959).

[451] *TP*, 323.

[452] *DW* I, 30-31 in *ESC*, 178-179.

note that a very similar resistance to strict dualities is also a salient characteristic of the teachings of Ibn al-'Arabi who, much like Meister Eckhart, intuits that the one God who is beyond all duality is found in and through an experience of the *coincidentia oppositorum* or "coincidence of opposites" in the Godhead.[453] For Eckhart, the seeming opposites of "virgin" and "wife" actually become complementary as in his perspective on the ideal relationship between the contemplative and active states.

As virgin/wife, the truly detached soul bears fruit unceasingly.[454] Because of the virgin/wife's perpetual likeness to Jesus, the virgin soul receives and conceives Jesus forever. In Sermon 6, *Justi vivent in aeternum* ("The just live forever"—Ws. 5:16), Eckhart speaks of the just human beings who have "gone out of themselves and who do not seek for what is theirs in anything." These, Eckhart says, "will live forever;" they live "eternally 'with God.'"[455] Eckhart also insists that it is also through the soul's likeness to Christ in its status as virgin and wife, that union is possible. In fact, for Eckhart, this process of receiving and conceiving Jesus also brings the virgin soul who is a wife to a level of equality with the Son and at the same time with the Father, as they each participate in the Son's "birth." On this equality in the process of the "birth of the Son" in the soul, Eckhart writes:

> Not only is the soul with him, and he equals with it, but he is in it, and the Father gives his Son birth in the soul in the same way as he gives him birth in eternity, and not otherwise. ...the Father gives birth to his Son without ceasing; and I say more: He gives me birth, me, his Son and the same Son. I say more: He gives birth not only to me, his Son, but he gives birth to me as himself and himself as me and to me as his being and nature.[456]

---

[453] For a discussion of the concept of *coincidencia oppositorum* in Ibn al-'Arabi (Ar. *jam' al-addad*), see *IW*, 63-64; *SPK*, 59, 67, 115, 116, 243, 288, and 375; *SDG*, 11, 73, 86, 184, 236-237, 311, and 358. For a discussion of the how the term applies to Eckhart, see Sells's analysis of the paradoxes of "self-containment" and "procession and remaining" in his *Mystical Languages*, 165.

[454] Cf. Ibn al-'Arabi's teaching about "perpetual creation," above, chapter 3.

[455] *ESC*, 187.

[456] *DW* 1, 109 in *ESC*, 187.

2. Detachment Is Not Withdrawal

If understood literally, Eckhart's concept of detachment can easily lead us to think that detachment is withdrawal from the world. For Eckhart, however, detachment does not entail withdrawal from the world in the sense of ignorance or insensitivity to all suffering, and the renunciation of responsibility for others. In fact, for Eckhart, the essence of detachment lies in the consistency that—whatever the condition and circumstances of our activity—we do what we do for the sake of God, and God alone. "When I was in a meditation," Eckhart relates, "and the poor people asked me for a cup of soup, the right thing for me is to leave my meditation and attend to the poor."[457] Thus, for Eckhart, real detachment means to be faithful to the will of God by always subordinating self-interest to the divine will. A detached person always has God wherever she or he may be—she or he in the bustling streets, or in the quiet of a monk's cell. A person who possesses the right focus and always has God as the object of his or her thoughts and actions must be careful to maintain this focus both within the sacred confines of a church and out in the chaos of the world.[458] Thus, for Eckhart, consistency is most fundamental to the meaning of detachment. In other words, when a person has God, nobody and nothing can foil her or him.

Eckhart's central meaning of his concept of detachment can be found by inference from his Sermon 16b ("*Quasi vas auri solidum ornatum omni lapide pretioso*"[459]) in which he describes the just or detached person, as someone who has "annihilated all created things and stands without distraction looking toward the eternal Word directly and who is formed therein and is reformed in justice."[460] Here again, for Eckhart, detachment never means withdrawal from the phenomenal world, but rather, as Milem argues, it "reflects the insufficiency of

---

[457] Cyprian Smith, *The Way of Paradox*, 66.

[458] *DW* V, *Die rede der underscheidunge*, 203, Cf. *ESC*, 79, see further *Com. On John* 14-22.

[459] Sirach 50:9 ("Like a vessel of hammered gold studded with all kinds of precious stones")

[460] *DW* I, 76, Sermon 16b in *TP*, 278.

creaturely goods in and of themselves. Since such goods are nothing without God, anyone practicing detachment has no regard for them."[461] Eckhart's concept of detachment, therefore, is a contemplative asceticism. "Contemplative" here does not mean to seek some kind of other-worldly "visionary experience." Instead, the Eckhartian contemplative ascetic sees the existence of the world within the divine being, and therefore without any rejection of the world.

According to Eckhart, the penitential practices usually associated with withdrawal from the world—frequent prayer, meditative exercises, kneeling, being disciplined, wearing hair shirts, lying on hard surfaces, fasting, charitable work, and the like—are perfectly legitimate and necessary to achieve detachment. The only caveat is to be aware of the danger of becoming attached to these practices—as if the practices themselves constitute detachment. For Eckhart, such activities can help the readers in their initial process of transformation, but only as an introductory or an opening into the essential process.[462] According to Eckhart, it is very easy for someone to be attached to the practice itself, so that she or he is possibly "getting the way [but] missing God."[463] In response to this line of thinking, some of Eckhart's critics and accusers felt that he was reducing the meaning and connection between practices (especially the sacraments) and the reception grace. They argued that because Eckhart's detachment is so all-encompassing, it even negates virtue along with good works as mere "means to an end." Anyone even vaguely familiar with Eckhart's writings knows that things like religious praxis and moral virtue were of paramount importance to the master. Indeed, if his behavior was less than impeccable, we can be sure his detractors would have called our attention to it. What these accusers are missing is Eckhart's refusal to speak about anything but God as absolute. As important as the sacraments are, they cannot, in Eckhart's mind, be placed on the same level as the only One who is Absolute.

---

[461] Milem, *Unspoken Word*, 163.

[462] *ST*, 56, Fox, *Breakthrough*, 451; Blakney, *Meister Eckhart*, 157, see also Frank Tobin, *Meister Eckhart, Thought and Language* (Philadelphia : University of Pennsylvania Press, 1986), 121.

[463] *DW* I, 227; *ST*. I,117; *ESC*, 183.

Some might mistakenly conclude that because Meister Eckhart cautions his hearers and readers about the abuse of penitential practices and the like, that the contemplative asceticism he is advocating is essentially half-hearted. For Eckhart, nothing could be farther from the truth. From his perspective, he is advocating the most radical form of asceticism because it demands, not that one renounces this or that possession or desire, but rather that one renounces one's entire self. The master concludes Sermon 12 ("*Qui audit me*"[464]) by insisting that "A person who [in detachment] remains in God's love should be dead to himself and to all created things, so that he gives as little attention to himself as he does to something a thousand miles away."[465] Notice that Eckhart does not describe the contemplative ascetic who cultivates true detachment as one who attempts to reject and completely withdraw from the world. Such an ascetic does not strive to treat him or herself and all created things as if they do not exist. For Eckhart, such an attempt is not radical asceticism, but is futile asceticism. It will not work and will only result in false detachment (i.e., attachment to detachment). Instead, the Eckhartian contemplative ascetic realistically and in a carefully balanced way, treats himself or herself and all created things—not as if they do not exist—but as if they are "a thousand miles away." In this manner, one becomes truly detached without the encumbrance of being attached to the impossibility of a total and complete withdrawal from self and world.

Because Eckhartian asceticism may be more realistic than the futile asceticism of withdrawal and negation, this does not mean that Eckhartian detachment is easy to attain. The master writes:

> Whoever were to forsake himself for an instant would be given everything. And if a person had forsaken himself for twenty years

---

[464] In the Latin Vulgate, Sirach 24:30-31 "Qui audit me non confundetur et qui operantur in me non peccabunt; qui elucidant me vitam aeternam habebunt." ("Whoever obeys me will not be put to / shame, / and those who work with me will / not sin. Whoever elucidates me / will have eternal life." Note that the NRSV numbers the Vulgate Sirach 24:30 as Sirach 24:22 and does not include the Vulgate Sirach 24:31 which reads, "Whoever elucidates me will have eternal life."

[465] *TP*, 270.

and then took himself back for an instant, he had never really forsaken himself at all. The person who has forsaken all and remains in this state and never for an instant casts a glance toward what he has forsaken and remains constant and unmoved in himself and unchanging, only such a person is detached. That we may remain as constant and unchangeable as the eternal Father, so help us God and eternal Wisdom. Amen.[466]

For Eckhart, true detachment does not lie in the *movement* of withdrawal, but rather in becoming immoveable as God is immoveable. To be detached is to be like a strong mountain, immovable against a little breath of wind.[467]

> True detachment is nothing else than for the spirit to stand as immovable against whatever may chance to it of joy and sorrow, honor, shame and disgrace, as a mountain of lead stands before a little breath of wind. This immovable detachment brings a man into the greatest equality with God, because God has it from his immovable detachment that He is God, and it is from his detachment that he has his purity and his simplicity and his unchangeability.[468]

Thus, according to Eckhart's treatise quoted above, the goal of detachment is not found in the movement of withdrawal. Instead it is found in a deep spiritual transformation which engenders a perfect inwardness. For Eckhart, once this transformation is achieved a person is free and ready to be a dwelling place of God. It is for this reason that, in Eckhart's mind, detachment enjoys superiority over the other virtues—because it frees one from creatures and it places a person on an equal ground with God in his utter simplicity. "I find no other virtues better than a pure detachment from all things," Eckhart writes, "because all other virtues have some regard for created things, but detachment is free from all created things."[469] And "I praise detachment above love," Eckhart continues, "because love compels me to suffer all things for God's love, yet detachment leads me to where I am

---

[466] *TP*, 270.

[467] Cyprian Smith, *The Way of Paradox, Spiritual Life as taught by Meister Eckhart* (New York: Paulist Press, 1987), 95.

[468] *ESC*, 288.

[469] *ESC*, 285.

receptive to nothing except God."[470] Elsewhere he writes: "Detachment forces God to me."[471]

3. Living without a "Why?"

Another important concept through which Meister Eckhart develops his central teaching on detachment is the notion of "living without a 'why?'" or *sunder warumbe*. For Eckhart, to "live without why" means to live and love as God lives and loves. In the words of Angelus Silesius (1627–1677), a physician and poet whom Eckhart influenced, "living without a 'why?'" is like a rose: *"Die Ros' ist ohn' warum, sie blühet weil sie blühet, Sie acht't nicht ihrer selbst, fragt nicht ob man sie siehet."* ("The rose [exists] without "why," she blooms because she blooms./ She pays no heed to herself, asks not if she is seen.")[472] For Eckhart, "living without a why" is a life in which one does not act for any conceived purpose, or for any reward, either temporal or eternal. In Sermon 5b (*"In hoc apparuit charitas Dei in nobis quoniam Filium suum unigenitum misit Deus in mundum ut vivamus per eum."*[473]), which takes as its scriptural text 1 John 4: 9, Eckhart writes about "living without a 'why?'":

> If anyone went on for a thousand years asking of life: "Why are you living?" life, if it could answer, would only say: "I live so that I may live." That is because life lives out of its own ground and springs from its own source, and so it lives without asking why it is itself living. If anyone asked a truthful man who works out of his own ground: "Why are you performing your works?" and if he were to give a straight answer, he would only say, "I work so that I may work."[474]

---

[470] *ESC*, 286.

[471] *ST*, III, 117-118.

[472] Angelus Silesius, *Der Cherubinischer Wandersmann* (Cherubinic Pilgrim) ed. by J. Schwabe, Basel, 1955, 35 quoted by *MP*, 245; see also John Caputo, "The Rose Is without Why," *Philosophy Today*, 15 (1971), 3–15. The translation is a modified version of Schurmann's.

[473] 1 John 4:9 ("God's love was revealed among us in this way: God sent his only Son into the world so that we might live through him.")

[474] *ESC*, 184; also cited in McGinn's "Theological Summary," 59.

It appears that, for Eckhart, this concept of "living without 'why?'" is closely linked with this passage in the first Johannine epistle. In I John 4:9, the writer of the epistle asserts that "God sent his only Son into the world so that we might live through him." The verse which immediately follows declares: "In this is love, not that we loved God but that he loved us and sent his Son to be the atoning sacrifice for our sins." In other words, the redemption wrought by the Son and the relationship of love which this redemption expresses is intrinsic to the divine nature and therefore has no "why?" or "wherefore?" The essence of God, and thus of all existence, is love and love—like the rose—has no purpose. Expounding on this very point, the master writes the following:

He who lives in the goodness of his nature lives in God's love; and love has no why.[475]

> It is proper to God that he have no "why or wherefore" outside or apart from himself. Therefore, every work that has a "why and wherefore" as such is not a divine work and is not performed for God. "He has made all things for himself" (Pr. 16:4). He who does anything that is not for God's sake does not have a divine work, since it has a "why and wherefore" which is foreign and different from God. It is not God and it is not divine."[476]

In a sermon on Romans 11:33–36,[477] Eckhart reflects on the meaning of Paul's classical Trinitarian doxology (in the Latin of the Vulgate): *quoniam ex ipso et per ipsum et in ipso omnia; ipsi gloria in saecula. Amen.* ("For all things are from him and through him and in him; glory be to him forever. Amen.")[478] Here Eckhart makes a subtle but critical distinction between, on the one hand, the proper understanding of the three prepositions of the doxology—"from," "through," and "in"—and, on the other hand, "for the sake of." Eckhart argues that there are three reasons why Paul did not add the expression "all things

---

[475] Sermon 28, *DW* II, 5 in McGinn, "Theological Summary," *ESC*, 59-60.

[476] *LW* II, ed. Konrad Weis, *Expositio Hibri Exodi*, n. 247, 201, *TP*, 120.

[477] *LW* 4, Sermon IV, I, *Ex ipso, per ipsum, et in ipso*, n. 21, 22.

[478] The original Greek reads: *hoti ex autou kai di autou kai eis autou ta panta; autoi he doxa eis tous aionas; amen.*

are *for the sake of* him" to this doxology. The first reason, according to Eckhart, is "because God and hence the divine man [i.e., truly detached person] does not act *for the sake of* a why or wherefore."[479] The second reason is "because all things do what they do in God, from him and through him, but God himself does all things in himself. 'In him' is not 'for the sake of.'"[480] The third and final reason Paul did not add "for the sake of" is "because that person really works for the sake of God who works from God, through God, and in God, just as the just man does just things or works justly, but not for the sake of justice insofar as 'for the sake of' is distinguished from 'of,' 'through,' and 'in.'"[481]

The master's point here—as difficult as it may be to perceive it—seems to be that any act of being with an ulterior motive, or any sense of instrumentality, is not an act of being from, through, or in God. Elsewhere, the master helps clarify this point when he writes: "I say truly: So long as you perform your works for the sake of the kingdom of heaven, or for God's sake, or for the sake of your eternal blessedness, and you work them from without, you are going completely astray. You may well be tolerated, but it is not the best."[482] From Eckhart's perspective, then, to "live without a 'why?'" is not at all a matter of living in some studied holy ignorance, not asking any questions about one's existence. If this were the case, Eckhart himself would be the worst offender against such a principle. By the same token, living "without a 'why?'" is not life lived in rejection of, or withdrawal from, any sense of purpose or goal. Instead, living "without a 'why?'" is life lived in utter detachment from all such things, realizing that to be attached to any of these things is to be separated from God.

Put in slightly different terms, the soul that is able to "live without a why" has no need to justify its existence; it simply appreciates the fact that it is alive. Amy Hollywood calls this ethics of "living without a 'why?'" an "apophatic ethics," which, for her, is grounded in Eckhart's

---

[479] *TP*, 207; my italics.
[480] *TP*, 207.
[481] *TP*, 207.
[482] *ESC*, 183.

apophatic theology and anthropology.[483] Specifically on this ethics of "living without a why," McGinn also remarks "Nothing could [be] simpler than living *ane warumbe*[484] to those who have reached detachment; nothing seems stranger to those who are still caught in the toils of attachment and who act for any purpose other than God. Eckhart does nothing to lessen the paradox...."[485]

Eckhart himself further elaborates on this concept:

> As long as you perform your deeds for the sake of the kingdom of heaven or for God or your eternal salvation, in other words for an external reason, things are not truly well with you. . . . Truly, when people think that they receive more in warmth, devotion, sweet rapture, and in the special grace of God than by the heart or in a stable, all you are doing is taking God, placing a coat around his head and pushing him under a bench. Whoever seeks God in ways, he takes the ways and loses God, who is hidden in ways. But whoever seeks God without ways, takes him as he is in himself: and the human being lives with the Son, and he is life itself.[486]

4. Poverty, Breakthrough, and Union

The concept of "living without a 'why?'" is closely linked with Ekhart's image of the *pauperes spiritu* or "poor in spirit" of the Matthean beatitudes (Mat. 5:3). In his commentary on this beatitude, Eckhart sharply criticizes the common understanding of what it means to be "poor in spirit." For Eckhart, the essence of spiritual poverty is detachment. The detached person is spiritually "poor" in that he or she "wants nothing," "knows nothing," and "has nothing."[487] Eckhart is highly critical of those who believe that the essence of spiritual poverty lies in one's devotion to "penances and outward practices." He also contends that it is inadequate to define the spiritually poor person as one who wills nothing—one who "never fulfills his

---

[483] Amy Hollywood, *The Soul as Virgin Wife: Mechthild of Magdeburg, Marguerite Porete, and Meister Eckhart* (Notre Dame: University of Notre Dame, 1995), 193.

[484] In Eckhart's work, *ane warumbe* is a synonym for *sunder warumbe*.

[485] Bernard McGinn, *The Mystical Thought of Meister Eckhart*, 154.

[486] *DW* I, 227 in *ST*, I, 117; *ESC*, 183.

[487] *ESC*, 199-201; *ST*, II, 269-270.

own will in anything, but that he ought to comfort himself so that he may fulfill God's dearest will."[488] Of such people Eckhart writes:

> Such people are in the right, for their intention is good. For this let us commend them. May God in his mercy grant them the kingdom of heaven. But I speak in the divine truth when I say that they are not poor men, nor do they resemble poor men. ... I say they are donkeys who have no understanding of divine truth. They deserve the kingdom of heaven for their good intention, but of the poverty of which we want to talk they know nothing.[489]

Furthermore, Eckhart says:

> So long as a man has this as his will, that he wants to fulfill God's dearest will, he has not the poverty about which we want to talk. Such a person has a will with which he wants to fulfill God's will, and that is not true poverty. For if a person wants really to have poverty, he ought to be as free of his own created will as he was when he did not exist.[490]

The two quotations above show that the real "poor" person is really one who truly "wills nothing," not even a reward, however exalted. This is because she or he is free from her or his own will, and identified completely with the will of God. In order for a person "to become poor in his will," Eckhart insists, "he must want and desire as little as he wanted, and desired when he did not exist."[491] The phrase "when he did not exist" here means the state before creation, when all souls were still in the unitive state, which is pre-existent. Poverty requires that one must be as free of the created will, as free, Eckhart says, as one was when one was not. Eckhart uses the word *ledic*, which means "free" or "emptiness" in the sense of "unattached, unencumbered."[492] For Eckhart, again, the soul should remain empty; by emptying the soul, he reminds the readers and the hearers, to "let God be God" within the ground of the soul. Hence Eckhart's inter-

---

[488] Sermon 52, *Beati pauperes spiritu* in *ESC*, 199; *ST*, II, 270; *MP*, 215.

[489] Sermon 52, *Beati pauperes spiritu*, *ESC*, 199-200; cf. *ST*, II, 270; *MP*, 215.

[490] Sermon 52, *Beati pauperes spiritu*, *ESC*, 200; *ST*, II, 270-271; *MP*, 215.

[491] Sermon 52, *Beati pauperes spiritu*, *ESC*, 200; *ST*, II, 270-271; *MP*, 215.

[492] *MP*, 11; Cf. McGinn, The Mystical Thought of Meister Eckhart, 132, 136.

pretation of Matt 21:12, in which Jesus drives the merchants out of the temple. For Eckhart, the Temple is the soul, which needs to be emptied of images and conceptions in order for God to dwell in: "When the temple becomes free of hindrances, that is from attachment to self and ignorance," Eckhart asserts, "then it is so radiantly clear ... that no-one can match its radiance but the uncreated God alone."[493]

Elaborating further on poverty Eckhart writes:

> I have often said . . . that a man should be so free of all things and all works, both interior and exterior, that he might become a place only for God, in which God could work. Now I say otherwise. If it be the case that man is free of all created things and of God and of himself, and if it also be that God may find place [*sic*] in him in which to work, then I say that so long as that is in man, he is not poor with the most intimate poverty. . . Poverty of spirit is for a man to keep so free of God and all his works that if God wishes to work in the soul, he himself is the place in which he wants to work.[494]

Here Eckhart is moving beyond the notion of emptying oneself in order to make a place for God. As long as there is a self which longs for God to dwell in it, the person has not achieved true poverty. Only when the person is completely emptied can God then become the place in which God dwells and works. It is unquestionable that Eckhart is here formulating the most radical kind of emptiness and poverty imaginable, and that he signals the radical nature of his teaching by employing the paradox that it is only when a person is "free of God and all His works" that he or she can be one with God. Here, describing his own experience, Eckhart declares "God's ground is my ground and my ground is God's ground. Here I live on my own as God lives on His own."[495] This poverty of self is the precondition of union with God. "I would have you know," Eckhart says, "that to be empty of creatures is to be full of God and to be full of creatures is to be empty of God."[496] For Eckhart, true

---

[493] Davies, *Selected Writings*, 155; quoted by Almond, "Doing Violence," 6.

[494] *ESC*, 202; *ST*, II, 273-274; *MP*, 218.

[495] *ESC*, 183, see, John D. Caputo, *The Mystical Element in Heidegger's Thought* (Ohio University Press, 1978), 100.

[496] H. C. Lea, *A History of the Inquisition*, vol. I (New York: Russell and Russell, 1958), 343; see also *Meister Eckhart*, trans. by R. B. Blakney (New York: Harper

"poverty" desires neither God nor eternity, for a perfectly detached person is someone who strives for a self and God that are "empty of God." Eckhart writes:

> When I stood in my first cause, there I had no God, and there I was the cause of myself; there I wanted nothing, and I desired nothing, for I was an empty being and a knower of myself in the joy of truth. There I wanted myself and wanted no other thing; what I wanted I was, and what I was I wanted, and here I stood empty of God and all things.[497]

"When I stood in my first cause," Eckharts says, "I was the cause of myself." The phrase, "the cause of myself," would be commonly understood to be referring to God. So is Eckhart claiming to have become God? The answer is a fairly certain, "no." When Eckhart says, "I was the cause of myself," he is engaging in apophatic discourse in order to speak of reality beyond the realm of dichotomous rational thought.[498] What he is trying to evoke in his hearer or reader is a glimpse of reality in which all distinctions between cause and effect collapse. Thus the otherwise absurd statement—"I was the cause of myself"—becomes the only accurate statement possible concerning the reality of the experience. In fact, what makes this statement true is that it means neither that Meister Eckhart is God, nor that he is not God. What it means is that the person has attained that state of radical poverty which thus "allows God to be God."[499]

Another important component of Eckhart's central teaching on detachment—one which is closely related to the concept of poverty is his concept of "breakthrough" (*durchbreechen*). In Sermon 52, Eckhart

---

Torchbooks, 1957), 85, cited by David E. Linge, "Mysticism, Poverty and Reason in the Thought of Meister Eckhart," *Journal of the American Academy of Religion*, XLVI, 4, 479.

[497] *DW* II, 492: 3-7 in *ESC*, 200; *MP*, 216.

[498] On Eckhart's and other mystic's use of apophatic discourse, see Michael A. Sells, *Mystical Languages of Unsaying*.

[499] I derive this expression directly from Eckhart's notion of "letting God be God" which I will discuss below in section five of this chapter.

stresses that it is in the experience of breakthrough that one finds "the most intimate poverty."

> In the breaking-through, when I come to free of will of myself and of God's will and of all his works and of God himself, then I am above all created things, and I am neither God and creature, but I am what I was and what I shall remain, now and eternally. Then I receive an impulse that will bring me up above all the angels. Together with this impulse, I receive such riches that God, as he is "God," and as he performs all his divine works, cannot suffice me; for in this breaking-through I receive that God and I are one. Then I am what I was, and then I neither diminish nor increase, for I am then an immovable cause, that moves all things. Here God finds no place in man, for with this poverty man achieves what he has been eternally and will evermore remain. Here God is one with the spirit, and that is the most intimate poverty one can find.[500]

The "breakthrough" of which Eckhart is speaking marks a non-spatial transition from an ontology of duality, where distinctions between "things" are part of the structure of reality, to an ontology of non-duality where there are no selves or concepts but only the God who is beyond all concepts, images, and relationships. This is the God who is no longer the object of perception, but the ultimate Subject of all perception. How is this breakthrough attained? Here we must pay close attention to the deeply Aristotelian nuances of the passage just quoted. Here we find Eckhart speaking yet again about the "empty-ing" of the will. This time, however, he stresses that the will needs to be emptied in order to receive an "*impulse* that will bring me up above the angels."[501] It seems that McGinn's use of the term "impulse" in this translation is probably not as felicitous as Quint's "impression."[502] This is because, as Sells notes, Eckhart is here alluding to the Aritsto-telian "sense faculty that can receive a new sense impression only when it is empty of previous impressions."[503] Sells goes on to point out that, according to the Aristotelian metaphysics with which the

---

[500] *ESC*, 203.

[501] My italics.

[502] *DW* II, Sermon 52, *Beati pauperes spiritu*, 504-505.

[503] Sells, *Mystical Languages*, 167.

master is working: "[L]ike a wax seal that cannot receive an imprint unless empty of previous imprints, the soul cannot receive the image or formal emanation unless it is empty of will and images."[504] The breakthrough, then is that moment in which the soul *reverts* to its pre-existent state when it was imprinted with the will of God. In this state, the human soul—filled completely by God's will and thus with no separate identity of its own—is eternal, achieving "what [it] has been eternally and will evermore remain."

In this vein, McGinn refers to breakthrough as a "spiritual death to our created being" which is rooted in "the total abandonment of self and all things, God and all creatures."[505] It may be helpful to note the very close affinity between this Christian concept of the death of the soul and the Sufi concept of *fana'*—the "passing away" on "non-becoming" of the self (*nafs*). This is especially true since Sufi concepts of *fana'* also involve the notion of a return to a primordially pure *tawhid*, when, on the Day of *Alast* (see Q 7:172), all of humanity recognized God's unity without compromise.

This "return" to the pre-existent state so central to Meister Eckhart's conception of the breakthrough is also conceived of in terms of a metaphorical "ascent" to the Godhead and thus to absolute unknowability. Not uncharacteristic of the apophatic nature of so much of his mystical discourse, the master also conceives of this "ascension" in terms of a "descent" to the *grunt* or "desert" of no-thing-ness.[506] To experience such an ascent/descent there can be no medium between the soul and the Godhead. Even the intellect must be left behind. "You ought to sink down out of all your your-ness," exhorts the master, "and flow into his his-ness, and your 'yours' and his 'his' ought to become one 'mine,' so completely that you with him perceive forever his uncreated is-ness, and his nothingness, for which there is no name."[507]

---

[504] Sells, *Mystical Languages*, 167.

[505] McGinn, *The Mystical Thought of Meister Eckhart*, 145.

[506] On Eckhart's use of term in his teaching of spiritual transformation, see Bernard McGinn, "Ocean and Desert as Symbol of Mystical Absorption in the Christian Tradition," in *Journal of Religion* 74 (1994), 155-181.

[507] *DW* III, 443: 4-7 in *ESC*, 207; cf. *ST*, II, 333.

It is in intimate connection with his idea of breakthrough that Eckhart develops his notion of union. He expounds on his understanding of union via breakthrough in Sermon 6 ("*Justi autem in perpetuum vivent*"[508]) where he has occasion to comment on 2 Cor 3:18. The verse reads, "And all of us, with unveiled faces, seeing the glory of the Lord as though reflected in a mirror, *are being transformed* into the same image from degree of glory to another; for this comes the Lord, the Spirit."[509] Here Eckhart uses the Eucharistic imagery of "transubstantiation," to illustrate the transformation of human to divine, and created to uncreated. "When in the sacrament bread is changed into the body of our Lord," Eckhart writes, "however many pieces of bread there were, they still become one body. . ... What is changed into something else becomes one with it. I am so changed into him that he produces his being in me as one, not just similar. By the living God," Eckhart continues, "this is true! There is no distinction."[510] Thus, according to Eckhart, a detached person, then, becomes wholly "transubstantiated" and united with Christ. As he further explores the mystery of union, Eckhart asks: "What is life?" He answers: "God's being is my life. If my life is God's being, then God's existence must be my existence and God's is-ness is my is-ness, neither less nor more."[511] Eckhart even goes so far as to say: "And if I did not exist, God would also not exist. That God is God, of that I am a cause; if I did not exist, God too would not be God."[512]

---

[508] Wisdom 5:15 (NRSV); 5:16 (Vulgate) "The just live forever...." Here I have substituted "just" for the NRSV "righteous" because most translations of Eckhart into English use "just" and "justice" instead "righteous" and "righteousness."

[509] My italics.

[510] *DW* 1, Sermon 6, 111 in *ESC*, 188.

[511] *DW* 1, Sermon 6, 266; *ESC*, 187; cf. Blakney, *Meister Eckhart, A Modern Translation*, 180; also *ST*, II, 134.

[512] *ESC*, 203. I have removed the quotation marks which the translator originally placed on the references to "God" in this passage. Here, I am following the wisdom of Michael Sells who has the following to say about this type of editorial interpolation: "These 'inverted commas' may seem innocuous. After all, modern editions of classical texts commonly add punctuation and capitalization, which themselves can become controversial in cases of syntactical ambiguity. From the perspective of this study [on apophatic discourse in the writings of Eckhart and

For Eckhart, in fact, union is closer than co-mingling as in the example of pouring a drop of water into a cask of wine, where even though the water and wine are mixed, each still exists independently and distinctly. For Eckhart, union erases all such distinctions such that the Eucharistic co-mingling of water and wine—wherein the human being comes "to share in the divinity of Christ who humbled himself to share in our humanity"[513]—is interpreted as such a radical divinization of the soul in the fullness of the divine being that no distinction remains between the soul and God. "God must," Eckhart says, "pour the whole of himself into [the detached] man, or else he is not God... God must pour out the whole of himself with all his might so totally into every man who was abandoned himself that God withholds nothing of his being or his nature or his entire divinity."[514] Interweaving his notion of true spiritual poverty with his understanding of union, Eckhart writes:

> As the soul becomes more pure and bare and poor, and possesses
> less of created things, and is emptier of all things that are not God,
> it receives God more purely, and it is more totally in him, and it
> truly becomes one with God, and it looks into God and God into
> it, face to face, as it were two images transformed into one.[515]

One of Eckhart's most striking metaphors for union is that of the fire and the wood. "When fire works," the master writes, "and kindles wood and sets it on fire, the fire diminishes the wood and makes it unlike itself, taking away its coarseness, coldness, heaviness and dampness, and turns the wood into itself, into fire, more and more like to it. But," he continues,

---

other mystics], the selective interpolation of inverted commas into editions and translations amounts to a censorship of the fundamental principle of apophatic discourse" (*Mystical Languages*, 188-189).

[513] Here, I am referring to the prayer uttered by the priest in the New Roman *Ordo*, as he pours a drop of water into the chalice filled with wine. As far as I know, Meister Eckhart himself does not use this image of the mingling of water and wine in the Eucharist.

[514] *ESC*, 197.

[515] *ESC*, 222.

neither the fire nor the wood is pacified or quieted or satisfied with any warmth or heat or likeness until the fire gives birth to itself in the wood, and gives to the wood its own nature and also its own being, so that they both become one and the same unseparated fire, neither less nor more.[516]

Using this metaphor of fire and wood, Eckhart emphasizes the way in which the soul loses its separate identity in God in the way the wood loses its separate identity in the fire. It is important to note, however, that Eckhart does not see destruction here as much as he sees creative transformation, represented in his metaphor by the image of the fire "giving birth to itself in the wood." The wood, like the human being, empties itself so that it can receive and conceive the essence of the fire. Far from being a nihilistic approach to the human self, this metaphor tries to convey the sense in which God's giving birth to Godself in the human soul does not entail the soul's destruction but rather the soul's transformation into its ultimate fulfillment. Turning once again to a comparison with the Sufi concept of *fana'*, we can see another similarity here. Although *fana'* is most frequently translated as "self-annihilation," it denotes a positive transformation of the soul such that the individual who undergoes the experience of "self-annihilation" can return to a new existence (in the state of *baqa'*) which perfectly reflects the divine unity.

Eckhart develops his teaching of the indistinctness of union in a number of other places in his writing. In his Sermon 7, Eckhart, again, uses the image of the oneness of body and soul to explain better his concept of indistinct union. "My body and my soul," Eckhart writes, "are united in one being, not just in one act, as my soul unites itself with the eye in the act of seeing."[517] In another sermon, Eckhart underscores this indistinction, and asserts that the soul does not unite with God but that it *becomes one* with God.[518] According to Eckhart, this indistinction of identities is dynamic and never static. "This identity,"

---

[516] *ESC*, 222.

[517] *DW* 1, Sermon 7, *Populi eius*,119; *TP*, 253.

[518] *DW* 3, Sermon 64, *die sele die wirt ain mit gotte und nit veraint*, 86 in *ST*, II, 225; my italics.

McGinn, asserts, "is a dynamic identity."[519] In this case, McGinn writes on another occasion, "Man must make a pilgrimage into the desert within [God] in order to encounter the wilderness of the hidden Godhead. The human being is then more than united with God: it is simply One with God without any distinction."[520]

At this juncture it should be remembered that, for Eckhart, the experience of God and union is not separated from daily life; the experiences of God and union are intrinsic to daily life. According to both Eckhart scholars, McGinn and Kieckhefer, when Eckhart talks about "union," he does not mean a mystical rapture that occurs beyond our daily life. But rather, it is a particular appreciation and consciousness of our common daily life. In fact Eckhart intends his approach to mystical union to function as a critique of "aspects of the religious fervor of his time, a criticism that may well have been forgotten by some of his followers."[521]

For Eckhart, there is no separation between the monastic, clerical, and religious life, on the one hand, and everyday life, on the other. For him, as Ruffing insists, "mysticism does not equal haphazard one-time experiences but an entire process within a person's life."[522] McGinn's definition of mysticism in Christianity as "part of its belief and practices that concerns the preparation for, the consciousness of, and the reaction to what can be described as the immediate or direct presence of God,"[523] is especially crucial to a complete and accurate understanding of Eckhart's mysticism. For Eckhart the goal of spiritual transformation is not contemplation, but rather the result of it, which has to be reflected in everyday life.

---

[519] Bernard McGinn, *The mystical thought of Meister Eckhart*, 48.

[520] Bernard McGinn, "The God Beyond God," *The Journal of Religion* 61 (1981), 5.

[521] Bernard McGinn, "The God beyond God," 18. See also Richard Kieckhefer, "Meister Eckhart's Conception of Union with God," *Harvard Theological Review* 71 (1978), 224- 225.

[522] See *Mysticism and Social Transformation*, ed. Janet K. Ruffing (Syracuse University Press, 2001), 7.

[523] Bernard McGinn, *The Foundation of Christian Mysticism*, Vol. I of *The Presence of God: A History of Western Christian Mysticism* (New York: Crossroad, 1991), xvii.

If we recall his interpretation of the story of Martha and Mary (discussed above) we see that, for Eckhart, Mary—the contemplative who rejects the quotidian—is still spiritually imperfect and immature. It is only when the contemplative blossoms in activity, as it does in Martha, that one can attain spiritual maturity and perfection. Kieckhefer describes the union of Eckhart's sober spirituality as "habitual union."[524] Habitual union is not a union that is experienced only by elite mystics via their extraordinary experiences of rapture, but rather, it is an experience open to every devout Christian in the course of his or her everyday life. One example of Eckhart's perspective on habitual union (as opposed to ecstatic union) can be found in one of the "counsels" he gives regarding frequent reception of the Eucharist.

> When a man is so disposed, he never receives the precious Body of our Lord without receiving extraordinary graces, and the oftener, the greater profit to him. Yes, a man might receive the Body of our Lord with such devotion and intention that if it were already ordained for him to come into the lowest order of angels, he might by so receiving on that one occasion be raised up into the next rank. Yes, you could receive him with such devotion that you might be seen in the eighth or in the ninth choir. And therefore, if there were two men alike in their whole lives, and one of them had received the Body of our Lord once more often than the other, through that he could appear like a shining sun in comparison with the other, and could receive a singular union with God.[525]

Through most of his sermons, Kieckhefer asserts, Eckhart avows that "his hearer's [and reader's] habitual union with God is every bit as good and holy as the ecstatic union stressed in more traditional contemplative literature."[526] According to some scholars, Eckhart is advocating a "new mysticism" which encourages people not to withdraw from the world but rather to live in the world, yet not be part of it. Linge, for example, calls this type of mysticism an "activist mysticism of dynamized silence."[527] In McGinn's words: "Eckhart preached

---

[524] Kieckhefer, "Meister Eckhart's Conception of Union with God," 208.

[525] *ESC*, 273.

[526] Kieckhefer, "Meister Eckhart's Conception of Union with God," 224.

[527] Linge, "Mysticism, Poverty and Reason," 483.

the possibility of a radical new awareness of God, in rich and often difficult terms, not to the clerical elite of the schools, but to women and
men of every walk of life."[528] In fact, McGinn points out that Eckhart's
use of the German vernacular is a strong indication of his attempt to
"democratize"[529] mysticism, making it accessible not only to the religious, but to the non-religious as well. In this respect, Eckhart is roughly six hundred years ahead of his time in his anticipation of the Second
Vatican Council's articulation of the "universal call to holiness."[530]

It is also important to note how, in certain respects, Eckhart's
reflections on union are very important to this dissertation's broader
concerns with how the teachings of our two masters relate to the
issues of religious diversity and interfaith dialogue. Like Ibn al-'Arabi
who is very fond of quoting an earlier Sufi's (al-Junayd al-Baghdadi)
metaphor of "color," Eckhart too uses a similar metaphor and couples
it with a metaphor of the "eye." Developing these metaphors of
"color" and the "eye," the master writes: "because [the eye] is free of
all colors, it therefore recognizes all colors."[531] This means that the
detached person (i.e., one who is "poor" of color), is united with God
(i.e., who is both colorless and full of colors). Through indistinct
union with God, the detached person can look upon creation with
the eye of God, thus not only seeing every color but understanding
the nature of every color as well. Writing in his sermon on the "poor
in spirit," Eckhart declares: "To be poor in spirit means that as the eye
is poor and deprived of color, and is able to apprehend every color, so
he is poor in spirit who is able to apprehend every spirit, and the Spirit of all spirits is God."[532]

The implications of this perspective for thinking about religious
diversity and interfaith dialogue have the potential to be profound and
far-reaching. Using the metaphor of color in a way very similar to that
of Ibn al-'Arabi, Meister Eckhart is suggesting that an integral dimen-

---

[528] McGinn, ed., *Meister Eckhart and The Beguine Mystics*, 10-11.

[529] McGinn, ed., *Meister Eckhart and The Beguine Mystics*, 10.

[530] *Lumen Gentium*, sec. 39.

[531] *ESC*, 220.

[532] *ESC*, 220.

sion of achieving the pinnacle of Christian spiritual transformation is the ability to understand the nature of all diversity in the world—including the diversity of religions—as it springs from the one Creator.

5. Pray to God to Be Free of God

In his sermon Eckhart writes, "When I went out from my own free will and received my created being, then I had a God, for before there were any creatures, God was not God, but he was what he was. But when creatures came to be and received their created being, then God was not God in himself, but he was God in the creature."[533] From this sermon we can deduce that, for Eckhart, God exists only in relation to creation. In other words, God (who is, by nature and to a significant degree, a function of creation) is distinct from the Godhead (a word signifying what cannot be signified, i.e., in McGinn's gloss, "the God beyond God"[534] which is God in Godself, or the Godhead [*Gotheit*]). In certain ways this concept is deeply analogous to Ibn al-'Arabi's "God created by believers," a comparison we will explore in some detail in chapter five.

It is the profound mystical intuition yielding awareness of a divine reality which is absolutely unknowable, but which stands behind all of what we know of God, that becomes the basis for one of Eckhart's most (in)famous exhortations of detachment: "So therefore let us pray to God that we may be free of God and that we may apprehend and rejoice in that everlasting truth in which the highest angel and the fly and the soul are equal—there where I was established, where I wanted what I was and was what I wanted."[535] Here Eckhart's prayer is a plea that he can be "free of God." According to Milem, the soul's appeal to be "free of God" is by no means to indicate that the soul has no God. It does not suggest, as some might suspect, that Eckhart is playing

---

[533] *DW* II, Sermon 52, *Beati pauperes spiritu*, 492 in *ESC*, 200; see also sermon "Blessed are the Poor" in *MP*, 216. I have deleted the quotation marks around *God*.

[534] *ESC*, 31, 35, 37, and 42

[535] *DW* II, *Beati Pauperes Spiritu*, 493-494 in *ESC*, 200; See also *MP*, 216. Once again, I am deleting the quotation marks surrounding the second reference to *God* in this passage.

with the fire of atheism.[536] Rather, what Eckhart is doing here is making an attempt to describe and actualize the soul in its purest state—the state of, as Milem puts it, "simply wanting what [she] already is."[537]

Although its spirit can be found throughout his work, the phrase "pray to God to be free of God" comes from Eckhart's Sermon 52 on the Matthean beatitude of the "poor in spirit" (already discussed extensively in this chapter). This statement describes what is necessary if a person is to be detached from any belief, concept, or word that creates a barrier between the soul and God. Indeed, it is only when the soul is annihilated and has been "freed of God" Eckhart declares that, "The eye in which I see God is the same eye in which God sees me. My eye and God's eye are one eye and one seeing, one knowing and one loving."[538] In fact, the prayer above expresses the "paradoxical condition of the soul as distinct and indistinct from God."[539] Indeed, the plea to become "free of God" must be understood in light of an important statement found in another sermon (and already quoted above in section four of this chapter): "When I stood in my first cause, then I had no God."[540] Thus, his prayer to be free of God is "a prayer to return to this state," where there was no distinction between God and the soul.[541]

Dorothee Soelle, a German liberation theologian who is very much inspired by Eckhart, views Eckhart's statement "let us pray to God to free us from God," as a "petition by [Eckhart] for liberation

---

[536] See Schurmann's discussion of Eckhart and atheism in the former's *MP*, 117-118.

[537] Bruce Milem, *The Unspoken Word, Negative Theology in Meister Eckhart's German Sermons* (Washington DC: The Catholic University of America Press, 2002), 32.

[538] Sermon 12, TP, 270. This phrase of Eckhart resonates—almost literally—with a well known hadith qudsi: "...wa ma yazalu 'bdi yataqarrabu ilayya bi l-nawafil hatta uhibbahu fa idha ahbabtuhu kuntu sam'ahu alladhi yasma'u bi-hi, wa basarahu alladhi yubsiru bi-hi, wa yadahu alladhi yabtishu bi-ha wa rijlahu allati yamshi bi-ha "... My servant continues to draw near to Me with acts of supererogation, such that I love him. When I love him, I am the hearing with which he hears and the sight with which he sees, and the hand with which he strikes, and the foot with which he walks." See Ezzedine Ibrahim and Denys Johnson-Davies, trans., Forty Hadith Qudsi (Beirut: Dar al-Qur'an al Karim, 1980), 104-105.

[539] Milem, *The Unspoken Words*, 170.

[540] *ESC*, 200.

[541] Milem, *The Unspoken Words*, 170.

from all things that limit God." [542] One has to be very cautious, however, not to read back into the writings of this thirteenth- and fourteenth-century mystic anachronistic resonances with Marxist political theory.[543] Although there are oftentimes many political implications of mystical teaching that go overlooked by the typical student of mysticism, it is a stretch to argue that Eckhart's apophatic prayer was intended as an exhortation to rebel against ecclesiastical authority. It is, rather, a broader call to beware the dangers of spiritual arrogance according to which we easily mistake God for God. This is an arrogance to which people at all levels of the church hierarchy and laity are susceptible. What Eckhart is doing with his prayer is calling all Christians to the absolute humility of spirit required for detachment. He is calling on believers never to tire of striving to move beyond God in order to "break through" into the desert, the *grunt*, where one must yield oneself and thus "conceive" the God of singularity beyond all perception and identity.

An important piece of the prayer to be "free of God" is Eckhart's emphasis on God as ultimately unnameable and nondefinable. In Sermon 53, the master writes, "[W]e should learn not to give any name to God, lest we imagine that in so doing, we have praised and exalted him as we should; for God is 'above names' and ineffable."[544] Furthermore, he writes, "In the scripture God is called by many names. I say that whoever perceives something in God and attaches thereby some name to him, that is not God."[545] Indeed, for Eckhart, the use of apophatic language is essential to his concept of detachment which is "letting be," and "letting God be God." When the master says to "be free of God," he alludes, as Soelle asserts, that "a God who does not exceed God is not a God. God imprisoned in a certain language, lim-

---

[542] Nancy Hawkins, "Conversations with Meister Eckhart and Dorothee Soelle," in *The theology of Dorothee Soelle*, ed. by Sarah K. Pinnock (Harrisburg, PA : Trinity Press International, 2003), 178.

[543] Matthew Fox, for example, mentions that Erich Fromm and Ernst Boch "invoke Eckhart as a forerunner of the Spirit of Karl Marx." See Fox, 2. See also Fox, "Meister Eckhart and Karl Marx: The Mystic as Political Theologian" in *Listening* (Fall 1978), 233-257.

[544] Sermon 53, *ESC*, 205.

[545] *ESC*, 205.

ited by certain definitions, known by certain names that have established certain socio-cultural forms of control, is not a God but becomes instead a religious ideology."[546] For Eckhart, a person is not to attach to "God" but to break through into the naked "God beyond God," or in the word of Angelus Silesius a person "must move still higher than God, into a desert."[547] In fact, according to Eckhart, for a detached person, the result of her or his breakthrough is the "disappearance of God" (*got entwirt*),[548] whereby, at the same time, she or he will return to her or his state where she or he was and where there was no God. Schurmann says, "[detachment] makes man reach for the origin, but for such a man there is no longer any God. "God" is the opposite of the creature, but if there are no created men to invoke him, God must vanish as God. There is then nothing other than the unknowable desert prior to the threefold. In the origin, everything is origin."[549]

Eckhart's unwillingness to name God as an absolute stems from his deep philosophical conviction that "even pure being cannot be attributed to God."[550] For Eckhart, every absolute attribute ascribed to God, as Caputo asserts, is merely "relative to something else in the discursive chain."[551] For some scholars, Eckhart's negative theology is analogous either to the radical negation of Zen Buddhism, or to contemporary European thinkers like Heidegger and Derrida.[552] John Caputo, for example, "find[s] in Meister Eckhart a great medieval

---

[546] Dorothee Soelle, *Theology for Skeptics: Reflections on God* (Minneapolis: Fortress Press, 1995), 38 cited by Hawkins, Conversations with Meister Eckhart, 180.

[547] Silesius, *Der Cherubinischer Wandersmann*, 61, quoted by *MP*, 246.

[548] Meister Eckhart, Sermon *Nolite timere eos*, Pf. 180, 18, quoted by *MP*, 246.

[549] *MP*, 114.

[550] Meister Eckhart, *Predigt*. 9; *DW* 1. 145: 5-7 in *ST*, II, 150; *TP*, 256.

[551] See Caputo, "Mysticism and Transgression: Derrida and Meister Eckhart," *Derrida and Deconstruction*, ed. Hugh J Silverman (New York and London: Routledge, 1989), 32.

[552] See MP; Schurmann, "The Loss of origin in Soto Zen"; D. T. Suzuki, *Mysticism: Christian and Buddhist* (New York: MacMillan, 1961); Hans Waldenfels, *Absolute Nothingness: Foundation for a Buddhist-Christian Dialogue* (New York: Paulist Press, 1976); Caputo, *The Mystical Element*; Caputo, "Mysticism and Transgression," Caputo, *Radical. Hermeneutics: Repetition, Deconstruction, and the Hermeneutic Project* (Bloomington : Indiana University Press, 1987)

deconstructive practice."[553] Further, Caputo asserts that "When [Eckhart] prayed aloud for God to rid him from God he was blowing the whistle on metaphysical theology—plain and simple.[554]

In developing such theories, one must be very careful not to force Eckhart into a category he explicitly rejects. In the same way that he rejects the one-sidedness of ascetic withdrawal as an immature stage in one's spiritual development, Eckhart would be likely to reject categorizing his "project" as "deconstructionist." Is a certain kind and degree of deconstruction necessary for true spiritual awareness? Eckhart would agree wholeheartedly. Eckhart recognizes all processes of "transformation" as deconstructionist in nature. But Eckhart's deconstruction is not for its own sake, but rather for the sake of a new creation. It is, in other words, a sacramental type of deconstruction which allows the ultimate reality that always was and always will be—and thus which is itself completely immune to "deconstruction"—to emerge by the power of divine grace. Unlike a secular deconstructionist who may claim that there is no stable meaning, and that all meaning is subject to deconstruction, Eckhart derives relatively stable meaning from scripture in order to bring the believer to the realization that God, Godself, lies beyond all meaning. This fact, however, this *grunt* of all existence, does not call into radical question the meaning of scripture or the teachings of the faith, but in turn, ratifies and strengthens them.

6. Pathless Path

One final concept through which Eckhart develops his central teaching on detachment is that of "the pathless path." In one sermon Eckhart describes the way to full realization of the Godhead as a path which is "free and yet bound, raised aloft and wafted off almost beyond self and all things, beyond will and images."[555] Focusing on Peter's famous confession of faith in Christ of Matthew 16:13-19, Eckhart uses him as an example of someone who had himself not seen God "bare [directly],"

---

[553] See Caputo, "Mysticism and Transgression," 31.

[554] Caputo, "Mysticism and Transgression," 32-33.

[555] *DW* 3, sermon 86, *Intravit Jesus in quodam castellum*, 486; *TP*, 341.

but as one who "had certainly been drawn up by the power of the heavenly Father above all created powers of comprehension to the rim of eternity." When he makes his startlingly accurate identification of Jesus as "Messiah [i.e., "Christ"], the Son of the living God" (16:16), Jesus responds by saying: "For flesh and blood has not revealed this to you, but my Father in heaven" (16:17). By envisioning Peter having gained this knowledge from the Father while standing on the "rim of eternity," Eckhart imagines Peter having been "clasped by the heavenly Father with tempestuous strength in a loving embrace, his spirit gaping upward unawares, carried beyond all human comprehension in the power of the heavenly Father."556

The master deems this mode of encountering God the mode of the "pathless path" because it is a "way" or "journey" to God that itself is immediate and direct. It does not entail *unmediated* experience of the Godhead, for it is still a path. It is, however, a path that needs no traversing—a path that one undertakes instantaneously and that instantaneously takes one to the "rim" (but no further). While the other disciples still struggle on the "first path" of "seeking God in all creatures"557 (i.e., their response to Jesus's question "Some say John the Baptist, but others Elijah, and still others Jeremiah or one of the prophets" 16:14), Peter bypasses this route, going directly to the rim of eternity and learning the truth without any process or delay whatsoever. This is the sense in which Peter is on the "pathless path"—that path which ranks higher than the first.

The highest path is not the "pathless path," but rather a path that "is called a path and yet is a being-at-home. It is to see God immediately in [God's] ownness."558 It is on this third, and most exalted of paths, that one hears Christ speak these words:

> "I am the way, the truth, and the life" (Jn. 14:6). One Christ, one Person; one Christ, one Father; one Christ, one Spirit; three, one; three: way, truth, and life; one beloved Christ in whom all this is. Outside this path bordering it are all creatures acting as means. To

---

556 *TP*, 341.
557 *TP*, 341.
558 *TP*, 341.

be led into God on this path by the light of his Word and to be embraced by the love of the Spirit of them both—this is beyond anything one can express in words. Now listen to something astounding. How wondrous to be within and without, to grasp and to be embraced, to see and to be what is seen, to hold and to be held: This is the final end where the Spirit remains at rest in the unity of blissful eternity.[559]

If the "pathless path" sounds paradoxical and apophatic in nature, then the "path that is a being-at-home" is even more paradoxical and thus more expressive of an encounter that is truly unmediated. Why is this the highest "path" for Eckhart? The answer can be found in his recognition of both the practical necessity and practical danger of "paths." The practical necessity lies in the fact that we all need "paths" in order to undertake our "journeys" of spiritual transformation. They are, in a very real sense, both as useful as they are unavoidable. The practical danger, however, lies in the equally real fact that the "stuff" of the path can easily become mistaken for the goal of the journey. Eckhart himself warns: "[W]hoever seeks God in a special way, gets the way and misses God."[560] Like his plea "to be free of God," discussed above, this teaching of the "pathless path" and the path that is a "being-at-home" seems also to stem from overriding concern in his central teaching on detachment: that nothing be mistaken for God—most of all, God, Godself.

---

[559] *TP*, 341.

[560] ST, I, 117 (from In hoc apparatuit caritas dei in nobis [Predigt, 5b, Largier, 70].

Chapter V

IBN AL-'ARABI AND MEISTER ECKHART—
SYNTHESIZING A COMPARATIVE
MYSTICAL CONVERSATION

IBN AL-ʿARABI AND MEISTER ECKHART— SYNTHESIZING A COMPARATIVE MYSTICAL CONVERSATION

To date, there are certain scholars who have worked on comparing the mystical teachings of both Ibn al-ʿArabi and Meister Eckhart. Some have already been referred to in this work and others will be referred to below. These comparisons have, by and large, been either very general in nature,[561] or focused specifically on one mystical and/or philosophical issue such as "transformation" of the self[562] or apophatic discourse.[563] The comparative mystical conversation that this chapter aims to construct, albeit in rudimentary form, is aimed at providing the necessary material—one might even say "nodes"—for the eventual development of a new, more mystically-based, matrix for Christian-Muslim dialogue. The specific contribution of this chapter, therefore, is in its selection of five points of conversation between the two masters and its presentation of these points as vital material for the eventual development of the new matrix (to be discussed in the next and final chapter). These "points of conversation" will be closely connected, and in many ways governed and shaped by the two major themes of the teachings of the two masters (i.e., the self-disclosure of God and detachment) explored in the two preceding chapters.

---

[561] E.g., Reza Shah-Kazemi, *Paths to Transcendence: According to Shankara, Ibn Arabi, and Meister Eckhart* (Bloomington, Ind. : World Wisdom, 2006); Ian Almond, "Divine Needs, Divine Illusions: Preliminary Remarks Toward a Comparative Study of Meister Eckhart and Ibn AlʿArabi," *Medieval Philosophy and Theology* 10, (2001).

[562] James Royster, "Personal Transformation in Ibn al-ʿArabi and Meister Eckhart," *Christian-Muslim Encounters*, Eds. Yvonne Y. Haddad and Wadi Y Haddad (Tallahassee: University Press of Florida, 1995).

[563] Michael A. Sells, *Mystical Languages of Unsaying* (Chicago: University of Chicago Press, 1994)

This chapter will begin with two preliminary sections on the orthodoxy of the two masters (to be discussed fully in the final chapter) and a general overview of the two masters in comparative perspective, followed by five sections, each of which articulate a specific point of conversation between the masters which has special relevance for the construction of a new matrix for Christian-Muslim dialogue.

1. A Note on the Orthodoxy of Ibn al-'Arabi and Meister Eckhart

In his polemical critique of Indian thought, Albert Schweitzer proposes a dichotomy of the basic types of mysticism. Following Weber's typology of "inner-worldy" and "world-rejecting" asceticism,[564] Schweitzer distinguishes between an "abstract mysticism" which concerns itself with philosophical constructs having to do with questions of ontology, and a "mysticism of reality" which is rooted in the practical living-out of the ethical imperatives of one's religious convictions.[565] The problem with such a typology is that it implies that a mysticism which centers around philosophical reflection and a mysticism which is rooted in daily ethical and spiritual practices are mutually exclusive. In the case of Ibn al-'Arabi and Meister Eckhart, nothing could be farther from the truth. Although both mystic masters are well known for their philosophical expressions of the esoteric nature of being, both are deeply immersed in lives of extraordinary personal observance of practices identified with exemplary ritual and moral behavior.

There is a very important reason why it is crucial to emphasize this point at the outset of a chapter which focuses on placing some teachings of these two mystic masters into synthetic conversation with one another. It has to do with the fact that the teachings this chapter will discuss are often seen to be abstractions which have very little to do

---

[564] Max Weber, *The Sociology of Religion*, Ephraim Fischoff, tr., fourth edition (Boston, MA: Beacon Press, 1993), 166.

[565] William F. Goodwin, "Mysticism and Ethics: an Examination of Radhakrishnan's Reply to Schweitzer's Critique of Indian Thought" in *Ethics* vol 67, no. 1 (October, 1956), 33.

with the mainstream religious practices of either Islam or Christianity. In fact, it is on the basis of such an impression that most of the "orthodox" condemnations of these two mystics rest. What this chapter hopes to accomplish, however, is not only to place abstract ideas from two religious thinkers in conversation with one another, but to do so without forgetting that these ideas were intimately connected to the realities of either mainstream medieval Muslim or mainstream medieval Christian identity. This will set the stage for the next chapter which will focus, in large part, on a rediscovery of the orthodoxy of both Ibn al-'Arabi and Meister Eckhart. At this juncture, it is also important to note that placing some of the central teachings of these two mystic masters in conversation with one another is in no way an attempt to identify a "middle ground" which is distinct from the orthodoxies of their respective traditions. Instead, this conversational process is designed both to demonstrate the ways in which each of the two masters help illuminate the teachings of the other, and to help us to understand with more precision and clarity exactly the ways in which each set of teachings is rooted in orthodox Islamic and orthodox Christianity doctrine, respectively.

2. The Two Masters in Comparative Perspective

There are various opinions and interpretations of Ibn al-'Arabi. Many critics have referred to him as a "Sufi Gnostic," a "Neoplatonist," a "*hadith* scholar," a "philosopher," and, of course, as a "mystic." Titus Burckhardt, for example, considered Ibn al-'Arabi to be a "fundamentally Platonic thinker."[566] Unlike Burckardt, however, Ibn al-Abbar (d. 1260), one of Ibn al-'Arabi's biographer, referred to him more as a "*muhaddith* or scholar of the sayings of the Prophet."[567] Ian Almond remarks that, although Richard Netton and Henry Corbin consider Ibn al-'Arabi in the same schools as the Persian mystic Suhrawardi— though Corbin himself recommended that it will be appropriate to put

---

[566] See Alexander D. Kynsh, *Ibn 'Arabi in the Later Islamic Tradition*, 34-35, quoted by Ian Almond, *Sufism and Deconstruction* (London and New York: Routledge, 2004), 12.

[567] Almond, *Sufism and Deconstruction*, 12.

Ibn al-'Arabi, in this case his *Futuhat*, in the Shiite tradition than in the Sunni[568]—Majid Fakhry puts Ibn al-'Arabi and al-Ghazali together as representative of "synthesis and systematization."[569] Almond goes on to suggest that "one of the primary sources of Ibn al-'Arabi's thought" was Ibn Masarra, and most importantly Empedocles.[570]

Different language is probably what accounts for the wide diversity of opinions among scholars about the kind of thinker Eckhart was. Different scholars have portrayed him as a mystic and an anti-mystic, a scholastic and an enemy of scholasticism, a follower of Thomas Aquinas and an opponent of Aquinas. As mentioned by Schurmann, "each generation has produced its own interpretation of Eckhart's works in accordance with its own ideological movement."[571] Thus, for example, Eckhart is called the "father of German speculation" in the German philosophy of the nineteenth century. While Hegel regarded him as a reconciler of faith and science, Schopenhauer saw him as the founder of transcendental idealism; and even Schelling found in Eckhart's works a closely resemblance to his own philosophy of revelation. One must also remember that scholars from outside the Christian tradition have found in Eckhart a spiritual master, e.g., some Buddhists discover in his preaching elements of their own teachings.[572] He is even considered a point of encounter between Eastern and Western traditions. And Marxists have also adopted Meister Eckhart.[573] Scholars like Erick Fromm and Ernst Bloch "invoke Eckhart as a forerunner of the spirit of Karl Marx."[574] He also has been described as a medieval environmentalist; as a feminist and

---

[568] H. Corbin, *Creative Imagination in the Sufism of Ibn 'Arabi*, 26; Richard Netton, *Allah Transcendent: Studies in the Structure and Semiotics of Islamic Philosophy, Theology and Cosmology* (Richmond: Curzon Press, 1994), 269.

[569] Almond, *Sufism and Deconstruction*, 12.

[570] The *Encyclopedia Britannica* , quoted by Almond, *Sufism and Deconstruction*, 12.

[571] *MP*, xi

[572] See for example Ueda Shizuteru, "Nothingness" in Meister Eckhart and Zen Buddhism, in *The Buddha Eye, an anthology of the Kyoto School*, ed.by Frederick Franck (New York: Crossroad, 1982), D. T. Suzuki, *Mysticism: Christian and Buddhist* (New York: Harper, 1957).

[573] *MP*, 2.

[574] Ernst Bloch, *Atheism in Christianity* (New York: Herder and Herder, 1972), 62ff; Erick Fromm, *To Have or To Be?* (New York: Harper & Row, 1976), 59, quoted by

a misogynist, as a medieval Hegelian; a Marxist, and Heideggerian; as a precursor to Luther, a Christian Buddhist, a Christian atheist, a flagrant heretic, and a loyal Catholic.[575]

Although there is no shortage of opinions about Ibn al-'Arabi and Meister Eckhart which portray them in a dizzying number of different lights, a review of the major studies of the two do identify at least one important intellectual tradition that both share at a deep level. Neoplatonic vocabulary plays a central role in the vocabulary of both mystic masters, although each gets his Neoplatonism from different sources: "Eckhart was a reader of Proclus and Dionysius" while "Ibn al-'Arabi was a reader of Plotinus."[576]

The marked influence of Neoplatonism in the work of both these masters does not mean that this was the major influence of their thought. Each was selectively influenced by a variety of philosophical traditions and each interprets Neoplatonic ideas that it would be a gross oversimplification to conclude that any and all affinities between the thinking of Ibn al-'Arabi and Meister Eckhart are the result of a

---

Matthew Fox, *Breakthrough: Meister Eckhart's Creation Spirituality in New Translation* (New York, London, Toronto, Sydney, Auckland: Doubleday, 1980), 2.

[575] Bruce Millem, *The Unspoken Word, Negative Theology in Meister Eckhart's German Sermons* (Washington D. C.: The Catholic University of America Press, 2002), 3. Report on Eckhart scholarship past and present can be found in Ingeborg, *Degenhardt, Studien zum Wandel des Eckhartbildes*, Leiden: Brill, 1967; Tony Schaller, "Die Meister Eckhart Forschung von der Jahrhundertwende bis zur Gegenwart." *Freiburger Zeitschrift für Philosophie und Theologie* (1968), 15: 262-316, 403-26; Tony Schaller, "Zur Eckhart-Deutung der letzen 30 Jahre," *Freiburger Zeitscrift für Philosophie und Theologie* 16: 22-39 (1969), Wolfram Malte Fues, *Mystik als Erkenntnis?: Kritische Studien zur Meister Eckhart-Forschung* (Born: Bouvier, 1981); Niklaus Largier, "'Intellectus in deum ascensus': Intellekttheoretische Auseinander-setzungen in Texten der deutchen Mystik," *Deutsche Vierteljahrsschrift für Literaturwissenschaft und Geistesgeschichte* (1995), 69: 423-71; Alois M. Haas, *Mystic als Aussage: Erfahrungs, Denk und Redeformen christlicher mystic* (Frankfurt am Main: Suhrkamp, 1996), 336-410, and Kurt Ruh, *Die mystik des deutschen Predigerordens und ihre Grundlegung durch die Hochscholastik*, Vol. 3 of *Geschichte der abendlandischen Mystik*, Munich: C H. Beck (1996): 220-35.

[576] Ian Almond, "Divine Needs, Divine Illusions," *Medieval Philosophy and Theology* 10 (2001), 264. Richard Netton even calls Ibn al-'Arabi "the Meister Eckhart of the Islamic tradition," (Netton, 293).

single Neoplatonic outlook. Also—as emphasized briefly above and as will be discussed extensively in the final chapter—the fact that both masters can be categorized, to a certain degree, as Neoplatonic in their thinking, does not in any way diminish the centrality of canonical scripture for each of them. For Ibn al-ʿArabi, there is no higher authority than the Qurʾan, and the same is true of the Bible for Meister Eckhart. Indeed, it is to the subject of each master's hermeneutical approach to the canonical scripture of his respective tradition that we will now turn as the first in a series of key points of the mutual conversation into which the teachings of Ibn al-ʿArabi and Meister Eckhart can be placed.

3. Scriptural Hermeneutics

In one of his well-known essays on biblical hermeneutics, Michael Fishbane notes that the tradition of rabbinic mystical exegesis known as *Sod*[577] turned on the principle that the words of sacred scripture speak to the reader "without ceasing." Thus, Fishbane asserts, "There is a continual expression of texts; and this reveals itself in their ongoing reinterpretation. But *Sod*," Fishbane emphasizes, "is more than the eternity of interpretation from the human side. It also points to the divine mystery of speech and meaning."[578] Fishbane goes on to speak about the "prophetic task" of "breaking the idols of simple sense" and restoring "the mystery of speech to its transcendent role in the creation of human reality." He asserts that one of the primary functions of the mystical exegete—individuals like Ibn al-ʿArabi and Meister Eckhart— is "to continue this prophetic mission." It is "in the service of *Sod* [i.e., mystical exegesis]," that mystical exegetes like our two masters mediate "a multitude of interpretations" as "they resist the dogmatization

---

[577] In his essay entitled, "The Teacher and the Hermeneutical Task: a Reinterpretation of Medieval Exegesis," Fishbane makes reference to the four-fold typology of medieval scriptural interpretation common to both the Jewish and Christian traditions. For Jewish exegetes, this typology took the form of the acronym PaRDeS, where P=*Peshat* (the literal meaning); R=*Remez* (the allegorical meaning); D=*derash* (the tropological and moral meaning); and S=*Sod* (the mystical meaning). See Michael Fishbane, *The Garments of Torah: Essays in Biblical Hermeneutics* (Bloomington, IN: Indiana University Press, 1989), 113.

[578] Fishbane, *Garments*, 120.

of meaning and the eclipse of the divine lights of speech." Taking our lead from Fishbane, we can assert that, as mystical exegetes, our two masters seek to "transcend the idolatries of language" and to condemn "hermeneutical arrogance in all its forms...."[579]

In their respective approaches to canonical scripture, both Ibn al-'Arabi and Meister Eckhart fulfill the role of mystical exegete as Fishbane interprets it for us. They believe unequivocally in an infinitely readable Text, and they champion this infinite readability in the hopes of combating the "idolatries of language" and "hermeneutical arrogance." According to Ibn al-'Arabi, each word of the Qur'an—not to mention its verses and chapters—has an unlimited meanings, all of which are intended by God. Correct recitation of the Qur'an allows reader to access to new meanings at every reading. "When meaning repeats itself for someone reciting the Qur'an, he has not recited it as it should be recited. This is proof of his ignorance."[580] In fact, Ibn al-'Arabi regards the words of language as symbolic expressions, subject to the interpretive efforts, which he calles *ta'bir* (lit. the act of "crossing over"). Thus, for him the truth of the interpretive effort presents itself in the act of crossing over from one state to another, and under this interpretation, difference becomes the root of all things since for the thing to be in a constant state of crossing is for it to be constantly differentiated, not only from other things, but also from itself.[581]

For Eckhart, though the biblical text may well have a progressively infinite number of meanings, unlike Ibn al-'Arabi, he rarely discusses the act of interpretation itself.[582] Nonetheless, the material of ideas in Eckhart's sermons and treatises is received doctrine from Scripture, tradition, and contemporaneous scholasticism. When one considers

---

[579] Fishbane, *Garments*, 120.

[580] *Fut.* IV, 367. 3.

[581] *Fut.* II, 518. 12. Indeed, Ibn al-'Arabi was what Bruce Lawrence calls "a deep-sea diver in the Ocean of the Qur'an." (See Bruce Lawrence, *The Qur'an, A Biography* (New York: Broadway, 2006), 109.

[582] In his "Divine Needs, Divine Illusions," Ian Almond writes that both Ibn al-'Arabi and Meister Eckhart have "a common tendency to reinscribe popular phrases and stories from the Qur'an and the Bible into their own thought-systems by imposing radically different interpretations upon them" (278).

the degree to which Eckhart quotes canonical, authoritative sources and their authoritative interpretations, it is difficult to imagine that Eckhart's aim was to depart significantly from orthodox mainstream theology. In fact, Eckhart never rejects the significant of a direct literal interpretation of the sacred writings. Instead what he is doing is searching for a deeper sense. Eckhart says, "[I]n interpreting the Scripture, it is always important to elucidate the hidden meaning under the letter."[583] Indeed, mystics have always declared that their thought is at the heart of the religion. And in fact, as Caputo notes, Meister Eckhart "rewrites the words of Scripture, turns and twists the most familiar sacred stories, reinterprets the oldest teachings in the most innovative and shocking ways."[584]

4. Oneness of Being

As discussed in chapter three, one of the central metaphors used by Ibn al-'Arabi to articulate his teachings about the self-disclosure of God is the metaphor of the Breath of Merciful (*nafas al-rahman*). For Ibn al'Arabi, this metaphor speaks of the pulse of creation, the dynamic life-force of the universe—always originating and always returning to God as its ultimate source. It is ever-blowing, both annihilating and re-creating in each and every moment of existence. The term "unity of Being" (*wahdat al-wujud*), has, over time, been interpreted as the concept that best captures the overarching ontological implications and insights of some of the central metaphors of Ibn al-'Arabi's teaching, such as the metaphor of the Breath of the Merciful. In fact, for many, it is the first concept that comes to mind should they be asked to summarize Ibn al-'Arabi's doctrinal position on the

---

[583] Prologue of the *Liber parabolarum Genesis*, *LW* I, 447, 4-9. Konrad Weiss, "Meister Eckharts Biblische Hemeneutik" in *La Mystique Rhenane* (Paris, 1963), 95, cited by *MP*, 10. For Eckhart's hermeneutics see also Donald Duclow, "Hermeneutics and Meister Eckhart," in *Philosophy Today* 28 (1984), 36-43.

[584] John D. Caputo, "Mysticism and Transgression, Derrida and Meister Eckhart," in *Derrida and Deconstruction*, ed. Hugh J Silverman (New York and London: Routledge, 1989), 35.

nature of Reality.[585] The concept of *wahdat al-wujud* is taken to mean that there is only one Being, and that all existence is nothing but the manifestation of that One Being (Being's Self-disclosure). When Ibn al-'Arabi explains his statement that Being is one, "he provides one of the most sophisticated and nuanced expression of the 'profession of God's Unity' (*tawhid*) to be found in Islamic thought."[586] According to this concept "the purpose of human existence, within such a system of thought, is for the human soul to 'realize' its own divine origins through a gradual, ascending return to God via a series of spiritual stages and stations."[587]

For Ibn al-'Arabi, *wahdat al-wujud* is an obvious, unavoidable ontological fact. The Arabic triliteral root from which *wujud* is derived is *WJD* which has the base sense of "finding." Literally, therefore, *wahdat al-wujud* can be translated as the "oneness" or "unity of finding." What this implies is that the search for God as "other" does not entail a discovery of an irresolvable dichotomy between creation and the Creator (between the one who searches and the One who is found), but rather a discovery that all of creation is a stunning manifestation of the oneness of the divine Being that ultimately admits no duality. According to Chittick, understanding the word *wujud* as "finding" carries with it the important sense of awareness and consciousness. So understood as

---

[585] Indeed he is known as the founder of the school of the Oneness of Being (*Wahdat al-wujud*), and the idea permeates his works, though he does not employ this exact term. See *SPK*, 79. Claude Addas says that the term *wahdat al-wujud* seems to have been used for the first time by Sadr al-Din al-Qunawi, one of Ibn al-'Arabi's closest student, and eventually, through the intermediary of others, it become the standard description designating Ibn al-'Arabi's metaphysics (*QRS*, 232).

[586] *SPK*, 79. For an introduction to the history of the usage of the term *wahdat al-wujud* among Ibn al-'Arabi's followers, see Chittick, "Rumi and Wahdat al-wujud," in Amin Banani, Richard G Hovannisian, and Georges Sabagh, eds., *Poetry and Mysticism in Islam : the Heritage of Rumi* (New York : Cambridge University Press, 1994); William C. Chittick, "Wahdat al-Wujud in Islamic Thought," *Bulletin of the Henry Martyn Institute of Islamic Studies*, 10 (1991), 7-27; Souad al-Hakim, *Al-Mu'jam al-Sufi: Al Hikma fi Hudud al-Kalima* (Beirut, 1401/1981); Alexander Knysh, "Ibrahim al-Kurani (d. 1101/1690), An Apologist for Wahdat al-Wujud, *Journal of the Royal Asiatic Society*, 3rd series, 5 (1995), 39-47.

[587] Almond, *Sufism and Deconstruction*, 14.

"finding," *wujud* is not just "to exist" or "to be", but it is "to be alive" and "to be aware." No wonder Ibn al-'Arabi always reminds the readers of this fact, by referring to the quranic verses "Everything in the heavens and the earth glorifies God" (57:1)."[588] In other words, all the elements of the created order are alive (i.e., exist) precisely to the extent that they are aware of and bear witness to the divine Being.

While it is certainly true that Ibn al-'Arabi is best known for his contributions (however controversial) to Islamic ontological speculation, his "main concern," as Chittick reminds us, "is not with the mental concept of being but with the experience of God's Being, the tasting (*dhawq*) of Being, that 'finding' which is at one and at the same time to perceive and to be that which truly is."[589] For Ibn al-'Arabi, being is an unconditionalized absolute (*mawjud la-bi-shart*)[590] beyond all duality or multiplicity, but it has in itself infinite modalities, some of which constitute the appearance of the phenomenal world. As the self-manifestation of Being the phenomenal world is the place where the One Being reveals itself continuously, without ceasing, in an infinity of its own forms. It is as the Qur'an says, "Each day he is upon some task"(55: 29) and "the task being the changes which he causes to occur in the engendered things (*akwan*)"[591] Thus, the only reality that the phenomenal world has is an overflowing modality of the One Being. It should be noted, however, that the multiplicity of the phenomenal world never affects the unity of Being in its creative act, rather it represents its various degrees and states. God's Self-disclosure, then, only constitutes a facet of the Absolute-God who is One in His

---

[588] William Chittick, "Presence with God," *The Journal of the Muhyiddin Ibn 'Arabi Society*, Vol. XX (1996), 1.

[589] *SPK*, 3.

[590] In fact, Ibn al-'Arabi's use of *wujud la bi-shart* rather than *wujud bi-la shart* is a case in point, The subtle difference here is that, while the former connotes an abstract reality plain and simple, the latter connotes a process of abstracting reality and thus subtly and cleverly calls attention to the fact that all that we, as human beings, think about God, are essentially projections rooted in our experience. This is very much in line with the warning in Ibn al-'Arabi's thinking not to idolize our conceptions of God as absolutely synonymous with the Reality that is God in God's ultimately unknowable essence.

[591] *Fut.* III, 198. 28; *SPK*, 100.

existence and many in His manifestations. It appears as a plurality of particulars because of the structure and nature of human cognition itself and the finitude of human consciousness.[592] For Ibn al-'Arabi, "God has effects manifest within the cosmos; they are the states within which the cosmos undergoes constant fluctuation (*taqallub*). This is a property of His name "Time" (*dahr*)."[593] Besides this limited perspective, what we are actually encountering is not many separate things or individuals but the infinite manifestations of the One and Only Being. This is why that, as stated above, the cornerstone of Ibn al-'Arabi's mystical philosophy of knowledge is that the *raison d'être* of humankind is to return to the vision of original unity; this is the fundamental human project. This is what is called *tawhid*.

In fact, for Ibn al-'Arabi the many aspects of the phenomenal world are an effect of the existential *tajalli* in the manifold modes of manifestation. For Ibn al-'Arabi, nothing can exist outside of the One.

Meister Eckhart's ontology is strikingly similar, in some respects, to that of Ibn al-'Arabi. Meister Eckhart's identification of God as All-Inclusive Being is the proposition in his thought which has deep analogical connections with Ibn al-'Arabi's assertion of the oneness of Being. In Eckhart's teaching, especially in his concept of "breakthrough" discussed in chapter four, "oneness" admits no distinction; it is Absolute and prior to all differentiation.[594] Creatures, according to Eckhart in his *Parisian Questions*, receive their being from God, who Himself is beyond being. For Eckhart, insofar as creatures have being, God is not, or insofar as God is, creatures are nothing.[595] In the *Three-*

---

[592] T. Izutzu, *Creation and the Timeless Order of Things, Essays in Islamic Mystical Philosophy* (Ashland, Oregon: White Cloud Press, 1994), 10-11.

[593] *Fut.* III, 315. 11, 16; *SPK*, 100.

[594] In his book, Bernard Muller-Thym mentions that there are "a number of characteristic pre-Socratic positions" in Eckhart's ontology. See his *The establishment of the University of Being in the Doctrine of Meister Eckhart of Hochheim* (New York, London: Institute of Medieval Studies, 1939), 5.

[595] See Meister Eckhart, *Parisian Questions and Prologues*, trans. and intro. Armand A. Maurier (Toronto: Pontifical Institute of Medieval Studies, 1974). He also said, "God considered as nothing, when existence is ascribed to creatures." See, *TP*, 396.

Part Work, Eckhart argues that *Esse Deus est* (Being/Existence is God),[596] which clearly distinguished God from created being.[597] In both his German and Latin works, Eckhart refers many times to God as undifferentiated existence, or *esse simpliciter* or *indistinctum*, such that God is in some way beyond *esse*.[598] Eckhart here is speaking about all creatures' dependence on God. Their being is "on loan" from god. Once again, the point here is that, apart from God, creatures are absolutely nothing. It does not mean by this that creatures do not exist. It means that they do not exist independently of God. Eckhart writes "All creatures are pure nothing. I do not just say they are insignificant or are only a little something: they are pure nothing. Whatever has no being, is not. Creatures have no being because their being depends on God's presence."[599] Eckhart also quotes Avicenna's Metaphysics 8.6, that "What every being desires is existence and the perfection of existence insofar as it is existence. . . Therefore that which is truly desired is existence."[600] Thus, for Eckhart, "no single being is existence, nor does any possess the root of existence."[601] The essential dependence of the creature on God also can be seen in another of Eckhart's sermons:

> What it possesses it does not have from itself as something that inheres in it, but that it has begged it and received it as something that is continually on loan. It has it in passing, as a reception, and not like a received quality given by its superior active cause.[602]

In fact, contrary to what some may conclude, when Eckhart says *Esse est Deus*, he is not denying the being of creatures. Rather, he intends precisely to "establish the being of creatures."[603] The creature does not have being in itself, its being is in God, who is the source of

---

[596] See, Eckhart, *Opus Tripartium Prologi*, ed. Hildebrandus Bascour (1935), II, 4.4-5.

[597] *Esse indistinctum, esse simpliciter versus esse hocet hoc, esse formaliter inhaerens* ; see *ESC*, 33.

[598] *ESC*, 32.

[599] *TP*, 250.

[600] *TP*, 250.

[601] *TP* 175.

[602] *ESC*,103.

[603] Muller-Thym, *The establishment*, 5.

all being. In other words, creatures are utterly nothing in themselves. "It is in virtue of the presence of God, *esse*, to creature, that the creature has the name of being."[604]

Like Ibn al-'Arabi, therefore, for Eckhart, no creatures have being, since being belongs only to God. If anything has being, its being is derivative. Thus, all creatures—with respect to their creaturely nature—and conceived apart from God, are mere nothings. As one might expect, it was statements such as these which were interpreted by certain ecclesiastical authorities of Eckhart's day as dangerous. In fact, as was the case with Ibn al-'Arabi, Eckhart's attempts to assert God's nature as "All-Inclusive" led to a perception that his theology was essentially pantheistic. This misreading of Eckhart, however, seems to be based on the erroneous assumption that he is equating existence, in every respect, with God, and God, in every respect, with existence. But, like Ibn al-'Arabi, Eckhart is saying that nothing can truly exist outside of God, and all existent phenomena exist only insofar as they are within God. For Eckhart, as for Ibn al-'Arabi, the danger of idolatry comes not primarily from the possibility of lapsing into crude pantheism, but rather from the opposite—from the temptation to think of creatures as possessing independent being. "Every created being," Eckhart writes, "taken or conceived apart from and as distinct in itself from God is not a being, but is nothing."[605] As God is one, then all are one, "not in the sense of being the sum total of all that is, but rather as the ground of all that is."[606] Eckhart says, "God touches all things and remains untouched. God is above all things an instanding [*sic.*] in Himself, and this standing in Himself sustains all creatures. . . . He is the ground and the incirclement [*sic.*] of all creatures."[607] Furthermore, in his *Commentary on Exodus*, Eckhart explores God, "the All-Inclusive" as follows,

> With his whole being God is present whole and entire as much as in the least things as in the greatest. Thus the just person who loves

---

[604] Muller-Thym, *The establishment*, 7.

[605] *Commentary on Exodus*, Chapter 15, verse 1 in *TP*, 55.

[606] Elizabeth Brient, *The Immanence of the Infinite* (Washington DC: The Catholic University of America Press, 2002), 155.

[607] *ST*, I, Sermon 24 (b), *vidi supra montem agnum stantem etc.* 193.

God in all things would seek in vain for something more or greater when he has some little thing in which the God whom he loves alone to the exclusion of everything else is totally present. There is no "greater" or "less" in God nor in the One; they are below and outside God and the One. And thus someone who sees, seeks, and loves what is more or less is not as such divine. This is the meaning of the axiom in the Book of the Twenty-Four Philosophers: "God is the infinite intellectual sphere with as many circumferences as centers and whose center is everywhere and circumference nowhere, he is entire in his least part.[608]

Perhaps Eckhart's single most important attempt to clarify the difference between his theology of radical divine oneness, on the one hand, and pantheism, on the other hand, is his gloss of the statement, "God is the One, the All-inclusive," as signifying *not* that God's being is "the sum total of all that is, but rather [that it is]…the ground of all that is." [609]

5. Naming God

The One or the Ultimate, for Ibn al-'Arabi, is the Essence (*dhat*), God in Godself. Sometimes he refers to the One as *al-Haqq*, signifying the fact that it is intrinsically unrelated to any created thing. In this case, it is unknowable and unnameable, "independent of the worlds, nondelimited (*mutlaq*) by any attribute whatsoever."[610] This Essence, in this sense, is said to be *ankar al-nakirat*, that is, "the most indeterminate of all indeterminates."[611] According to Ibn al-'Arabi, only negative statements can be made of Him since any positive propositions would be necessarily limiting and constitute a definition of That which is indefinable. According to Ibn al-'Arabi, "He who supposes he has knowledge of positive attributes of the divine Self (*sifa nafsiyya thubutiyya*) [*sic.*] has supposed wrongly. For such an attribute would define (*hadd*) Him, but His Essence has no definition."[612]

---

[608] *Commentary on Exodus*, Chapter 16, verse 18 in *TP*, 75.
[609] Brient, *The Immanence of the Infinite*, 155.
[610] *SPK*, 109.
[611] Toshihiko Izutzu, *Sufism and Taoism*, 23.
[612] *Fut.* II, 619. 15; *SPK*, 58.

To know something means to find it, and to find something means to set conceptual limits to it. God, therefore—as construed by the human heart through genuine experience of the *nafas al-rahman*— can be found; God can be the object of the "finding" (*wujud*) of the human subject. Not so the Essence. The Essence is paradigmatically unlimited, therefore, it cannot be found. If it cannot be found, then it cannot really be known. Indeed, according to Ibn al-'Arabi, there is a dimension of the "Majesty of God" (*jalal*) that is beyond the grasp of human conceptualization.

The reason why, for Ibn al'-Arabi, speculative thought is inadequate as a means for the knowledge of God is, quite simply, its finitude. All speculative thought "narrows and limits a 'Divine Vastness' (*al-tawassu' al-ilahi*)."[613] Ibn al-'Arabi maintains:

> He who restricts the Reality [to his own belief] denies Him [when manifested] in other beliefs, affirming Him only when He is manifest in his own belief. He who does not restrict Him does not deny Him, but affirm His Reality in every formal transformation, worshipping Him in its infinite forms, since there is no limit to the forms in which He manifests Himself.[614]...[t]he intellect restricts and seeks to define the truth within a particular qualification, while in fact the Reality does not admit of such a limitation. It is not a reminder for the intellectuals and mongers of doctrinal formulations who contradict one another and denounce each other . . . *and they have no helper*. (3: 91)[615]

Hence, when Ibn al-'Arabi criticizes theologians and philosophers as idolatrous (*mushrikun*), it is because "they mistake their perspective for the bird's eye view, their singular interpretation for the final exegesis."[616] According to Ibn al-'Arabi, the reflective thinkers tried to constrain the Essence to their limited perception, which simply entails moving "from veil to veil."[617] Both stories of the encounter between Ibn Rushd and Ibn al-'Arabi, and between Moses and Khidr (discussed

---

[613] Ian Almond, *Sufism and Deconstruction*, 10.

[614] *BW*, 149, *Fusus al-Hikam*, 121, quoted by Almond, *Sufism and Deconstruction*, 16.

[615] *BW*, 150, *Fusus al-Hikam*, 122, quoted by Almond, *Sufism and Deconstruction*, 16.

[616] Ian Almond, "Divine Needs, Divine Illusions," 267-268.

[617] *Fut.* IV, 105. 3; *SPK*, 230.

above in chapter one), also is an important illustration of how critical it is to recognize that, at some point, reason is just another veil or obstacle which has to be removed in order to come to perfect knowledge.[618]

Indeed, as already mentioned in the previous chapter, God's Self-manifestation is both infinite and never repeated, it is a perpetual and constant flow. Based on this perspective, it is understandable that Ibn al-'Arabi considered speculative thinking as a "fetter,"[619] because it attempts to fetter perpetual flow of God's Self-manifestation, which means delimit the undelimited Essence:

> In the view of Verifiers, the Real is too exalted "to disclose Himself in a single form twice or to two individuals." The Real never repeats anything, because of His non-delimitation of the Divine Vastness, since repetition amounts to constraint (*dhiq*) and delimitation.[620]

For Ibn al-'Arabi, an over-emphasis on speculative thinking and formulation leads to a kind of rationalism which results in confining the Essence. This is why Ibn al-'Arabi sees, as asserted by Almond, so many theologians and philosophers as people who impose "a banality and a predictability upon God," and by doing this, at the same time, they undertake "a way of fossilizing God's dynamic flexibility."[621] It is very important to recognize that this does not mean that Ibn al-'Arabi is hostile to everyone who assigns attributes to God; the human being cannot hope to relate to God without formulating and reflecting upon God's attributes. What it does mean is that, within the framework of such formulation and reflection, the human being *must* maintain the ultimate ineffability of Reality. Ibn al-'Arabi says, "A [true] definition of the Reality is impossible, for such a definition would depend on the ability to [fully] define every form in the Cosmos, which is impossible.

---

[618] In these stories, Ibn Rushd and Moses represent those who possess only exoteric knowledge, especially of the Law, Ibn al-'Arabi himself and Khidr are presented as embodiments of the esoteric knowledge of the saints.

[619] In the *Futuhat* Ibn al-'Arabi points to the root meaning of the term *aql* (reason) closely connected to *iqal* (fetter), *Fut.* III, 198. 33 in *SPK*, 107.

[620] *Fut.* II, 657. 13 in *SPK*, 111.

[621] Almond, *Sufism*, 18.

Therefore, a [complete] definition of the Reality is impossible."[622] Again, Ibn al-'Arabi emphasizes on the unknowability of the Essence:

> Were the Essence to make the loci of manifestation (*mazahir*) manifest, It would be known. Were It known, it would be encompassed (*ihata*). Were It encompassed, It would be limited (*hadd*). Were It limited, It would be confined (*inhisar*). Were It confined, It would be owned (*mulk*).[623]

In criticizing speculative thinkers who cannot transcend the rational faculty (*'aql*), Ibn al-'Arabi is attempting to highlight the serious risks involved in creating a system of doctrinal formulations which purport, however implicitly, to encompass the Essence. An example of this would be the theological systems of the Ash'arites, which make certain claims about the Essence through positive attributions (i.e., so-called "kataphatic" discourse), all the while ignoring the inherent inadequacy of these attributions.

As was the case with his teachings regarding the oneness of Being, Ibn al-'Arabi's objections to naming and thus "fettering" the infinite God, have their own deep analogical connections to Eckhart when the latter speaks of those who "want to see God with the same eyes with which they look at a cow . . ." For Eckhart, these people "love [the cow] for the milk and the cheese and for their own profit."[624] Caputo aptly summarizes this aspect of Eckhart's teachings when he describes Eckhart's position as follows: that "to call God 'creator' was just to mark Him off in terms of 'creatures'; to call Him 'cause' was to mark Him off from 'effects'; to call Him 'good' was to name Him in refer-

---

[622] *BW*, 74.

[623] *Fut.* II, 597. 19; *SPK*, 60.

[624] *MP*, 102. In fact, like Maimonides, Eckhart, in this case, expresses the fear that people who desire of the knowledge of God ultimately for their own worldly purposes only. This is a common theme in the *Guide for the Perplexed*, where Maimonides rebukes the sophists who derive [from the scriptures] inferences and secondary conclusions' in order to exploit the "multitude who listen to these utterances." See A Hayman and J. Walshe, *Philosophy in the Middle Ages* (Indianapolis: Hackett Publishing Co., 1973), 377.

ence to the will; and to call Him 'true' was to give Him a name relative to the intellect."[625] Throughout his several sermons, Eckhart says,

> [W]hen people think that they are acquiring more of God in
> inwardness, in devotion, in sweetness and in various approaches
> than they do by the fireside or in the stable, you are acting just as
> if you took God and muffled his head up in a cloak and pushed him
> under a bench.[626]

> [Y]ou are acting just as if you were to make a candle out of God in
> order to look for something with it. Once one finds the things one
> is looking for, one throws the candle away.[627]

The quotations above allude to the fact that, for Eckhart, to name
God means to treat God as an object according to one's own human
purposes and one's own human blueprints. In fact, he strongly denies
any depiction of God by saying, "whatever we say God is, He is not;
what we do not say of Him, He is more truly than what we say He is."[628]
And "whatever fine names, whatever words we use, they are telling lies,
and it is far above them. It is free of all names, it is bare of all forms,
wholly empty and free, as God in Himself is empty and free."[629] This is
the reason why Eckhart, as a deeply apophatic theologian, profoundly
distrusts the desire to name and describe God—certainly to a much
greater extent than Ibn al-'Arabi. A very important influence on Eckhart's stance on the unnameability of God is the seminal medieval Jewish philosopher and religious thinker Moses Maimonides. Like Maimonides, Eckhart asserts that "nothing affirmative is properly and aptly
said about God, but only insuitably said."[630] This "insuitability" does

---

[625] John D. Caputo, "Mysticism and Transgression: Derrida and Meister Eckhart," in
Derrida and Deconstruction, ed. Hugh J Silverman (New York and London:
Routledge, 1989), 32, Caputo here is referring to Eckhart's sermon 52, *Beati paupers
spiritu*, see ESC, 200-3.

[626] *ESC*, 183; cf. *ST*, I, 117.

[627] Sermon 4, *Omne datum optimum et omne donum perfectum desursum est* (Jm. 1: 17),
DW I, 69, 2-4; *TP*, 250; Meister Eckhart, *An Introduction*, 173; *ST*, 284; also
quoted by *MP*, 113.

[628] *ST*, I, 237.

[629] *ESC*, 180.

[630] *MP*, 58.

not, for Eckhart, imply the illegitimacy of formulations about God. Rather, it is meant to critique those who are eager to take these formulations far beyond their capacity. For Eckhart, God is "unnamable to us because of the infinity of all existence in him," though, paradoxically, we also can assert that he is "omninameable."[631] Eckhart says,

> Unsophisticated teachers say that God is pure being. He is as high above being as the highest angel is above gnat. I would be speaking as incorrectly in calling God's being as if I called the sun pale or black. God is neither this nor that.[632]

Quoting Maimonides who says "nothing is in the Creator but the true, perfectly realized simplicity,"[633] in his *Commentary of Exodus*, Eckhart declares that anyone who absolutely "attributes positive denominations to the Creator sins in four ways,"[634]

> First, because the intellect and the apprehension of the one grasping something of this sort about God is "limited." Second, because such a person "makes God participate," that is, he understands him as having parts, and not as perfectly realized simplicity, or else as "participating," that is, he makes him participate and share something with the creature. Third, because "he apprehends God as other than [God] is"; and fourth, because such a person removes God's existence from his heart, "even if he does not know it."[635]

Thus, for Eckhart, "the finest thing that we can say of God is to be silent concerning him from the wisdom of inner riches,"[636] and "as long as the soul has God, knows God and is aware of God, she is far from God."[637]

It can be concluded that, with regard to God, the One All-Inclusive, the Essence, *al-Haqq*, both Ibn al-'Arabi and Eckhart maintain an apophatic dialectic approach. For Ibn al-'Arabi, since the Essence

---

[631] McGinn, *The Mystical Thought of Meister Eckhart*, 99.

[632] *TP*, 256; Eckhart, *Predigt.* 9; *DW* 1. 145: 5-7; *ST*, II, 150.

[633] Maimonides, *Guide for the Perplexed*, a modern edition, I. 60, cited by *TP*, 97.

[634] *TP*, 97.

[635] *TP*, 97.

[636] Davies, Selected Writings, 236.

[637] Davies, *Selected Writings*, 244.

has no attributes, It has no definition; for Eckhart, God is much closer to what is not said than what is said. Ibn al-'Arabi calls the Essence "the One"; for Eckhart, the Godhead (*Gotheit*) is the "solitary One." Nevertheless, if Eckhart explicitly refers to the Absolute as "Beyond Being", there is no such explicit term in Ibn al-'Arabi's teaching. What Eckhart asserts as "Beyond Being," however, is none other than what Ibn al-'Arabi calls "Being."

In the chapter on Moses in *Fusus al-hikam*, Ibn al-'Arabi mentions that "[True] guidance means being guided to bewilderment (*hayra*), that he might know that the whole affair [of God] is perplexity, which means perturbation and flux, and flux is life. There is no abatement and cessation, but all is being with no non-being."[638] In fact, for Ibn al-'Arabi all paths to God ultimately end in bewilderment (*hayra*) and perplexity.

It is because of this perplexity that Ibn al-'Arabi is saying that the philosophers and theologians can make no ultimate proposition about the Real. Not unlike the great jurist, theologian, and Sufi before him— Abu Hamid al-Ghazali (d. 1111 ce)—Ibn al-'Arabi is insisting that philosophers and theologians recognize the limitations of their respective intellectual enterprises. Ibn al-'Arabi often cites the verse, "God warns you about His Self" (3:28, 30) which he interprets very often in light of the prophetic saying: "Reflect (*tafakkur*) upon all things but reflect not upon God's Essence."[639] Elsewhere Ibn al-'Arabi writes, "None knows God but God."[640] According to Ibn al-'Arabi, the Qur'an 3:28, 30 "alerts us to the form of the veil within which the Real discloses Himself. Then He transmutes himself from it into another veil. In reality, there is nothing but passage from veil to veil, since no divine self-disclosure ever repeats itself. Hence the forms must be diverse, while the Real is behind all of that. We possess nothing of Him but the name Manifest, whether in a vision or a veil. As for the name Nonmanifest, it remains forever Nonmanifest."[641] Furthermore he maintains,

---

[638] *BW*, 254, *Fusus al-Hikam*, 200, also cited by Almond, *Sufism*, 21.

[639] *SPK*, 62.

[640] *Fut.* II, 69. 35; *SPK*, 62.

[641] *Fut.* IV, 105. 5; *SPK*, 230.

If you insist only on His transcendence, you restrict Him,
   And if you insist only on His immanence you limit Him.
If you maintain both aspects you are right,
   An Imam and a master in the spiritual sciences.
Whoso would say He is two things is a polytheist,
   While the one who isolates Him tries to regulate Him.
Beware of comparing Him if you profess duality,
   And, if unity, of making Him transcendent.
You are not He and you are He and
   You see Him in the essence of things both boundless and limited.[642]

6. God Created by the Believer versus the Godhead

I would like to preface this section with a word of caution regarding both masters' use of terminology to speak about the God that is beyond God (i.e., for Ibn al-'Arabi, *al-Haqq* or "the Real" and for Meister Eckhart, *Gotheit* or the "Godhead"). In both cases these expressions are employed as signifiers which signify that which is beyond signifying and thus which defies *all* signification. As such, they can be used as linguistic "placeholders" for that which cannot be "held," but they can never be in any way mistaken to actually determine and name what they appear to be signifying.

For Ibn al-'Arabi "when a person rationally considers God, he creates what he believes in himself through his consideration. Hence he considers only a God which he has created through his consideration."[643] Thus, here, Ibn al-'Arabi alludes to the two different dimensions of the human experience of God. The first is the "God created by the believers," or the "God of Belief," which changes according to the predisposition of the believer.[644] The second is the Godhead, the unknowable Essence. Contrary to common caricatures of Ibn al-'Arabi's teachings, there is nothing wrong with the "God of Belief," *providing that the believers themselves are always conscious of the degree to which this experience of God is conditioned in significant ways by their own limited and particu-*

---

[642] *BW*, 75; Ibn al-'Arabi, *Fusus al-Hikam*, 70.

[643] *Fut.* IV, 143.2, *SPK*, 360.

[644] *BW*, 282.

lar consciousness. Caputo demonstrates an analogous mode of thinking in Meister Eckhart:

> The divine names just keep referring back to other names in the chain. We never get a name which really is God's own name, which really seizes upon God, and then, having done its duty, having delivered us into the inner chambers of the Godhead, quietly dissipates into thin air. Eckhart also kept warning us about the contingency of the signifier we deploy.[645]

Like Ibn al-'Arabi, Eckhart distinguishes between God as understood by the believers (the God we worship), on the one hand, and God as beyond images and concept, on the other hand, or between God and Godhead (*Gotheit*). In fact, like Ibn al-'Arabi, for Eckhart, the God who is the object of Christian worship and devotion is distinct from the indescribable Godhead. "God and the Godhead," Eckhart maintains,

> are as different from each other as heaven and earth . . . . God *becomes* as phenomena express him. When I existed in the core, the soil, the river, the source of the Godhead, no one asked me where I was going or what I was doing. There was no one there to ask me, but the moment I emerged, the world of creatures began to shout: "God!". . . . Thus creatures speak of God. . . . God acts. The Godhead does not. . . . The difference between God and the Godhead is the difference between action and non-action."[646]

Furthermore, like Ibn al-'Arabi, for Eckhart, the worshipped God (the God of the believer) is "partly human construction, she/he exists only in relation to the worshipping community." [647] Eckhart writes, "when I stood in my first cause, then I had no God, . . . but when I went out from my own and received my created being, then I had a God, for before there were any creatures, God was not God, but he was what he was. But when creatures came to be and received their created being, then God was not God in himself, but he was God in

---

[645] John D. Caputo, "Mysticism and Transgression," 32.

[646] Blakney, *Meister Eckhart, Modern Translation*, 225-6.

[647] John Hick, "Ineffability," *Religious Studies* 36 (United Kingdom: Cambridge University Press, 2000), 39-40.

the creatures."[648] Thus, Eckhart warns the believer "not to have a God who is just a product of his thought, nor should he be satisfied with that, because if the thought vanishes, God too would vanish. But one ought to have a God who is present, a God who is far above the notion of men and of all created things."[649]

Analogues to Eckhart's statement above, Ibn al-ʿArabi argues that "the Essence, as being beyond all these relationships, is not a divinity. Since all these relationships originate in our eternally unmanifested essences, it is we [in our eternal latency] who make Him a divinity by being that through which He knows Himself as Divine. Thus, he is not known [as God] until we are known."[650] Again, like Ibn al-ʿArabi, for Eckhart the Christian God is "a manifestation in human terms of the ultimate divine reality, and that, as manifest, He exists only in relation to his worshippers."[651]

Although both Ibn al-ʿArabi and Eckhart have deeply analogous ideas about the God created by believers and the Godhead, it is important to recognize that they develop these ideas along somewhat distinct tracks which are not coincidentally related to the distinctiveness of their signature teachings on the self-disclosure of God and detachment, respectively. For Ibn al-ʿArabi, the God created by believers is a matter of perspective—it is not something to outgrow spiritually, but something to be appreciated for the ways in which it participates in the self-disclosure of God. As for Eckhart, Almond would maintain that for this Christian mystic master—who (in)famously prays to God to be delivered from God—the God created by the believer is little more than a lower means to a higher end, a "Wittgensteinian ladder which, once we have climbed, we have to kick away from under us."[652] But Almond is too extreme in this interpretation. Eckhart is not suggest-

---

[648] *ESC*, 200. Here I am removing all inverted commas surrounding the word *God* to prevent the unintended "censorship" of apophatic discourse. See chapter four (above), sec. 4, note 98.

[649] *ESC*, 253.

[650] *BW*, 92.

[651] John Hick, "Ineffability," *Religious Studies* 36 (United Kingdom: Cambridge University Press, 2000), 39-40.

[652] Almond, "Divine Needs," 267.

ing the impossible; he is not suggesting that we purge ourselves from the God created by the believers, but rather that we be *detached* from our conceptualizations of God, lest we fall into idolatry in the name of championing orthodoxy. For Ibn al-'Arabi, the attempt to deny the role our conceptions of God play in *God's self-disclosure* is to violate the oneness of being by suggesting that there is any aspect of our experience in which it is not possible to "find" God. For Eckhart, it is *detachment* from—and not disavowal of—our concepts of God that plays a crucial role in facilitating the "breakthrough" to the Godhead. This is just one example of the governing role played by the major themes of each of the masters' work. In fact, I would argue quite strongly, that each of the points of conversation enumerated in this chapter cannot be fully understood within the context of each masters' teachings without reference back to the themes exposited in chapters three and four.

For both our masters, one of the fruits of recognizing the difference between God and the "God of the believer" is the ability to see with the eye of God. With this eye, one is able to look upon the diversity of the created order with a perspective infinitely broader than that of the "God of the believer," the role of which is to convince the believer not to look outside of the "box," so to speak, of his or her tradition for any truth. As is evident above in chapter four, the degree to which the two masters seem to use metaphors of color has to do with the mystical assertion that one of the gifts of becoming "one with" God is the ability to see and understand the nature of the diversity in creation through the lens of the divine unity from which this diversity stems.

7. Transformation of the Self

There are many paths in the journey to God, but first, it should be noted that in Ibn al-'Arabi's teaching, the seeker can only go as far as the door. When he or she reaches the door, he or she can knock as often as he or she likes, but God decides when and if He will open it.[653] And it is also very important to note that, for both Ibn al-'Arabi and Meister Eckhart,

---

[653] This image of opening the door explains the meaning of the title of the Shaykh's magnum opus, *Futuhat al-Makiyya*, "The Meccan Opening/Revelation." See *IW*, 8.

"the performance of the orthodox rites is taken for granted as one of the foundations of path of transcendence and is not abandoned at any point."[654] The question that this section will address is what, for Ibn al-'Arabi and Meister Eckhart, is the nature of the transformation that the seeker undergoes in the process of his or her journey.

Describing the process whereby one attains transformation or "opening," (*fath*) Ibn al-'Arabi says,

> When the aspiring traveler clings to retreat and invocation of God's name, when he empties his heart of reflective [i.e., speculative] thoughts, and when he sits in poverty, having nothing, at the door of his Lord, then God will bestow upon him and give him something of knowledge of Him, of the divine mysteries, and of the lordly sciences. . . . That is why Abu Yazid has said, "You take your knowledge dead from the dead, but I take my knowledge from the Living One who does not die."[655]

Ibn al-'Arabi also says that a person must withdraw and flee from those affairs which divert him from this situation, so that God may unveil his insight and his sight.[656] He writes:

> Every seeker of his Lord must be alone with himself with his Lord in his inmost consciousness, since God gave man an outward dimension (*zahir*) and an inward dimension (*batin*) only so that he might be alone with God in his inward dimension, and witness Him in his outward dimension within the secondary causes, after having gazed upon Him in his inward dimension, so that he may discern Him within the midst of the secondary causes. Otherwise, he will never recognize Him. He who enters the spiritual retreat (*khalwa*) with God does so only for this reason, since man's inward dimension is the cell of his retreat.[657]

---

[654] Shah Reza-Kazemi, *Path to Transcendence, according to Shankara, Ibn Arabi, and Meister Eckhart* (Bloomington, Ind. : World Wisdom, 2006), 198.

[655] *Fut.* I, 31. 4 quoted by *IW*, 8; On Ibn al-'Arabi's teaching of transformation see also, Chittick, "Belief and Transformation: Sufi Teaching of Ibn al-'Arabi," *The American Theosophist* 74 (1986).

[656] *Fut.* III, 265. 17, *SPK*, 158.

[657] *Fut.* III, 265. 17, *SPK*, 159.

In his experience of transformation, Ibn al-ʿArabi distances himself from all created things. Thus, the seeker is instructed to remain free of all that might distract him or her from the divine, to detach from the mundane world in order to know God. It should be noted, however, that "fleeing to God," in this case refers to the flight from ignorance to knowledge.[658] In fact, Ibn al-ʿArabi comes close to God by means of a knowledge which both impels him to deeper discovery, and at the same time keeps him grounded in the practice of most of his fellow Muslims. Speaking about fleeing from ignorance to knowledge, however, unlike theologians and philosophers who uses reason as their essential means, for Ibn al-ʿArabi, "these kinds of knowledge are useful and good, but they can become obstruction to gaining the most real and useful of knowledge, which is taught by God Himself."[659] Moreover, for Ibn al-ʿArabi, knowledge which can guide one to God must by nature be connected to practice. Ibn al-ʿArabi says, "God's deceiving (*makr*) the servant is that He should provide him with knowledge which demands practice, and then deprive him of practice."[660] Of this practice, Ibn al-ʿArabi says that it encompasses both inward and outward activities:

> There is an outward practice, which is everything connected to the bodily parts and an inward practice, which is everything connected to the soul (*nafs*). The most inclusive inward practice is faith in God and what has come from Him in accordance with the words of the Messenger, not in accordance with knowledge of it. Faith embraces all acts which are to be performed or avoided.[661]

This commitment to practice, to strict observance of the divine commandments, is what Ibn al-ʿArabi refers to as "undertaking acts of obedience," in the course of which it is also essential for the seeker to "abandon those of his individual desires which detract from his felicity."[662] Thus fidelity to the Shariʿa plays the role of pivotal catalyst

---

[658] *Fut.* III, 265. 1, *SPK*, 158.

[659] See Q. 18: 65, *Fut.* II, 370. 4, *SPK*, 148.

[660] *Fut.* II, 529. 34; *SPK*, 151.

[661] *Fut.* II, 559. 20; *SPK*, 152.

[662] *Fut.* II, 558. 34.

in the transformation of the seeker into a deeper awareness of and dedication to the Real.

Like Ibn al-'Arabi, throughout his sermons Eckhart also talks about an analogous process of transformation (i.e., "attaining to the presence of God") which relies very heavily on the principle of detachment or "poverty." Kazemi asserts that both Ibn al-'Arabi and Meister Eckhart elaborate in great detail the concept of detachment "dialectically, in order to distinguish between the volitive 'poverty' which relates more to the moral and affective aspect of detachment, and an ontological 'poverty,' the ground of which is the effacement of the ego."[663] In sermon 52: *Beati paupers spiritu*, Eckhart, mentions people who are "attached to their own penances and external exercises;"[664] as "donkey" or "asses" "who do not grasp the actual meaning of divine truth."[665] They believe that they have achieved poverty of the will in their conceit that they, through their many devotional practices, they have conformed their own wills to God's will, thus rendering the human will and the divine will indistinguishable from one another.[666] For Eckhart, however, true poverty of the will comes in the pursuit of utter detachment from one's will, no longer ascribing reasons to explain one's actions, but simply acting, without imagining one's actions to have significance in the eyes of God. This attitude toward the will is an integral part of the "living without a why" (*sunder warumbe*) that is the fruit of genuine detachment.

In a similar sense, as stated by Kazemi, Ibn al-'Arabi differentiates between "slavehood" (*'ubudiya*) and "servitude" (*'ubuda*) "in order to show that the perfect [human being] is subsumed within the latter quality rather than possessed of the former, with such possession implying personal affirmation prior to subordination to the Absolute."[667] Being subsumed in *'ubuda*, however, does not involve a rejection of the creation in the transformation that is so central to the

---

[663] Kazemi, *Path to Transcendence*, 212.

[664] *ESC*, 199.

[665] *MP*, 214, Cf. *ESC*, 200.

[666] *ESC*, 199.

[667] Kazemi, *Path to Transcendence*, 212.

quest to find God, but rather a detachment from the illusion that the human self is the active agent in this transformation, and a growing awareness that the transformation of the self is a work accomplished by God using any means (i.e., any element of the created order) God pleases. Since, for Ibn al-ʿArabi, "God never ceases gazing upon the entities of the possible things in the state of their nonexistence,"[668] "withdrawal" from the world or "renouncing everything other than God" is best understood, not as something the human self can actually accomplish, but rather the attitude the human self must adopt to be open to the annihilative transformation that can come from God and God alone.[669] Because, according to the Islamic tradition that is the source of Ibn al-ʿArabi's teaching, "the whole cosmos is constantly singing God's praises," withdrawal from the world, in the literal sense, is actually "impossible and undesirable, since to renounce the cosmos is to renounce the possibility of increasing one's knowledge of God."[670] Thus, the analog in Ibn al-ʿArabi's thought to the principle of "detachment" in Eckhart—Ibn al-ʿArabi's "flight to God"—is not a flight away from one thing towards another, since there is nothing in existence but God.

The actual meaning of this withdrawal can be depicted in Ibn al-ʿArabi's teaching, when he asks, "From whom dost thou flee and there is nought in existence but He?" Ibn al-ʿArabi, in fact, warns that it is necessary to be wary of separating God from the world and fleeing to a divinity of one's own imagining. The cause of this imaginary flight, Ibn al-ʿArabi says, "is the lack of tasting (*dhawq*) of the things" and "the fact that the one who flees heard in the recitation (of the Qurʾan) (Q 51:50) "So flee to God!" This verse is correct except that the one who is fleeing did not pay attention to what is mentioned in the following verse, that is, His words, "And set not up with God another God." Had he known this completed verse, he would have known that God's words, "So flee to God!" refer to the flight from ignorance to knowledge. The situation is one and unitary."[671]

---

[668] *Fut.* III, 263. 16, 35, 265. 1; *SPK*, 157.

[669] *SPK*, 157.

[670] *SPK*, 157.

[671] *Fut.* III, 263. 35; *SPK*, 58.

In sum, the genuine (as opposed to the imaginary) "flight" to God is a metaphor for an inner transformation which opens one's being to the fullness of the divine self-disclosure in every aspect of phenomenal existence.

In the spiritual retreat, both mystics regard ecstatic mystical vision as a relative attainment which "must be transcended by realization of the Absolute as one's own innermost identity."[672] In Eckhart's language, this realization is the continual *durchbruch* or "breakthrough" that follows detachment and the "birthing of God" respectively. In the language of Ibn al-'Arabi this realization is the "opening" referred to (in the plural) in the title of his magnum opus, *Futuhat*. According to Chittick, this term is a near synonym for "unveiling," "tasting," "witnessing," "divine effusion," "divine self-disclosure," and "insight."[673] The way to achieve this opening is through self-discipline. In this respect Ibn al-'Arabi quotes the Qur'an: "Be godfearing [i.e., be scrupulous in fulfilling the commandments of God] and God will teach you" (Q 2: 282). According to Ibn al-'Arabi, God will prepare the seeker for God's teaching, and this preparation will involve a transformation which will "entail his complete absorption in putting the revealed Law into practice and invoking (*dhikr*) the name of God under the teacher's (*shaykh*) guidance." The seeker needs *khalwa* (spiritual retreat) and *jalwa* (presence in society) at the same time.[674] "Unveiling comes to them in their retreats when the divine lights dawn within hem, bringing sciences purified of corroding stains."[675]

Because of the relativity of mystical vision, for Ibn al-'Arabi, it is necessary for the seekers not to think of the station of blissful or ecstatic experience as their journey's end. In addition, they must refrain from seeking rewards or gifts from God in order to gain realization in God Himself. In a deeply analogous manner, Meister Eckhart also insists that no image from any vision, however exalted or beatific, is to remain, not even the image of Christ. It is to be resisted and excluded.

---

[672] Kazemi, *Path to Transcendence*, 200.

[673] *SPK*, xii.

[674] *SPK*, xii.

[675] *Fut.* II, 600. 3; *SPK*, xii.

Eckhart says "So leave all images and unite with the formless essence,"[676] and "Go right out of yourself for God's sake, and God will go right out of Himself for your sake! When these two have gone out what is left is one and simple. In this One the Father bears His Son in the inmost source."[677] In fact, Eckhart's crucial concept of "breakthrough" (*durchbruch*) refers to "the soul's penetration beyond the Trinity into the divine wilderness, or Godhead beyond God."[678] It "rejects all created things, and wants nothing but naked God, as He is in Himself. It is not content with the Father or the Son or the Holy Spirit, or with the three Persons so far as each of them persists in his properties."[679]

This is closely linked with the concept of *sunder warumbe* (living without why), as discussed in chapter four, where Eckhart says: "As long as you perform your deed for the sake of the kingdom of heaven or God or your eternal salvation, in other words for an external reason, things are not truly well with you. . . . Whoever seeks for God in a particular way, takes that way and misses God, who is hidden in ways. But whoever seeks God without a way, will find Him as He is in himself."[680]

For Ibn al-'Arabi, the result of the transformation of the self is the perfect human being, whose heart is the polished mirror which reflects, as perfectly as possible, the attributes of God. For Eckhart, the result of the transformation of the self is the Nobleman who has experienced the birth of Son in the soul and broken through to the Godhead. He and only he can say, "God and I, we are one. I accept God into me in knowing; I go into God in loving."[681] Eckhart declares:

> God and I are one. Then I am what I was, and then I neither diminish nor increase, for I am then an immovable cause that moves all things. Here God finds no place in man, for with this poverty man achieves what he has been eternally and will evermore remain.

---

[676] *ST*, 128.

[677] *ST* I, 118.

[678] Lanzetta, *Other Side of Nothingness, Toward a Theology of Radical Openness*, (Albany, State University of New York Press, 2001), 21.

[679] *ESC*, 198.

[680] *DW* I, 227; *ST*, I, 117; *ESC*,183.

[681] *ESC*, 188; see also 203, and see also McGinn, *The Mystical Thought of Meister Eckhart*, 10-11.

Here God is one with the spirit, and that is the most intimate poverty one can find.[682]

For Eckhart, man has two natures, body and spirit, the outer
man and the inner man. It is the inner man which is called the Nobleman, "a new man, a heavenly man, a young man, a friend."[683] The
Nobleman or the Just Man is also one who acts properly, appropri-
ately, within whatever conditions that may prevail. Quoting from the
institutes of Justinian, Eckhart says, "That man is just who gives
everyone what belongs to him."[684] Thus, the just are "those who give
God what is his, and the saints and the angels what is theirs, and their
fellow man what is his."[685] This quality of appropriateness in daily living is the Just Man's way of honoring God, possible only in the total
absence of ego, of any vestige of a separate self-sense. Those honor
God, Eckhart asserts, "who have wholly gone out of themselves, and
who do not seek for what is theirs in anything. . . , who are not looking beneath themselves or above themselves or beside themselves or
at themselves, who are not desiring possessions or honors or ease or
pleasure or profit or inwardness or holiness or reward or the kingdom of heaven."[686]

The Nobleman, according to Eckhart, is the "Only-Begotten
Son of God whom the father generates from all eternity."[687] Describing the process of "birthing" of the Son in the soul, Eckhart mentions
that there is a prerequisite condition; it is that one must honor God
in absolute selflessness and absolute humility. "If God is to enter, the
creature must exit."[688] When the condition of emptiness and silence
prevailed, the birth of the Son in the soul may take place. Here the
spiritual journey becomes a medium for Eckhart's apophatic lan-

---

[682] *ESC*, 203.

[683] *ESC*, 240.

[684] *ESC*, 185.

[685] *ESC*, 185.

[686] *ESC*, 185.

[687] *ESC*, 79.

[688] Richard Kieckhefer, "Meister Eckhart's Conception of Union with God," *Harvard Theological Review* 71 (July-October, 1978): 21 f.

guage as the soul is exhorted to break through, to free itself from God. Eckhart says:

> The Father gives birth to His Son without ceasing; and I say more: He gives birth not only to me, his Son, but he gives birth to me as himself and himself as me and to me as his being and nature. In the innermost source, there I spring out in the Holy Spirit, where there is one life and one being and one work.[689]

Thus, in its ground or being, the Godhead is in an eternal process of begetting in two directions, "outward" toward the Trinity, and also "inward" toward its own deeper ground as an "unknown stillness without name."[690]

The other major category according to which Meister Eckhart discusses the return of the soul to its Origin is the breakthrough (*durchbruch*) to the Godhead. What we are referring to in the teachings of our two masters as "transformation of the self," many typically refer to as mystical "union"—a union in which consciousness continues, but which somehow, according to conventional understanding, *nullifies* the condition of individuality. For his part, Eckhart hearkens back to his pre-existence in which there is no duality between self and God—a state in which God is "all in all." The ideal transformation of the self constitutes a return to a state in which there is no longer a dichotomy (i.e., between self and God) to be reconciled in "union." Some scholars, however, are correct in pointing out the inadequacy of terms like "union" to describe the transformations of which both Ibn al-'Arabi and Meister Eckhart speak. The same fundamental point can also be found in Ibn al-'Arabi. When he is detached from his contingent dimension, he realizes that he himself is God, and at the same time that he also transcends God. This is very similar to Eckhart's assertion that in his first cause and final return he "has no God." Thus, in both cases, there is the claim to have not only realized a transcendent identity, but also to have realized in this identity a degree that surpasses the level of the personal God.

---

[689] *ESC,* 187.
[690] Lanzetta, *Other Side of Nothingness,* 40.

8. Moving Toward a New Matrix for Christian-Muslim Dialogue

The question now before us is what relevance this synthesized conversation between our two mystic masters might have for enhancing and facilitating deeper, and perhaps more fruitful, contemporary Christian-Muslim dialogue. I will argue—primarily in the next and final chapter—that this relevance lies in the potential of this conversation to provide us with "nodes" for a new matrix for dialogue. The work that lies before us before we move into the next chapter and its exploration of the key issues involved in moving toward the creation of such a matrix is to identify, in a preliminary way, how each of the points of conversation between the two masters analyzed above can be construed as a potential node for this new matrix. We should, however, make one important methodological observation before proceeding any further.

The five points of conversation are all closely related and overlap with one another because the teachings of the two masters are fully integrated. This is because no one element of Ibn al-'Arabi's teaching does integrally relate to another. The same can be said for Meister Eckhart. The reason for enumerating, in this chapter, five points of conversation is to help organize and better illustrate the mutual complementarity of the two masters' teachings, not to somehow reduce the complexity of these teachings to a few simple and distinct theses.

With respect to scriptural hermeneutics, both masters appear to be convinced in the infinite potential for meaning inherent in the nature of divine revelation, especially in the form of sacred scripture. Such an understanding of the nature of scripture can be invaluable in dialogue because it demands that the person of faith not only take a stance of conviction within the teachings of his or her sacred texts, but also that they realize that this conviction—however deep it may be—does not restrict or exhaust in any way the potential meaning of these texts. There is also an additional sense in which the insights of the masters with respect to the infinite readability of scripture have particular relevance to dialogue. If dialogue is authentic and brings about authentic transformation, then the encounter with the religious other should have some effect on our religious self-understanding, and therefore on our own readings of our own texts.

With respect to oneness of being, when one recognizes—as our two masters do—an underlying unity to all of existence, a self-disclosure of the one Creator in all of the created order, then the work of dialogue between people of different faiths—especially Christians and Muslims—should not be about proving where God is and is not in one another's beliefs and practices. Rather, it should be about discerning *how* and *where* we can find God in the beliefs and practices of others.

With respect to naming God, out of the depths of their monotheistic faiths, both masters are very concerned that, as human beings—beings blessed with a special relationship to the Source of all Being—we never lose sight of our own limitations vis-à-vis God. These limitations take many forms, one of which is the inherent inadequacy of our various languages and modes of discourse, and the limited understandings regarding God—who is ultimately and essentially beyond understanding—that they convey. All too often, dialogue breaks down, or cannot begin because of a certain hubris with respect to our understandings of God. In the context of the encounter with the other, how many Christians are Christian because they feel that Christianity contains the "best" or "highest" understanding of the divine? How many Muslims are Muslim for the same reason? I am not suggesting that the insights of the two masters regarding this issue of the "naming of God" should be interpreted to encourage relativistic thinking as a solution to this hubris. Such a reading of the masters would entail a gross distortion of their own epistemological frameworks and religious worldviews. Instead, what I am suggesting is that our masters demand that we adopt postures of profound humility as we stand before—and, I would add, *as we articulate to others*—our most deeply and passionately held beliefs and doctrinal formulations. All the piety and passion one could possibly muster will not change the fact that our languages about God admit serious inadequacies and that, if we are to be truly faithful believers, we have to let "God be God" both within and beyond our various doctrinal formulations regarding Him.

Closely related to, in fact springing from, the naming of God is the idea of God created by the believer versus the Godhead. Where naming God speaks directly to issues of language and discourse and their inherent limitations, God created by the believer versus the Godhead, is a broader warning from our masters that we must always be aware of the ways in which we all, as human beings with limited understanding and perception, inevitably create God in our own image. There is no point in arguing about the legitimacy of this process because there is no way to escape it. As Stewart Guthrie points out in his *Faces in the Clouds*, anthropomorphization of one form or another appears to be part of the hardwiring of human cognition. The point the masters are trying to make, however, is how important it is—if we are to avoid idolatry—to strive tirelessly to see the human, created, and thus derivative nature of our faith traditions. This perspective is echoed, to a certain degree, by the Indonesian Muslim scholar Nurcholish Majid and his distinction between the concept of "secularism" and the concept of "secularization." For Majid, the former is a dangerous attempt to rid societies and cultures of significant religious influences while the latter is a positive form of "de-sacralization" and *tawhid* (i.e, avoiding *shirk* by recognizing the difference between what must be held as sacred in a culture and what must not).[691]

With respect to transformation of the self, in both Islam and in Christianity we are called to be "clay in the potter's hands." In classical Sufism, the quranic references to the three "selves" (i.e., the self-inciting to evil, the self-critical self, and the tranquil self or the self at peace) are taken as part of the revelation's teaching that being Muslim is a journey of faith in which, each minute of each hour of each day one is transformed into a better and better servant of God. In some ways, Christianity—particularly with its sacramental theology—places an even more overt emphasis on the need of the Christian to be "conformed to Christ" (Paul's Letter to the Romans) or to die to life lived "according to the flesh" and to rise to life lived according to the spirit. If dialogue is to have a meaning it must facilitate our becoming better and better human beings and witness-practitioners to the faiths we profess.

---

[691] Nurcholish Majid, "The Necessity of Renewing Islamic Thought and the Problem of the Integration of the Umma" in Charles Kurzman, *Liberal Islam: A Sourcebook* (New York: Oxford University Press, 1998) 286.

Chapter VI

TOWARDS A NEW MATRIX FOR CHRISTIAN-MUSLIM DIALOGUE: RE-DISCOVERING TRADITION

TOWARDS A NEW MATRIX FOR
CHRISTIAN-MUSLIM DIALOGUE:
RE-DISCOVERING TRADITION

This chapter will argue that the process of birthing a new matrix for interfaith dialogue requires, not necessarily a "re-inventing" of our religious traditions (as some may argue), but rather a re-discovery of our traditions. Such a rediscovery is oriented toward employing the full richness of our respective religious heritages in order to interpret our traditions in the most vital and authentic ways for changing contexts. As for the challenge to rediscover our traditions, this chapter maintains that it entails at least five processes: (1) demonstrating that dialogue itself is an important component—especially given the increasingly pluralist nature of our societies throughout the globe—of orthodox or mainstream Islam and Christianity; (2) reevaluating the mystical dimensions of Islam and Christianity neither as marginal, as some would maintain, nor as the essential core of the traditions, as others would maintain (neither claim is historically accurate), but as rich and vital resources for the ongoing interpretation of each tradition; (3 and 4) articulating the ways in which our two medieval masters offer interpretations of the tradition which identify the scriptural rootedness, and thus the orthodoxy, of an openness and commitment to dialogue; and (5) without pretending to create the matrix (this is something which can only be accomplished in and through the praxis of actual communities from the two traditions which are committed to engendering this new matrix) reflecting on possible forms this new matrix may take with respect to contemporary issues and contexts and with an eye to the "nodes" enumerated and discussed in the previous chapter.

1. To Be Religious Is to Be Inter-religious

Interfaith dialogue is perhaps one of the most impressive and important religious developments of the twentieth century. It became the topic of the day, from the formal fora of academia to popular discussion in the cafés. Like any other phenomenon, it does not stand by itself. It emerged as a result of many factors. One of them, if not the most important, is what Gilles Kepel called the "crisis of modernity."[692]

With the exception of those who a priori reject forging relationships of understanding and trust between people of different faiths (i.e., the aim and stuff of "dialogue"), a lot of people assume that the intensity and quality of interfaith dialogue will increase in the future. Today, even, there is less discussion about the importance of the dialogue and more about what is the most appropriate approach/method for the dialogue, and how the dialogue can yield changes for the better in praxis and consciousness at the grass roots level, and not only at the academic or intellectual levels.

The most cursory glance at the history of religions tells us that, throughout most of recorded history, humanity has experienced a rich plurality of religions. From certain theological perspectives, this phenomenon is due to the manifold nature of divine revelation and of its human response in an astonishing variety of different cultures and historical contexts.[693] Many, however, are quick to point out that the contemporary globalizing context of religious pluralism is unlike any of its precursors in that never before have so many different religious communities and individuals existed in such close proximity to—and even interdependence on—one another. In fact, I would argue that the very existence of the fairly recent interfaith movement is an indication that today the world's religions are interacting on an unprecedented scale. If the shelves of bookstores from Chicago to Berkeley to New York, to Rome, to Istanbul, to my native Yogyakarta are any indication, there

---

[692] See Gilles Kepel, *The Revenge of God: The Resurgence of Islam, Christianity and Judaism in the Modern World* (Pennsylvania: The Pennsylvania State University Press, 1993), 191.

[693] Pope John Paul II in Assisi, 27 Oct. 1986   .

seems to be an increasing curiosity about other religions—sometimes positive, sometimes negative—as the phenomenon of reading each other's scriptures and religions seems to grow more popular.

Depending on our own socio-cultural location, those of us who engage in interfaith inquiry are variously inspired, perplexed, and—in some cases—even repulsed—by what we surmise as each other's insights and practices. Optimally speaking, we find that our various traditions share some of the same fundamental values that each of us cherish in our own religions, albeit expressed in different ways. We also realize that we are being challenged to articulate our own religious identities in an increasingly religiously plural setting where others are, in many ways, listening and asking questions of us as we do so. What this means is that whether we like it or not *to be religious today is to be interreligious*. That great pioneer of the modern discipline of the history of religions, Friedrich Max Muller once famously wrote, "He who knows one religion knows none," perhaps largely referring in his own scholarly context to those who aspired to become experts in the study of a particular religious tradition. Yet today, this dictum seems to have significance well beyond the membership of the American Academy of Religion and similar scholarly societies. In today's increasingly religiously plural social contexts, these words suggest not only that a failure to engage pluralism is an act of self-marginalization within our own social contexts. They also suggest that, without some understanding of the faith of our neighbor, the religious person (or community) living in a religiously plural society cannot even understand oneself (or itself).

Theological explanations of this plurality vary from tradition to tradition, as well as within a single tradition. In the Abrahamic faiths, such explanations tend to fall into two distinct, but not always mutually exclusive, categories. There are those explanations that attribute religious plurality either to ignorance of the truth, or perversity in the face of truth. And there are other explanations which suggest that religious plurality is somehow a part of the divine design to bring humanity together as one family before God. Suffice it to say that it is this second category of explanations that one most often finds at the theological heart of most efforts at interfaith dialogue.

In Islam, the Qur'an is the single most important source of inspiration for interfaith dialogue. It may be that the Qur'an is unique among the Abrahamic scriptures—and perhaps other scriptural texts as well—in the explicit manner in which it refers not only to dialogue between adherents of different faith-communities, but also to the divine ordainment of religious diversity, and, in consequence, to the spiritual validity of these diverse religious paths. Quranic discourse presents these paths as so many outwardly divergent facets of a single, universal revelation by the unique and indivisible Absolute.

There are at least two quranic verses which are frequently interpreted as the basis for an Islamic theology of religious pluralism which recognizes the degree to which such pluralism can be seen in a positive light. The first (*Surat al-Ma'ida*, 5:48) speaks of human communal, and perhaps therefore cultural and religious plurality, to be part of the divine design. The reason it offers for this plurality is so that different groups of human beings will "compete with each other in virtue."

The second (*Surat al-Hujurat*, 49:13) has a very similar theme. It suggests that God has "appointed" cultural and perhaps even religious diversity for the human race in order that human beings may be faced with the challenge of coming "to know each other" and striving with one another to be the "most honored in God's sight" by being the most God-conscious (*atqa*).

Rabbi Jonathan Sacks asserts that part of the creative genius of Rabbinic Judaism was that it pioneered not one, but two ideals of peace.[694] The first is the ultimate "messianic" peace in which all divisions among humankind will be dissolved and all tensions resolved. Perhaps the most well-known biblical text expressing this messianic ideal is Isaiah 11:6–9, beginning with the famous words, "The wolf shall live with the lamb, the leopard shall lie down with the kid, the calf and the lion and the fatling together, and a little child shall lead them." As beautiful as this vision may seem, for Sacks the genius of the biblical tradition lies not so much in developing the ideal of the messianic

---

[694] See Jonathan Sacks, *A Clash of Civilizations? Judaic Sources on Co-Existence in a World of Difference*, published on Sacks's website at http://www.chiefrabbi.org/dd/titlecontents.html.

peace, as it does in developing the idea of *darkhei shalom* or "the ways of peace" and *eviah* or "[the avoidance of] ill-feeling" as an "ideal of peace in an unredeemed world."[695] For Sacks, the genius of Jewish teachings regarding peace is that it complements the messianic ideal with a practical ideal of a "here-and-now peace which depends on different groups with incompatible ideals living graciously or at least civilly together, without attempting to impose its beliefs on others."[696]

From a Christian perspective, there have been many biblical passages attested in support of interfaith dialogue and peaceful coexistence (Gen. 1:27; Isaiah 56:1-7; Mark 9:40; Luke 9:50). In the meeting of religious leaders from all over the world which took place in Assisi in October of 1986, the late Pope John Paul II summarized a basic insight common to many Christian theologies of religious pluralism and dialogue when he said, addressing the assembly, "Religions are many and varied and they reflect the desire of men and women throughout the ages to enter into relationship with the Absolute Being."[697] In this address, John Paul echoed the teaching of the Second Vatican Council and its document *Nostra Aetate* that "the Catholic Church rejects nothing that is true and holy" in the other religions of the world.[698]

If we leave the realm of specifically Abrahamic discourse on religious pluralism and interfaith dialogue, we encounter those who—in ways which are more consonant with the epistemologies of certain forms of Hinduism and Buddhism than they are with traditional Abrahamic epistemologies—articulate a thesis of radical complementarity based on a perception of the contextual limitations and specifics of every human tradition. V. F. Vineeth argues that religions are life

---

[695] Sacks, *A Clash of Civilizations?*, 9. Sacks traces the roots of this non-messianic ideal of peace to Jeremiah 29 and the instructions to the Israelites now captive in Babylon: "Build houses and live in them; plant gardens and eat what they produce. Take wives and have sons and daughters, and do not decrease. But seek the welfare of the city where I have sent you into exile, and pray to the Lord on its behalf, for in its welfare you will find your welfare."

[696] Sacks, 10.

[697] Pope John Paul II in Assisi, 27 Oct. 1986.

[698] *Nostra Aetate* (October 25, 1965)

expressions of the experience of revelation in a given historical context. They are, therefore, limited by factors of history, culture, language, etc. If we are ever to transcend these limitations, each of us in our own limited traditions must aspire precisely to encounter other religious or cultural traditions. According to this view, no religious expression is complete and thorough. Thus, "one way to advance in the experience of the fullness [of truth] is to become more and more enriched by the contributions of complementary expressions."[699] According to Vineeth, with the encounter of a new religion, a concealed jewel of truth is now awakened, and a new potential comes to blossom. For example, Thomas Merton had a new interpretation of Christian Religious experience after his encounter with Buddhism.[700]

A person is enriched through encounter and dialogue. When one "shares" the experience of others, one is challenged to see things as others, experience them. Although we can never understand each other completely, we can still understand a great deal about each other.

Dialogue is learning of truths attained by others and coming back with those truths to enrich our own spirituality. It is called, in John S. Dunne's term, "passing over" from one religion and way of life to other's religion which may differ from our own religion. Then, we "come back," enriched by new knowledge and perspectives, not only adapted from other religious perspectives, but helpful for developing our own religious perspective.[701] Learning from other religions, not to be like others but to "come back" to understand our own faith in a new way, is the goal.

---

[699] V.F. Vineeth, CM, "Interreligious Dialogue: Past and Present. A Critical Appraisal," in *Journal of Dharma*, no 1, vol xix (Jan-March, 1994), 37.

[700] Vineeth, "Interreligious Dialogue", 37; cf. *The Asian Journal of Thomas Merton* (New York: New Direction Book, 1973), Cf. also Thomas Merton, *Mystics and Zen Masters* (New York, 1967); Knitter in his dialogical odyssey has the same experiences, when he encountered with Buddhism. See Paul Knitter, *One Earth Many Religions, Multifaith Dialogue and Global Responsibility* (New York: Maryknoll Orbis Books, 1995).

[701] John S. Dunne, The Way of All The Earth, An Encounter with Eastern Religions (London: Sheldon Press, 1972), xiv.

Theological and spiritual dialogue will be valuable only if accompanied by the courage of the participant to question and criticize her or himself when encountered by the core of the religious experiences of others. An encounter with other religions does not mean that a person sinks inside forever, forgetting to go out and back to her or his own religion. Nevertheless, as already mentioned, this "passing over" from one culture to other cultures, from one way of life to other ways of life, should be followed by the process called "coming back" with a new horizon to our own culture, way of life and our own religion. This is what we call "spiritual pilgrimage." Thus, "passing over" here means the courage to undertake the spiritual pilgrimage to other religions (*wonder land*) and to "come back" from the pilgrimage to our own religion (*mother land*) with a new perspective to enrich our own religion. "A creative dialogue is also possible only if there is a complete openness, and no preliminary assumption that one revelation . . . must be the yardstick for all others."[702]

2. Sufism and Christian Mysticism as Rich Resources for Interpreting the Traditions

A distinguished Catholic theologian Friedrich von Huegel (1852–1925) opines that all living religions embody a unity of three elements: the historical-institutional which addresses to mind and memory, the intellectual or analytic speculative, which is associates with reason and the mystical, intuitive-emotional which directs to the will and the action of love.[703] In almost the same manner, the scholar of Jewish mysticism, Gershom Scholem, says that religion develops in three stages, mythical, institutional and mystical.[704] These three elements have to be in a mutual and harmonious relationship in order for religion to flourish. Thus, as Scholem mentions, when one aspect is ignored in the expense of the

---

[702] John Macquarrie, "Christianity and Other Faiths," *Union Seminary Quarterly Review* 20 (1964), 43-44.

[703] Cited by Dorothee Soelle, *The Silent Cry, Mysticism and Resistance* (Minneapolis: Fortress Press, 2001), 1.

[704] See, Gershom Scholem, *Zur Kabbala und ihrer Symbolik*. translated by Ralph Manheim (New York : Schocken Books, 1965).

other, or when an unbalance of the application of these aspects occurred, conflict will be unavoidable.

It is very common, however, to hear voices from both traditions and from the academy in general who suggest that mysticism and mystical perspectives are the most central and authentic. S.H. Nasr, for example, asserts, that it is on the level of Sufi esotericism that "the most profound encounter [of Islam] with other traditions has been made and where one can find the indispensable ground for the understanding in depth of other religions today."[705] Indeed, Sufism has much to offer Muslims who are attempting to formulate a genuinely Islamic theology of religious pluralism. The Sufi is someone who is ideally able to go beyond the phenomenal world on her or his journey to God into the deeper and innermost experience of unity, thus, moving from a specific way of life into a more holistic one. The Sufi "leaves the many for the One, and through this very process is granted the vision of the One in the many."[706] Furthermore, according to Nasr, Sufism is as the "Centre where all the radii meet, the summit which all roads reach, and only such a vision of the Centre can provide a meaningful dialogue between religions, showing both their inner unity and formal diversity."[707] As erudite and as insightful as Nasr's perspectives are, the problem with this particular approach is that, for some Muslims, it over-emphasizes the centrality of Sufism and Sufi perspectives. If, indeed, Sufism is a rich source for the ongoing interpretation of the Islamic tradition, it cannot be taken as such outside of the connections between Sufism and other modalities of Muslim piety such as the spirituality of the so-called "Salafi" movements.

In a "schematic" and to some extent "simplistic" way, according to Chittick, the difference between Sufi and non-Sufi Islam is rooted in the "different perceptions of the fundamental trust of the Qur'an and the *Sunnah* of Muhammad."[708] So according to him, Muslims who understand religion to be something that has relevancy "primarily to

---

[705] Seyyed Hossein Nasr, *Sufi Essays* (London, 1972), 146.

[706] See Nasr, *Sufi Essays,* 146.

[707] Nasr, *Sufi Essays*, 150.

[708] *IW*, 3.

activity, they stress the *Sharia*"—the revealed law of Islam—"and they emphasize individual and social responsibilities toward God. Theologically this leads to a vision of God that emphasizes His transcendence and rigor," and most Muslims fit into this category.[709] But when these same Muslims, Chittick continues, "see their religion as rooted in inner attitudes such as love and compassion,"[710] they place a great deal of stress on the qualities that are necessary for the best of human relationships—relationships of trust, love, and mutual respect. Some might maintain that, theologically, this stress reflects the principle enunciated in the famous hadith qudsi, "My [i.e., God's] mercy takes precedence over My wrath." "The loving and gentle face of God is put forward rather than the stern and severe face. This softer and gentler form of Islam tends to be stressed by those Muslims who are inclined toward Sufi teachings."[711]

What Sufism offers those who seek to interpret Islam in ways that speak effectively and authentically to issues of religious pluralism is a view of religious diversity which is not necessarily negative and even, in some respects, positive. The argument of this book that mysticism offers both Muslims and Christians important resources for creating a new matrix for dialogue is not predicated on privileging mysticism over other modes of religious expression, but rather is predicated on the idea that, unless we commit ourselves to an honest and inclusive rediscovery of our traditions—one that entails recognizing the mainstream authority and force of truth in certain mystical teachings—we are truncating our traditions and turning our backs on the very resources that we need the most at this particular point in our history.

3. Ibn al-ʿArabi: Scripture, Orthodoxy, and Religious Diversity

As discussed in chapters one and two, Ibn al-ʿArabi and Meister Eckhart are figures who have been at the center of some controversy with-

---

[709] *IW*, 3.

[710] *IW*, 3.

[711] *IW* 3.

in their respective traditions. In light of this fact, it would not be surprising if some were to find the idea of using the thinking of controversial figures within each tradition as the source of a new matrix for
dialogue. To those who would have serious reservations about the use
of these two figures based on the controversial nature of certain aspects
of their thinking, I respond in two related ways. The first is to point
out that the greatest and most creative minds in the history of religions
have always been at the center of some controversy. From Maimonides to Augustine to Shankara to al-Shafi'i and Ibn Rushd, the historical record is replete with stories about the "trouble" caused by
particularly gifted religious geniuses.[712] The second is to say that if, in
the process of mining the riches of our traditions, we wish to assess
fairly and accurately the orthodoxy of a religious thinker, we need to
do so on the basis of a fair and open analysis of their teachings themselves and not on whatever propaganda may exist for or against the figure in question. When it comes to the figures of Ibn al-'Arabi and
Meister Eckhart and the way in which the teachings of each can be
seen as expressions of Islamic and Christian orthodoxy on the issues
of religious pluralism and interfaith dialogue, this process of fair analysis may be simpler and more straightforward than many would suspect.

For some, religious diversity may be viewed as a problem, but
it certainly is not for Ibn al-'Arabi and for the school of thought
that he established. In fact, Ibn al-'Arabi has an *explicit* theology of
religions in contrast to Meister Eckhart's *implicit* one. In Ibn al-
'Arabi's own words, "There are as many paths to God as there are
human souls." The reality, however, of how religious diversity has
been dealt with in Islamic history varies from context to context. To
generalize, it is not inaccurate to say that—much the same as the
case of Christianity (which tended, at least in the medieval period,
to be significantly less tolerant of intra- and interreligious diversity
than Islam)—some Muslim scholars have emphasized an exclusivist

---

[712] For orthodoxy and heresy in Medieval Islam, see Alexander Knysh, "'Orthodoxy'
and 'Heresy' in Medieval Islam: An Essay in Reassessment," *The Muslim World*, Vol.
LXXXIII, No. 1 (Jan. 1993).

approach, while others have emphasized a more open and inclusivist one. Ibn al-'Arabi seems to be the most sophisticated and profound thinker of this second category.

Ibn al-'Arabi's discussion of religious pluralism begins with the assertion that God Himself is the source of all diversity in the cosmos. Thus, divergence of beliefs among human beings ultimately stems from God:

> God Himself is the first problem of diversity that has become manifest in the cosmos. The first thing that each existence thing looks upon is the cause of its own existence. In itself each thing knows that it was not, and that it then came to be through temporal origination. However, in this coming to be, the dispositions of the existent things are diverse. Hence they have diverse opinions about the identity of the cause that brought them into existence. Therefore the Real is the first problem of diversity in the cosmos.[713]

According to Ibn al-'Arabi, this diversity of opinion is one of the many signs that, to paraphrase the famous hadith qudsi, "God's mercy takes precedence over His wrath." Thus, "Since God is the root of all diversity of beliefs within the cosmos, and since it is He who has brought about the existence of everything in the cosmos in a constitution not possessed by anything else, everyone will end up with mercy."[714]

One of the most important and striking features of Ibn al-'Arabi's teachings on the nature of the Real (*al-Haqq*) and its connection to religious pluralism is that they are thoroughly grounded in quranic exegesis. One of the most important verses upon which he bases these teachings is: "Then high exalted be God, the King, the Real! There is no God but He, the Lord of the noble Throne" (Q 23: 116). Commenting on this verse Ibn al-'Arabi says:

> This is the *tawhid* of the Real, which is the *tawhid* of the He-ness. God says, "We created not the heavens and the earth and all that between them, in play" (21: 116, 44: 38). This is the same meaning as His words, "What do you think that We created you only for

---

[713] *Fut.* III, 465, 23 in *IW*, 4.

[714] *Fut.* III, 465. 25 in *IW*, 4-5.

sport?" (23: 115). Hence, "there is no God but He" [in the above quranic passage] is a description of the Real.[715]

Here Ibn al-'Arabi is describing the way in which the verse in question (Q 23:116) speaks about a particular expression of the divine oneness. In doing so he makes two points that are critical for an understanding of his teaching on religious diversity. The first point is that the Qur'an reveals multiple dimensions of the divine oneness. Another way of putting this is to say that the Qur'an discusses more than one "type" of *tawhid*. In fact, according to Ibn al-'Arabi, there are thirty-six different types of *tawhid* found in the Qur'an. The dimension of divine oneness expressed in Q 23:116 is that of the "He-ness" of God or the degree to which the Real is God and God alone. The second point Ibn al-'Arabi is making in this brief commentary on Q 23:116 is that every element of phenomenal existence is a purposeful expression of the divine oneness (i.e., no aspect of creation exists as "play" or "sport.") For Ibn al-'Arabi, this includes the diversity of religions. Indeed, Ibn al-'Arabi affirms that the abundant quranic references to the plurality of religions is by no means a reference to an accident of fate, but is rather the nineteenth type of *tawhid* which the Qur'an most directly addresses in the following verse: "We never sent a messenger before thee [i.e., Muhammad] except that We revealed to him, saying, 'There is no god but I, so worship Me!'" (Q 21: 25). Commenting this verse Ibn al-'Arabi says:

> This is a *tawhid* of the I-ness . . . . It is like God's words, "Naught is said to thee but what was already said to the messengers before thee" (41: 43). In his verse God mentions "worship" (*'ibada*), but not specific practices (*a'mal*), for He also said, "To every one [of the prophets] We have appointed a Law and a way" (5: 48), that is, We have set down designated practices. The period of applicability of the practices can come to an end, and this is called "abrogation" (*naskh*) in the words of the learned masters of the *Shari'a*. There is no single practice found in each and every prophecy, only the performance of the religion, coming together in it, and the statement of *tawhid*. This is indicated in God's words, "He has laid

---

[715] *Fut.* II, 415. 18; *SPK*, 134.

down for you as Law what He charged Noah with, and what We have revealed to thee [O Muhammad], and what We charged Abraham with, and Moses, and Jesus: "Perform the religion, and scatter nor regarding it'" (42: 13). Bukhari has written in a chapter entitled, "The chapter on what has come concerning the fact that the religion of the prophets is one," and this one religion is nothing but *tawhid*, performing the religion, and worship. On this the prophets have all come together.[716]

What, then, is the distinction that Ibn al-'Arabi is making between Qur'an 23:116 and Qur'an 21:25? As he himself tells us, it is a distinction made between two expressions of *tawhid*. The first is an expression of *tawhid* in which God refers to Godself in the third person (i.e., as "He") and in which He makes mention of Himself as "King" (*al-malik*) and "The Real" (*al-haqq*), and also makes reference to His "Noble Throne" (*al-'arsh al-karim*). In a sense, this can be interpreted as the Qur'an's own use of the language of discursive or speculative theology which can only speak of God in the third person, and thus takes as its appropriate object the divine "He-ness" (*huwi-yya*). In 21:25, however, God expresses His oneness in the first person (i.e., as "I"). In this context, God makes reference to the Prophet Muhammad himself (the recipient of this specific revelation) in the second person singular, to all the messengers sent before Muhammad, and to acts of worship. For Ibn al-'Arabi, this verse is making a direct connection between the succession of messengers (and by extension the different forms that authentic religion takes) and acts of worship which ideally mediate a direct experience of the "I-ness" of God in which God acts as the subject beyond objectification. Thus, when one juxtaposes the two verses, one sees the divine oneness being expressed in two very different verbal modalities which reflect two very different human activities: the cognitive activity of speculative thought and the more affective experience of ritual worship. It is not that one modality is a more authentic expression of *tawhid* than the other, but rather that both represent two very important dimensions of *tawhid*.

---

[716] *Fut.* II, 414.13; *SPK*, 171.

As Ibn al-'Arabi more explicitly develops his teaching on religious diversity he builds upon a key insight conveyed by the second of the two verses analyzed above. For Ibn al-'Arabi, the succession of prophets and messengers, culminating in the messengership of Muhammad, which characterizes all orthodox Islamic perspectives in the history of revelation is one in which an underlying unity of encounter with the one and only God (i.e., the one immutable religion for which all of humanity for all time has been created) is historically expressed in a multiplicity of forms. In the master's own words: "The 'path of Allah' is the all-inclusive path upon which all things walk, and it takes them to Allah."[717] Thus, commenting on Bukhari's title, mentioned in the quotation above, "The chapter on what has come concerning the fact that the religion of the prophets is one," in which Bukhari uses an article in the word "religion" ("the religion", instead of a "religion"), Ibn al-'Arabi says,

> He brought the article which makes the word "religion" definite, because all religion comes from God, even if some of the rulings are diverse. Everyone is commanded to perform the religion and to come together in it. . . . As for the rulings which are diverse, that is because of the Law which God assigned to each of one of the messengers. He said, "To everyone (of the Prophets) We have appointed a Law and a Way [*shir'a wa minhaj*] ; and if God willed, he would have made you one nation" (5: 48). If He had done that, your revealed Laws would not be diverse, just as they are not diverse in the fact that you have been commanded to come together and to perform them. [718]

Thus, Ibn al-'Arabi is differentiating between *din*, which means primordial ideal religion and "path," or *shir'a wa minhaj* ("law" and "way"; or contextualized/historicized religion"). Although the "*din*" is always singular and unitive, the various "paths" or "laws" are numerous. "The paths to God are numerous as the breaths of the creatures," writes Ibn al-'Arabi, "since the breath emerges from the heart in accordance with the belief of the heart concerning Allah."[719] Such approach

---

[717] *Fut.* III, 410. 25, 411. 22; *SPK* 302-3.
[718] *Fut.* III, 413. 15; *SPK*, 303.
[719] *Fut.* III, 411. 22; *SPK*, 303.

endorsed by Ibn al-ʿArabi is very essential in enhancing interfaith dialogue and acceptance of different religious perspectives.

There is no way that the careful reader of Ibn al-ʿArabi can miss the fact that his teachings on the underlying unity of all human systems of belief and practice is part of an elaborate esoteric commentary on the first article of Islamic faith *"La ilaha illa Allah"* (there is no God except God). We can see a very direct example of this by returning briefly to his exegesis of Qurʾan 23:115.

> That within which the existence of the cosmos has become manifest is the Real; it becomes manifest only within the Breath of the All-Merciful, which is the Cloud. So it is the Real, the Lord of the Throne, who gave the Throne its all-encompassing shape, since it encompasses all things. Hence the root within which the forms of the cosmos became manifest encompasses everything in the world of corporeal bodies. This is nothing other than the Real Through Whom Creation Takes Place. Through this receptivity, it is like a container within which comes out into the open (*buruz*) the existence of everything it includes, layer upon layer, entity after entity, in a wise hierarchy (*al-tartib al-hikami*). So It brings out into the open that which had been unseen within It in order to witness it.[720]

Another quranic verse important to an understanding of Ibn al-ʿArabi's teaching on religious diversity is: "Everything is perishing except His Face [or Essence] (Q 28:88). This verse refers to the sense of the relativity of all things in the face of God, which is helpful in cultivating the humility necessary for openness to other perspectives and other stories of encounters with the divine. Equally important are quranic references such as:

> And unto God belong the East and the West; and wherever ye turn, there is the Face of God (Q 2:115).
> He is with you, wherever you are (Q 57:4).
> We are nearer to him [man] than the neck artery (Q 50:16).
> God cometh in between a man and his own heart (Q 8:24).
> Is He not encompassing all things? (Q 41:54).
> He is the First and the Last, and the Outward and the Inward (Q 57:3)

---

[720] *Fut.* II, 415. 20; *SPK,*134.

These verses express a profound sense of the immanence of the divine which, Ibn al-'Arabi rightly argues, are set in balance with those preeminent verses such as we find in *Surat al-Ikhlas* (Q 112) and the famous "Throne Verse" of *Surat al-Baqara* (Q 2:255) For Ibn al-'Arabi, the balance between the *tanzih* (transcendence) and *tashbih* (immanence) of God plays a major role in his thinking about religious diversity. *Tanzih* involves the fundamental assertion of God's essential and absolute incomparability "with each thing and all things."[721] It involves the assertion that His being transcends all creaturely attributes and qualities. At the same time, however, "each thing displays one or more of God's attributes, and in this respect the thing must be said to be "similar" (*tashbih*) in some way to God."[722] Thus, a certain similarity can be found between God and creation. Unlike traditionalist theologians, who opine that these two concepts are diametrically opposed and cannot exist together in harmony, for Ibn al-'Arabi, both *tanzih* and *tashbih* are in this sense compatible with each other and complementary. *Tanzih* and *tashbih* "derive necessarily from the Essence on the one hand and the level of Divinity on the other."[723] Out of this distinction, Ibn al-'Arabi challenges, that anybody who exercises and upholds *tanzih* or *tashbih* in its extreme form is either an ignorant man, or one who does not know how to behave properly toward God, because such extremes are attempts to delimit God's Absoluteness. To deny completely the authenticity of other religious "ways" is to insist that there is no divine self-disclosure to be found there. In doing so, one sets limits on God much in the same way as those who only know God through cognitive activity (which tends to place emphasis on transcendence) and not through affective experience (which can convey a profound sense of divine immanence). Only when one combines *tanzih* and *tashbih* in one's attitude can one be regarded as a "true knower" ('*arif*) of the Absolute.[724] Ibn al-'Arabi says,

---

[721] *SPK*, 9.

[722] *SPK*, 9.

[723] *SPK*, 69.

[724] Izutsu, *Sufism and Taoism*, 54.

When the Gnostics know Him through Him, they become distinguished from those who know Him through their own rational consideration (*nazar*), for they possess nondelimitation, while others have delimitation. The Gnostics through Him witness Him in each thing or in the entity of each thing, but those who know Him through rational consideration are removed far from Him by a distance which is required by their declaration of His comparability. Hence they place themselves on one side and the Real on the other. Then they call Him "from a far place" (Qur'an 41: 44).[725]

It is important to note that Ibn al-'Arabi's interpretation of *tanzih* and *tashbih* and how this relates to his teaching regarding the underlying unity of all religions is by no means restricted to medieval esoteric hermeneutics. The highly influential Salafi modernist thinker Rashid Rida offers an interpretation of the meaning of the word *islam* in the Qur'an which complements and supports Ibn al-'Arabi's approach to the question of religious diversity. The Qur'an declares, "Do they seek other than the religion of God, when unto Him submits whoever is in the heavens and the earth, willingly or unwillingly?" (Q 3:83). Here the Qur'an uses the word *aslama* based on the fourth form of the root *SLM* which has to do with the act of "submitting" to God. The word *islam* is the *masdar* or verbal noun from this same form and thus literally means "submission." As is the case in Q 3:19,[726] in this verse *islam* is identified as "the religion of God." According to Rashid Rida, understanding the word *islam* in the proper sense (i.e., writ large as "Islam") to refer to the doctrines, traditions and practices observed by Muslims, is a post-quranic phenomenon according to which *al-din* is understood in its social and custom-

---

[725] *Fut.* III, 410. 17; *SPK*, 110.

[726] Ibn al-'Arabi offers his own interpretation of 3:19 as follows: "Verily the true *din* with God is this *tawhid* which He has prescribed for Himself. His *din* is, therefore, the *din* of the submission of one's entire being . . . [to be a Muslim means that I have] severed myself from my ego and achieved annihilation in Him." In Pseudo-Ibn al-'Arabi ('Abd al-Razzaq al-Qashani), *Tafsir Ibn 'Arabi*, vol. 1 (Beirut: dar al-Sadr, n. d), 105, cited by Esack, *Qur'an, Liberation, and Pluralism, An Islamic Perspective of Interreligious Solidarity against Oppression* (Oxford, Oneworld, 1997), 127.

ary form.[727] For Rida, these forms of Islam, writ large, "which [vary] according to the differences which have occurred to its adherents in the way of uncritical acceptance, has no relationship with true *islam*. On the contrary," Rida writes, "it is subversive of true faith."[728]

Rida's interpretation of the quranic usage of the word *islam* is helpful in understanding the distinction Ibn al-'Arabi makes between the form and essence of revealed religion. Ibn al-'Arabi's interpretation of the scriptural story of Noah is clearly rooted in this distinction. In the *Fusus*, Ibn al-'Arabi says that the people of Noah are not entirely mistaken. For Ibn al-'Arabi, the idols that were worshiped by the people of Noah were in fact "the diversity of the names" understood by Ibn al-'Arabi as the Divine Names through which human beings become aware of the self-disclosure of God. The people of Noah committed "the sin of idolatry" not because they recognized the divine in a plurality of forms, but because of their ignorance that these forms are not deities in themselves, but rather concrete forms of the one God's self-manifestation. Their sin, therefore, was in their worship of these forms as independent entities apart from God. According to Ibn al-'Arabi, the idols are nothing other than God's self manifestations.[729] For Ibn al-'Arabi, the quranic verse: "And Thy Lord hath decreed that you should worship none other than Him" (Q 17: 23) does not mean, as it is usually understood, "that you should not worship anything other than God," but rather "that whatever you worship, you are thereby not (actually) worshiping anything other than God."[730]

In this sense, "idolatry"—as serious a sin as it is—can be nothing more than a matter of the worshipper's awareness and intention. Since there is no God but God, it is actually impossible to worship anything other than He. Some may well ask what impact such a distinction

---

[727] Muhammad Rashid Rida, *Tafsir al-Manar* (Beirut: Dar al-Ma'rifah), vol. 3, 361, cited by Farid Esack, *Qur'an, Liberation, and Pluralism*, 130.

[728] Rida, *Al-Manar*, 361, Esack, *Qur'an, Liberation, and Pluralism*, 130.

[729] Affifi, *Fusus, Com*, 39, see *BW*, 76, "The Wisdom of Exaltation in the Word of Noah."

[730] Affifi, *Fusus Com*, 39, Cf. also Ibn al-'Arabi, *Fusus al-Hikam*, ed. A. Afifi (Beirut: Dar al-Kutub al-'Arabi, 1946), 55/72, also cited by Isutzu, *Sufism and Taoism*, 59-60.

might have on the approach to the whole question of religious diversity. Does it matter, in other words, whether one asserts that idolaters are sinning because they are actually worshipping something other than God, or because, though they are worshipping God and cannot do otherwise, they sin in their lack of awareness of the true nature of their worship? The answer seems to be "yes." By locating the sin in the human being's intent, rather than in objective reality, one retains the necessity of discernment in intent and the meaningfulness of true worship versus idolatry, without the arrogance of believing that some human beings have an authentic relationship to God and others do not. In this way, not only is it possible to perceive degrees of authenticity in different forms of worship, but it also no longer guarantees that just because an individual or group adopts a particular form of worship, they are immune to idolatry.

There are many other aspects of Ibn al-'Arabi's thought that have direct relevance to what he has to say about religious diversity, but which, unfortunately, are too numerous to mention here.[731] The key thing to remember about Ibn al-'Arabi's teaching on religious diversity is that, although it is not in the least bit relativist (i.e., it never denies

---

[731] E.g., in the *Futuhat*, Ibn al-'Arabi gives a more explicit explanation for the esoteric unity of all revelation, which is, for him, is innate in every diversity. He quotes the verses 42: 13, which affirms that the law with which Muhammad is charged is the same as with which Noah, Abraham, Moses, and Jesus were charged. Then, Ibn al-'Arabi quotes from other verses, which mentioned further prophets, and concludes with verse 6: 90 saying: "Those are they whom God has guided, so follow their guidance." Then He says, "This is the Path that brings together every prophet and messenger. It is the performance of religion, scattering not concerning it and coming together in it. It is that concerning which Bukhari wrote a chapter entitled 'The chapter on what has come concerning the fact that the religion of the prophets is one'" (Ibn al-'Arabi, *Fut*. III, 413. 12 in *SPK*, 303). Ibn al-'Arabi also recommends to the seeker of God not to get fascinated with any one form of belief, but rather to try seeking the "knowledge that is inherent in God" (*ilm laduni*), and not to be imprisoned within ideologically closed ways of viewing the phenomenal world. This is why Ibn al-'Arabi can convey the following in a poem in his *Tarjuman al-Aswaq* (The Interpreter of Ardent Desires): "My heart has become capable of every form." According to Peter Coate, this aspect of Ibn al-'Arabi's worldview reflects "the perfect immensity of his metaphysics which makes it intrinsically antithetical to all forms of fundamentalism, cognitive or metaphysical" (Peter Coate, *Ibn 'Arabi and Modern Thought*, 15).

the superiority of Islam over the other religions of humanity), it abhors the arrogance and idolatry of suggesting that other religious ways are not somehow themselves manifestations of authentic human connections to the one source of all Being.

In the final analysis, Ibn al-'Arabi warns his fellow Muslims against restricting God to the form of one's own belief, a warning that is entirely in accordance with the thrust of so much quranic discourse:

> Beware of being bound up by a particular creed and rejecting others as unbelief! Try to make yourself a prime matter for all forms of religious belief. God is greater and wider than to be confined to one particular creed to the exclusion of others. For He says, "Wherever ye turn, there is the Face of God."[732]

> He who counsels his own soul should investigate, during his life in this world, all doctrines concerning God. He should learn from whence each possessor of a doctrine affirms the validity of his doctrine. Once its validity has been affirmed for him in the specific mode in which it is correct for him who holds it, then he should support it in the case of him who believes in it.[733]

In light of certain key quranic verses, Ibn al-'Arabi maintains that Muslims are commanded to believe in all revelations and not just in that conveyed by the Prophet of Islam. He writes:

> All the revealed religions are lights. Among these religions, the revealed religion of Muhammad is like the light of the sun among the lights of the stars. When the sun appears, the lights of the stars are hidden, and their lights are included in the light of the sun. Their being hidden is like the abrogation of the other revealed religions that takes place through Muhammad's revealed religion. Nevertheless, they do in fact exist, just as the existence of the lights of the stars is actualized. This explains why we have been required in our all-inclusive religion to have faith in the truth of all the messengers and all the revealed religions. They are not rendered null [*bâtil*] by abrogation—that is the opinion of the ignorant.[734]

---

[732] Ibn al-'Arabi, *Fusus al-Hikam*, 113, cited by *IW*, 176.

[733] *Fut.* II, 85. 11 quoted by *IW*, 176.

[734] Fut. III, 153. 12, quoted by *IW*, 125.

Thus, Ibn al-ʿArabi insists that one should not delimit God within just one of the many possible modes of divine self-disclosure. Instead, the true Muslim is a person who recognizes God in all revelations:

> So turn your attention to what we have mentioned and put it into practice! Then you will give the Divinity its due and you will be one of those who are fair toward their Lord in knowledge of Him. For God is exalted high above entering under delimitation. He cannot be tied down by one form rather than another. From here you will come to know the all-inclusiveness of felicity for God's creatures and the all-embracingness of the mercy which cover everything.[735]

Ibn al-ʿArabi alerts the believers not to fall into particularism—an admonition which resonates with the quranic dictum: "And they say: 'None enters paradise unless he be a Jew or a Christian.' These are their own desires. Say: 'Bring your proof if you are truthful.' Nay, but whosoever surrenders his purpose to God while doing good, his reward is with his Lord; and there shall be no fear upon them, neither shall they grieve."[736]

4. Meister Eckhart: Scripture, Orthodoxy, and Religious Diversity

Like Ibn al-ʿArabi, Meister Eckhart roots his teachings in sacred scripture. Also, like Ibn al-ʿArabi, Eckhart tends to interpret scriptural texts in more allegorical and mystical ways, not to replace more straightforward interpretations, but rather in order to supplement conventional interpretations by delving into the deepest meanings of the texts and by doing so with the aid of philosophical methods. In his *Commentary on John*, Eckhart asserts that "in interpreting this Word and everything else that follows my intention is the same as in all my works—to explain what the holy Christian faith and the two Testaments maintain through the help of the natural argument of the philosophers."[737] For Eckhart, the arguments of true philosophers are completely compatible

---

[735] *Fut.* II, 85. 20; *SPK*, 355-356.
[736] Qur'an 2: 112.
[737] "Commentary on John," *ESC*, 122-3.

with Christian teaching. According to Eckhart, "the truths of natural principles, conclusion and properties are well intimate for him 'who has ears to hear' (Mt. 13: 43) in the very words of sacred scripture, which are interpreted through these natural truths."[738]

Unlike Ibn al-'Arabi, however, Meister Eckhart has no explicit teaching on theology of religions. Nonetheless his mystical teaching has a number of very significant implications for an approach to the question of religious diversity which, analogous to that of Ibn al-'Arabi, is an example of how, through mystical insight, one can admit the presence of the divine in other religions, all the while remaining faithful to mainstream doctrine and practice. Just as Ibn al-'Arabi's teaching on religious diversity is rooted in his broader central teaching on the self-disclosure of God (exposited above in chapter three), the implications of Meister Eckhart's thought for Christian reflection on religious diversity are rooted in his central teaching on "detachment" (exposited above in chapter four). When talking about detachment Eckhart insists that when the mystic comes close to union with God, no image, however glorious, can be retained, not even the image of Christ. The soul should be empty of all images; only then can the real union take place. Quoting the Gospel of St John, Eckhart writes: "It is expedient for you that I should go away from you, for if I do not go away, the Holy Spirit cannot come to you" (Jn.16:7). He then proceeds to comment: "This is just as if he had said: 'You rejoice too much in my present form, and therefore the joy of the Holy Ghost cannot be yours.' So leave all images and unite with the formless essence."[739]

Thus, the detached person in Meister Eckhart's doctrine is someone who, in St.Paul's words, "count[s] all as dung" (Phil. 3: 8)—someone who does everything without a why and wherefore, only in God and for God. Eckhart's dictum in this regard is: "If God is to enter, the creature must exit."[740] Here, Eckhart is further rooting his reflections in orthodox tradition by referring to St. Augustine who famously said,

---

[738] *ESC*, 123.

[739] *ST*, I, 128.

[740] Richard Kieckhefer, "Meister Eckhart's Conception of Union with God," *The Harvard Theological Review*, Vol. 71 (1970), 210.

"Lord, I did not want to lose you, but I wanted to posses, along with you, the created thing which I crave; and that is why I lost you, because you do not want anyone to possess, along with you who are the truth, the falsehood and deceits of created things."[741] Eckhart warns his readers that a failure to detach from the creaturely becomes a source of idolatry. He argues that

> The least creaturely image that takes place in you is as big as God. How is that? It deprives you of the whole of God. As soon as the image comes in, God has to leave with all His Godhead ... Go right out of yourself for God's sake, and God will go right out of Himself for your sake! When these two have gone out what is left is one and simple. In this One the Father bears His Son in the inmost source.[742]

It is important to note here the differences and similarities between how Eckhart and Ibn al-ʿArabi conceive of idolatry. For Ibn al-ʿArabi the danger of idolatry comes in trying to assert that there are aspects of phenomenal existence in which no self-disclosure of the divine can be found. For Eckhart, the danger of idolatry lies in thinking that the divine can be found in *any* aspect or dimension of phenomenal existence. Yet both are asserting a radical doctrine of the oneness of God (as discussed above in chapter five). How can this be? Perhaps an answer lies in the fact that each is attempting to compensate for a certain lopsidedness in the dominant expressions of their respective orthodoxies. In the case of orthodox Islamic theology, the emphasis is on the transcendence (*tanzih*) rather than the immanence (*tashbih*) of the divine. In this context, if Ibn al-ʿArabi is to articulate a teaching of uncompromising oneness, he needs to compensate for the emphasis on transcendence by re-emphasizing immanence. In the case of orthodox Christianity, there is a certain emphasis on the immanence of the divine in both the doctrines of the Incarnation and those Trinitarian teachings having to do with the Holy Spirit. In this context, if Meister Eckhart is to articulate a teaching of uncompromising oneness, he

---

[741] "The Book of Divine Consolation," *ESC*, 214.

[742] *ST*, I, 118.

needs to compensate for this emphasis on immanence by re-emphasizing the divine transcendence.

In his teaching on the self-emptying that is necessary to attain detachment, Eckhart refers to St. Paul, who speaks of a complete transformation of the human being in Christ. In fact, Eckhart's sermons are replete with Pauline references to transformation. Such references include: "Do not be conformed to this world but be transformed by the renewal of your mind" (Romans 12:2); "Put off your old nature . . . and put on the new nature" (Ephesians 4:22-23); nothing counts "but a new creation" (Galatians 6:15); and "From now on, therefore, we regard no one from a human point of view; even though we once regarded Christ from a human point of view, we regard him thus no longer. Therefore, if anyone is in Christ, he is a new creation; the old has passed away, behold, the new has come" (2 Corinthians 5:16-17). In Eckhart's mystical language, the product of this transformation is the Noble Man—the truly just person who attains this righteousness precisely in his authentic detachment. Implicit in his ideal of the Noble Man is where we find Eckhart's implicit approach to religious diversity. Since the hallmark of the Noble Man, who is truly detached, is a constant striving to discover and treasure everything that is good in others, it follows that the Noble Man is one who is committed to discerning what is good and true in religions other than Christianity.

Of the Noble Man Eckhart writes:

> The true meaning of the Latin word for "man" is in one sense he who subjects himself wholly to God and surrenders everything that he is and that is his, and looks upward to God, not to what is his, which he knows to be behind him, below him, beside him. This is perfect and real *humility*, [my italics] which has its name from "earth."[743]

Such a transformation grounded in humility is essential to any genuine dialogue both within and between religious communities. Eckhart insists that "one who is not humble (*humilis*—'from the ground') is not

---

[743] *ESC*, 244.

a man, for the word 'man' (*homo*) is taken from 'ground' (*humus*)."[744] Eckhart's teaching of humility is based on the teaching of Jesus Christ, when he says, "Take my yoke upon you and learn from me for I am gentle and humble in heart" (Mt. 11: 29) and "For all who exalt themselves will be humbled and those who humble themselves will be exalted" (Lk. 14: 11). In addition Eckhart also refers to St. Bernard in his book *On Consideration*, who says "Humility is a good foundation on which the whole spiritual structure is erected and grows into a temple holy to the Lord."[745] He also cites St. Augustine[746] who refers to humility by saying that "this 'tower of strength in the face of enemy' (Ps. 60: 4) is as brilliant as any gem. You can have no virtue without it because it alone makes man subject to God and has him look upon God the way an inferior does a superior."[747] For Eckhart, the biblical basis for this conception of the Noble Man and his or her attitude toward others is the dictum: "Love your neighbour as yourself" (Lev. 19:18, Mt.22: 37-8, and Lk. 10: 27). In his Sermon 30, *Praedica verbum, vigila, in omnibus labora*, Eckhart says "if you love your own hundred marks more than someone else's, this is wrong."[748] Thus, Christians are those who do not seek to enjoy for themselves the advantages they have. They are those, in other words, who do not put their own "selves" in the first priority. Meister Eckhart reminds his listeners and readers to do nothing in the way of seeking personal benefit. Instead, he asks believers to denounce self-seeking, and put in its place service to others and to the world in general.[749]

---

[744] *ESC*, 158.

[745] St. Bernard, On Consideration, 3.2.6, cited in *ESC*, 158.

[746] McGinn suspects that it s perhaps an allusion to *City of God* 5. 19, cited in *ESC*, 158.

[747] *ESC*, 156.

[748] Sermon 30, *Praedica verbum, vigila, in omnibus labora*, in *TP*, 294. Cf. A Sermon for St. Dominic Day, Praedica Verbum, James M. Clark and John Skinner, *Treatises and Sermons of Meister Eckhart* (New York: Harper and Brothers, 1958), 60.

[749] It is curious that, although Eckhart's sermons are replete with references to "detachment" and "self-emptying" and saturated with Pauline references, he appears to make no reference to the locus classicus for Paul's theology of the connection between self-emptying (i.e., *kenosis*) and the love of others in Philippians 2:1-11.

Additional aspects of Eckhart's implicit approach to religious diversity can be found in his development of other important concepts closely related to detachment and the whole process of the mystical transformation of the self in which detachment plays such a central role. One of these concepts is that of *durchbruch* or "breakthrough" (discussed above in chapter four). For Eckhart, transformation into the Godhead via breakthrough is not a one-time event. "Therefore it is not enough to surrender self and all that goes with it once. We have to renew the surrender often, for thus we will be free and unfettered in all we do."[750] What this surrender entails, then, is a continual attempt to break into that state of consciousness in which the seeker can actually say: "God's is-ness is my is-ness."[751] Here "Distinctions are lost in God," as the title of one of the master's sermons proclaims. In this sermon he writes: "In this likeness or identity God takes such delight that he pours his whole nature and being into it. . . . it is his pleasure and rapture to discover identity, because he can always put his whole nature into it—for he is this identity itself."[752] As is so characteristic of his writing, Eckhart roots his doctrine of continual breakthrough (accompanied by "detachment" and "birthing") in Pauline scripture, and especially Paul's teaching that "We are eternally chosen in the Son."[753] Eckhart himself asserts that because of this eternal chosenness "we should never rest until we become that which we eternally have been in him; for the Father urges and prods that we be born in the Son and become the same thing that the Son is."[754] This process of being indistinct with God can happen when we can "let go" (*eigenschaft*) of the "spirit of merchandisers." Meister Eckhart makes reference to this spirit in his commentary on the story of Jesus cleansing the Temple of the moneychangers or "merchandisers" in Mt.

---

[750] Blakney, Meister Eckhart, A Modern Translation, 33.

[751] Blakney, *Meister Eckhart, A Modern Translation*, 180.

[752] Blakney, *Meister Eckhart, A Modern Translation*, 205.

[753] This is Eckhart's paraphrase of Ephesians 1: 4 ("just as he chose us in Christ before the foundation of the world...")

[754] Sermon 39, *Iustus in perpetuum vivet et apud dominum est merces eius*, DW, 2: 262, 263, in *TP*, 298.

21:21. The possible implications of Eckhart's teaching on the necessity of "letting go" the "spirit of the merchandisers" for an approach to religious diversity—and in particular interfaith dialogue—are simple and yet profound. For dialogue of any kind to be effective, the participants must be willing to "let go" of all manner of preconceptions, prejudices, and stereotypes, no matter how central they may have been for the participants in the past. It is only with a willingness to "let go" of these encumbrances, that the dialogue participants can "break through" to a new level of mutual understanding and a new reality. Following in line with Eckhart's teaching on the "letting go" of the "spirit of the merchandisers," "letting go" of prejudice is not something that occurs instantaneously, once and for all time. It is a "perpetual process" which must be cultivated as a *habitus*.[755] An Eckhartian perspective on interfaith dialogue, then, would no doubt insist that the participants be free from the "spirit of merchandisers;" for Eckhart, it is only when we are free that we are no longer constrained by the "why and wherefore" of our own agendas, and thus finally open to the presence of the O/other. It is important to note here that Eckhart would probably argue that this "letting go" must entail more than just prejudices and stereotypes. He would most likely insist that it also means "letting go" of some of our most deeply held beliefs—but *not* in the sense of rejecting or disavowing them. An Eckhartian approach to dialogue would not be a relativistic one whereby the participants would, at any point, be obliged to turn their back on, or even "bracket" their religious identities. Such an approach would, however, suggest that we must be willing to "let go" of our identities in order that we might arrive at a deeper understanding of them in light of our encounter with the other. What Meister Eckhart's is saying here is the more we stick and are attached to specific perceptions of reality, the farther we are, not only from the reality we perceive, but also from others who perceive the same reality in their own ways. Ultimately this means to persist in our

---

[755] I borrow this term from Pierre Bourdieu, *Outline of a Theory of Practice* (Cambridge University Press: 1977).

attachments and to persist in our disconnection from God; ultimately it means "getting the way and missing God."[756]

Using John Dunne's theory of "passing-over," interfaith dialogue based on Eckhart's teaching thus, begins from "letting go" in order to "pass over" into other religious traditions and to see both the other and the self in a new light. In "passing-over" one not only comes to a better understanding of the other, but one enters into a deeper and somewhat inexpressible understanding of one's own faith. "A receptive power cannot receive a form unless it is empty and free of other forms—the eye can only see color because it has no color of its own."[757] By way of this "letting go" participants in dialogue can "break through" and be transformed by truth. They can also then "come back" with new horizons of insight into their own tradition as it has been enriched by encounter with the other.

There is another aspect of Eckhart's thought which not only has striking implications for thinking about his approach to religious diversity, but very directly suggests what might be a key element of an Eckhartian theology of interfaith dialogue. This aspect centers around the important spatial metaphor of the *grunt*, which is a desert in which the soul must dwell if it is ever to give birth to God. According to McGinn, "*grunt* is a protean term at the center of Eckhart's mysticism, and consciousness of the *grunt*. . . is the foundation of his mystical preaching."[758] To the degree that this is the case it might also be said about the role of the concept of *grunt* in a theology of dialogue influenced by Eckhart's insights. It is often said that dialogue is a journey. If so, where does the journey lead? Does it lead right back to the starting point? If this were the case, there would be no transformation and thus no real dialogue at all. Does it lead, as some might have it to a "place in the middle" which is located within neither tradition and which feels like alien territory to participants from

---

[756] *DW* I, 227 in *ST*, I, 117; *ESC*, 183.

[757] McGinn, *The Mystical Thought of Meister Eckhart*, 133.

[758] McGinn, "The Problem of Mystical Union in Eckhart, Seuse, and Tauler," in *Miscellanea Medievalia, Meister Eckhart in Erfurt* (Berlin, New York: Walter de Gruyter, 2005), 545.

both of the traditions in dialogue? Or, might it lead the participants from each tradition, to a place which is as squarely located within their tradition as it is unfamiliar? It is quite plausible to interpret Eckhart's teaching about the *grunt* to suggest that within every religious experience within every tradition, there is a place where the spiritual seeker must finally come—and return to repeatedly—where new questions are articulated and new possibilities are just over the horizon.

For Eckhart, knowing nothing is a prerequisite for entering into the *grunt*, a synonym for the "desert," and into the unknowing which itself discloses a new experience. This action is essential to bring the soul into its source where blessedness consists, in order for God to dwell in the seeker. In the dialogue, when participants arrive at this *grunt*—within the parameters of their own tradition—they will receptively be open to an abundance of new possibilities of experience and interpretation. Experience and interpretation of otherness outside of the context of actual dialogic encounter is almost always very different from the experiences and interpretations of otherness which emerge out of a genuine encounter with the other. The implications of Eckhart's mystical theology for a theology of interfaith dialogue is that a crucial element of the dialogic experience is coming to the *grunt*—an internal "space" where receptivity and new possibilities of awareness are maximized. Eckhart refers to this state of being as the "pregnancy" of nothingness wherein, detached from all that is familiar, the seeker is filled with the potential to give birth to many things.

Like Ibn al-'Arabi, Eckhart does not allow his readers to believe that their beliefs are the end or goal of their journey, instead he insists that a realization of the ubiquitous presence of God is the goal. This resonates with the thought of Abraham Joshua Heschel when he writes:

> [R]eligion is a means, not an end. It becomes idolatrous when regarded as an end in itself. . . . To equate religion and God is idolatry. . . . Does not the all-inclusive God contradict the exclusiveness of any particular religion? . . . Is it not blasphemous to say: I

alone have all the truth and the grace, and all those who differ live in darkness, and are abandoned by the grace of God?[759]

Another feature of Eckhart's thought which gives us a deeper understanding of his implicit teaching on religious diversity is his dynamic interpretation of the doctrine of the Trinity and "God beyond God." If for Eckhart, the unity of God is trinitarian, then the unity inheres in a certain relational diversity which characterizes the Godhead. From this perspective, one might suggest that the reality of religious diversity represents different facets of the indeterminate Godhead in a determinate mode. The contemporary Christian theologian of religious diversity, Mark Heim, draws out the implications of Trinitarian theology for an understanding of the authenticity of a variety of religious forms and ends. In his groundbreaking work on a "Trinitarian theology of religious ends," Heim writes:

> Trinity provides a particular ground for affirming the truth and reality of what is different. Trinitarian conviction rules out the view that among all possible claimed manifestations of God, one narrow strand alone is authentic. Trinitarian conviction would rule out as well the view that all or most of these manifestations could be reduced to a single pure type underlying them. A simple exclusivism and a simple pluralism are untenable. There is an irreducible variety in what is ultimately true or of greatest significance. Christians can find validity in other religions because of the conviction that the Trinity represents a universal truth about the way the world and God actually are.[760]

5. Envisioning a New Matrix for Christian–Muslim Dialogue: Contemporary Challenges

The ultimate goal of this book is to help advance Christian-Muslim dialogue in general, and especially Christian-Muslim dialogue in my native Indonesia by attempting to introduce comparative mysticism as a new

---

[759] Harold Kasimow and Byron L. Sherwin, eds., No *Religion Is an Island: Abraham Heschel and Interreligious Dialogue* (Maryknoll, N. Y: Orbis, 1991), 14.

[760] Mark Heim, *The Depth of the Riches: A Trinitarian Theology of Religious Ends* (Grand Rapids, MI: William B. Eerdmans, 2001), 127.

matrix for this dialogue. Such an advance is important because the integrity of the Indonesian social fabric and its capacity to embrace pluralism depends to a very large extent on the degree to which people can become more aware of their own religious identity and the degree to which they are able to bring this identity into dialogue with others. If people can see clearly the various ways in which their faith traditions allow and even encourage understanding of the faith experience of religious others, then we will have developed a context for ourselves in which diversity can be affirmed and celebrated, and in which conflict prevention will begin to erode the need for conflict resolution.

The genesis of this project lies in my practice as an Indonesian Muslim scholar who teaches comparative history of religions to both Muslim and Catholic Christian students, and who also has been involved in the work of Interfidei (Institute for Interfaith Dialogue in Indonesia), a non-governmental organization dedicated to fostering harmonious relationships between the majority Muslim population and minority, especially Christian, Indonesian faith communities. In both of these ministerial contexts my primary task is to develop, with my academic and NGO constituencies, interfaith sensibilities which are sufficiently deep and sophisticated as to provide a basis for fruitful Christian-Muslim dialogue in an Indonesian context. Without a doubt, one of the most significant challenges I have faced in my ministry is to identify and help advance a discourse for Christian-Muslim dialogue which—without ignoring the importance of either Christian or Muslim doctrinal formulation—is able to move beyond the many *a priori* impasses presented by interpretations of doctrine which pay little attention to the important mystical insights of each tradition. In my experience so many opportunities for dialogue have been squandered by an initial fixation on superficial understandings of dialogically thorny theological constructs such as the Christian doctrine of the Trinity or the Islamic doctrine of the Qur'an as the word of God with no human interpolation.

What remains to be done in this final section of this final chapter is to help the reader envision the new matrix proposed in the title of the book by proposing scenarios—drawn in part from practical experience and in part from imagination—in which the conversation between our two masters can be adopted and adapted as a new and more fruitful framework for Christian-Muslim dialogue. To do this I will select a certain combination of some the key five points of conversation outlined in the previous chapter, and discuss what significance these points might have in approaching a certain "problem" in the dialogue. In doing so, I will be imaging these points as "nodes" of this new matrix, or *central principles* of the dialogue which provide the primary structural support for the matrix under discussion.

One of the larger problems facing participants in Christian-Muslim dialogue is the interpretation of certain biblical and quranic verses which are generally interpreted in highly exclusivist ways and often cited by the opponents of dialogue. The purpose here is to imagine the ways in which a matrix for dialogue which is centered around nodes derived from key points of conversation between our mystic masters can provide a framework for this dialogue which is more fruitful and more grounded in orthodox/mainstream tradition than those currently available. Let us begin with a review of these verses and then move on to envision an application of the proposed new matrix.[761]

The Qur'an does not only contain verses which clearly declare the divine ordainment of religious diversity, exhortations to engage in dialogue, and the presence of piety and righteousness in religions other than Islam. It also contains polemical verses. For example, the Qur'an says:

> O ye who believe, take not the Jews and the Christians for friends [or "guardians."] They are friends [or "guardians"] one to another. He among you who taketh them for friends [or "guardians"] is (one) of them. Truly, God guideth not wrongdoing folk (5:51).

---

[761] At this juncture, it is important to emphasize once again that my aim is *not* to create such a matrix. This can only be done in the context of actual praxis and, therefore, will obviously be influenced by many more interpretations of Ibn al-'Arabi, Eckhart, and the two traditions (i.e., Islam and Christianity) than I, as an individual scholar/practitioner, could possibly bring to bear. My aim here, rather, is to try to envision *provisionally* what such a matrix might "look like," i.e., how it might function to enhance the dialogue.

And the Jews say: Ezra is the son of God, and the Christians say: The Messiah is the son of God. That is their saying with their mouths. They imitate the saying of those who disbelieved of old. God fighteth them. How perverse are they! (9:30).

A common radically exclusivist interpretation of these verses is that Jews and Christians are corrupted peoples practicing corrupted traditions of worship and belief. As such, they can never be trusted to be "friends" to the believers. Moreover, these peoples are understood to be the enemies of the faithful since God himself "fights them" (*qatalahumu llahu*).

The New Testament has its own fair share of verses which have conventionally been interpreted in highly exclusivist ways. Such verses include those that: present Jesus as the "one [and only] mediator" between God and humanity (1Tim 2: 5); that there is "no other name under heaven" by which persons can be saved (Acts 4: 12); that "no one comes to the Father except through me [i.e., Jesus] (John 14: 6); that Jesus is the only begotten Son of God (John 1:14); and that whoever sees him sees the Father (John 14:7).[762] Hence Jesus is viewed as the only one who truly and fully reveals God. It is, in part, on the basis of verses such as these that Jesus is claimed to be the particular and unique savior of the world.

What the traditions of exclusivist interpretation of both these verses have in common is that they tend to be uninformed from within as well as from without. By "uninformed from within," I mean they are usually deaf to alternative interpretative possibilities from within their own tradition. By "uninformed from without," I mean they are usually articulated with little to no experience of genuine encounter with the

---

[762] See this discussion in Knitter, Paul, *No Other Name? A Critical Survey of Christian Attitudes Toward the World Religions* (New York: Maryknoll Orbis Books, 1985); Knitter, Paul, "The World Religion and the Finality of Christ: A Critique of Hans Kung's On Being A Christian," in *Interreligious Dialogue*, Richard W. Rousseau, ed. (Ridge Row Press, 1981); Kung, Hans, et al., *Christianity and The World Religions, Path of Dialogue with Islam, Hinduism and Buddhism* (New York: Doubleday, 1982); Young, Frances, "A Cloud of Witness," in *The Myth of God Incarnate*, John Hick, ed. (London: SCM Press, 1977).

other, or if there is experience of the other, it is short-lived and highly negative.

By applying some of the key points of the conversation of our mystic masters as a framework for exploring the significance of these verses, we can more clearly see the ways in which these orthodox teachers can help us develop a more fruitful dialogue focused on this subject. At this juncture, however, it is important to mention that the Ibn al-ʿArabi-Meister Eckhart matrix proposed here is by no means the only matrix that holds some promise of fruitfulness when it comes to Christian-Muslim dialogue. Rather, this matrix is proposed as one among many possibilities.

The point of conversation between the masters—what we will now refer to as a "node" of the matrix—that immediately comes to mind when faced with the problem of the quranic and biblical verses cited above is the *infinite potential for meaning* inherent in the nature of divine revelation. Within the context of the Ibn al-ʿArabi-Eckhart matrix for dialogue this important hermeneutical principle would by no means require an *a priori* dismissal of the more exclusivist interpretations of these verses. In fact, it would be a misuse of the matrix to load it with a particular political or philosophical agenda other than the foundational conviction that interfaith (and intra-faith) dialogue is inherently good and necessary for the welfare of the participating traditions as well as for the welfare of the human family in general. Rather, what this principle would do is remind the participants in dialogue who are aware of these verses and their exclusivist interpretations, that other possibilities for interpretation exist which may well be equally defensible within the context of the larger tradition and thus, depending on the authoritative consensus of the community of believers, may be equally or even more orthodox in nature.

As I see it, the Ibn al-ʿArabi-Eckhart matrix and its node of infinite potential of scriptural meaning, would encourage two complementary activities when faced with any scriptural text that posed a challenge (either positive or negative) for dialogue, cooperation, and mutual understanding and trust. The first of these activities would be to imitate the masters themselves by delving as deeply as possible into all the contextual resources available for interpreting these texts. This not only means reading quranic or biblical passages in light of other proximate and otherwise related quranic or biblical passages. It also means using all the available tools of historical research to uncover key elements of the original context of a given passage's revelation (in the case of the Qur'an) and a given passage's composition (in the case of the Bible). The second of these activities would also involve a certain imitation of the masters when it comes to their common valorization of experience and its importance in interpreting sacred scripture. In this case, the experience that would be most significant would be that of the encounter with the religious other. The matrix and its node of the infinite potential for meaning of scripture would encourage interpretations of all scripture—especially passages which purport to speak about the religious other—to be rooted in actual experience of that other. Simple reason dictates that any interpretation of what the Qur'an, for example, says about Jews and/or Christians is de facto faulty if it cannot stand in the face of a given Muslim's authentic relationships with Jews and/or Christians.

Another node of the matrix which is also pertinent in the case of scriptural interpretation is the node of the *oneness of being*. This node of the matrix dictates that God's presence and influence can be found in all traditions, thus, any interpretation of sacred scripture which suggests otherwise would be suspect. From the perspective of both Ibn al-'Arabi and Meister Eckhart and the respective orthodoxies each of them represents, no passage of the Qur'an or Bible should be interpreted to suggest that any group of people, by virtue of their beliefs and practices, live outside of a relationship with God. This does not mean that, according to this matrix, no distinction can be made between "believers," for example, and "unbelievers." It also does not mean that one tradition cannot be perceived of as superior, in certain ways, to another. What it does mean is that the hubris of decreeing God to be "here" and not "there," or "with us" and not at all "with you" cannot be accepted.

Of course, there are many other challenges encountered in the dialogue besides those of interpreting apparently exclusivist scriptural passages. Another example might be problems of interpreting either our own or others' doctrinal formulations. A primary illustration of this in Christian-Muslim dialogue is the Christian doctrine of the Trinity and/or the doctrine of the Incarnation and the Muslim doctrine of *tawhid*. Although some expect the dialogue to resolve such fundamental doctrinal differences as this one, this is by no means the purpose of the matrix. Here is where the masters' idea of the "naming of God" can be helpful. Given the importance of our doctrinal formulations to the integrity of our respective traditions, we must never fall into the arrogance of believing either that these formulations are equivalent with the reality (i.e., God) of which they speak, or the arrogance of believing that they amount to little more than disposable conjecture in our quest for the truth. Through the node of the matrix that has to do with the "naming of God" we hear our two masters asking us never to lose sight of our creaturely limitations —especially the inherent inadequacy of our modes of discourse to convey an understanding of God. Another way of putting this is to say that we do not preserve the integrity and sacredness of our doctrinal formulations by absolutizing them in such a way as to exclude all others. Rather we preserve this integrity and sacredness precisely by humbly recognizing that the deepest understanding of these inherently limited linguistic formulations must leave room for validating and dignifying the religious experiences and formulations of others, no matter how different they may be from our own.

Also, to the extent that we lose a sense of humility with respect to our doctrinal formulations, we also lose a sense of humility as we stand before our traditions and thus run the risk of lapsing into idolatry by mistaking our traditions for God. Through the node of the matrix that has to do with the distinction between "God created by the believer," on the one hand, and the "Godhead," on the other, the two masters remind us that however passionately we may believe in the articles of our faiths or however passionately and devoutly we may perform their rituals, the moment we begin to use these beliefs and practices as weapons to establish the dominance of the self over others is the moment we mark ourselves as servants of our own egos rather than of God. Of course, because all the nodes of a matrix are deeply interrelated, it should come as no surprise that the effects of the nodes mentioned above are directly connected to the only node we have failed to mention thus far—the node involving the transformation of the self. By interpreting scripture with a hermeneutic of the infinite potential of meaning, by never forgetting the oneness and ubiquitousness of the divine Being, by recognizing the limitation of our theological language and our success distinguishing between the "God" we create and the ultimately ineffable Godhead, we truly plumb the depths of our relationship to God by opening ourselves to the goal at the heart of both Islam and Christianity: to transform the believers into better and better beings, more deeply committed to the service of God and one another.

CONCLUSION

Speaking of God Without Speaking for God

Diversity of religions, cultures, ethnicities, languages, etc. is an existential reality; it is a fact of our phenomenal world, both on a global scale as well as on the level of local societies. Of course, this diversity is nothing new. It is as old as human existence. Equally old is the series of conflicts that appears to have been such an integral part of the human experience of diversity. In one part of the quranic creation story,[763] God declares that He is about to "place a vicegerent on the earth." The angels object asking, "Will You place on the earth [another being who] will spread corruption and shed blood in it, while we praise and glorify You?" Although God responds by saying, "I know what you do not know," it appears that the angels have a deep and accurate insight into the future of humanity. But what is it that God knows about humanity that the angels do not know? Perhaps it is our capacity for knowledge of the truth, wisdom, and compassion? Perhaps it is our capacity to repent from the evil that we do and set out on another path? Indeed, in the quranic story of the original fratricide, when Qabil/Cain was shown by the raven (*al-ghurab*) how to bury his brother's corpse, he is overcome with regret for the great crime he has committed (*fa asbaha min al-nadimin*).

The Qur'an's dominant meta-narrative of human history is not one of ever-increasing violence, moral degradation, and decay, but of a progressive divine revelation and guidance delivered to humanity through the medium of great prophets and messengers who embody human perfection and who invite all human beings in their communities and beyond to fulfill their destiny by perfecting their own lives. Through Qabil's/Cain's regret over the murder of his brother Habil/

---

[763] Q 2:30.

Abel, the reader of the Qur'an is meant to recognize that God intends the human heritage to be one molded, not by the example of mutual hostility represented by Qabil/Cain, but rather by the example of Habil/Abel who prefers to accept death rather than disobey God and raise his hand against his brother Qabil/Cain (*la in basatta ilayya yadaka li-taqtulani ma ana bi-basitin yadiyya ilayka li-aqtulaka; inni akhafu Allaha rabba al-`alamin*). What the angels do not know about Adam is that, despite the fact that he and his descendents will have the capacity to do great evil, their divinely ordained purpose—a purpose toward which God will relentlessly guide humanity—is one of life lived in harmony with one another and with all creation.

Although there are many other verses of the Qur'an that are far more frequently cited as being in support of dialogue (e.g., Q 49:13 and 5:48), the story of Habil/Abel and Qabil/Cain very powerfully conveys the message that the divinely ordained paradigm for human relations is not one of rivalry, envy, and murder, but rather one of fear of God manifest in a deep and abiding respect for one's fellow human beings and an abhorrence of violence. What is interesting is that this paradigm of peace through dialogue and understanding is as prevalent in "Athens" (i.e., Hellenistic philosophy) as it is in "Mecca" and "Jerusalem" (i.e., quranic and biblical traditions). The story of the death of Socrates memorializes in a pagan idiom the Habili/Abelian virtue of preferring nonviolent dialogue and understanding over violent conflict, even at the cost of one's life. In a way, then, Habil/Abel and Socrates stand as martyrs for dialogue, both for those who locate themselves within the quranic and/or biblical traditions and for those who see themselves more as humanists without a particular religious affiliation.

The one principal difference between the mythical/historical context of Habil/Abel and Socrates, on the one hand, and the one in which we now live, on the other, is the stunning scope and intensity of human diversity that is the hallmark of the globalizing present. Although they lived in very different historical and demographical circumstances, Ibn al-`Arabi and Meister Eckhart developed ideas on their experience of God that have great relevance for contemporary Muslims and Christians as we reflect—amidst a diversity that seems to become more complex each day—on our sacred duty to live with respect for and in harmony with one another.

Though the teachings of both Ibn al-`Arabi and Meister Eckhart are not entirely original—though each are indebted to predecessors who struggled with similar questions—both are, nonetheless unique and special in terms of the powerful ways in which they expressed their respective understanding of how the one God relates to a created order of what seems like infinite multiplicity. Both masters have been accused of being heretics who stand in defiance of their respective orthodoxies an orthopraxies. Throughout our discussion in this dissertation, however, we have seen how both masters are deeply rooted in the orthodoxies and orthopraxies of their respective religious traditions, all the while attempting to demonstrate what more these traditions have to offer.

I do not, however, have unrealistic expectations. Although, as a historian of religions and a theologian, I will argue to the bitter end for the orthodoxy and orthopraxy of these two masters, I have no illusions that centuries of polemic against, or simply ignorance of, what these masters teach can be undone overnight, by one book. But my intent is not to articulate the nodes of a new matrix for dialogue among staunchly "Salafi" (i.e., so-called "Wahhabi") Muslims and conservative Evangelical Christians. Indeed, my intent is not principally to "convert" other Muslims and Christians to my way of thinking about these masters. Rather, I have set out in this book to offer to those who are disposed to dialogue and who are, at the same time, very committed to their traditions, a way in which to anchor their dialogic disposition squarely within these traditions. This is not exactly "preaching to the choir" because many people who are disposed to dialogue have never really begun to "sing." At the same time, I am not preaching to those who would never even consider "entering the church." While I am well aware of social contexts in which the "choir" is not very large and in which there are not many people in the category between the "choir" and those who want no part of dialogue. In my native Indonesia, however, and in other countries where there are large or majority Muslim populations (e.g., Turkey and India) this "in-between" category is quite substantial. Indeed, there are many

Muslims (and Christians) hungry for a new matrix for dialogue—an effective way to root their coming to terms with religious diversity squarely within the orthodoxies and orthopraxies of their traditions.

Before summarizing, by way of conclusion, what I believe to be the unique contribution of my efforts in this book, I would like to pause here and underscore the fact that, to be true to the visions of our two masters, we should try, as much as possible, to avoid rigidly categorizing ourselves according to any popular three-fold typology such as exclusivist, inclusivist, and pluralist[764] or others. For any honest rediscovery of tradition such as the one we attempt to outline in the last two chapters above, it is crucial that we remain as open and dialogic as possible *within* our traditions. While it is important to recognize who are kindred spirits are, it is by no means a corollary to dismiss those who may not understand or who may actively oppose our efforts. The Habilian/Abelian paradigm is clear: if we are committed to dialogue, we must be willing to make the sacrifices necessary to see to it that we do not allow any of the dialogues we help create to become just another political instrument of exclusion and demonization. Although we must always speak *of* God and strive to get right what it is we say, we must be careful never to presume to speak *for* God. To do so would be—especially in the eyes of our two masters—blasphemy of the highest order. It would constitute an embrace of that very distinctive brand of religious arrogance which is no less than the highest form of idolatry.

The first two chapters of this book were designed to introduce the reader to the extraordinary lives and legacies of Ibn al-ʿArabi and Meister Eckhart. Such an introduction serves two purposes. The first is to convey a sense of who these two great thinkers were *within their distinct socio-historical contexts*. To present the thinking of these two masters without a serious look at their respective biographies and the role played by their respective contexts in shaping who they were, would be intellectually irresponsible. It would cheat the reader out of

---

[764] See Diana Eck, *Encountering God: A Spiritual Journey from Bozeman to Banaras*, second edition (Boston: Beacon Press, 2003).

the important opportunity to see that these great mystics were men of "flesh and blood" who were products of their context, and yet at the same time spoke in ways that undoubtedly have trans-contextual significance within their respective traditions and even across them. It would also cheat the reader out of the information necessary to find weaknesses in some of my arguments and interpretations, thus restricting the utility of my presentation.

The third and fourth chapters are attempts to synthesize "within"— to distill from the very complex thought of each of the masters, some of their most important and distinctive concepts. In the case of Ibn al-`Arabi, I chose his teaching on the "Self-disclosure of God" as the central organizing principle of his thought and the one which would be most relevant to a comparison with the thought of Meister Eckhart. In the case of Meister Eckhart, I did the same, focusing on his pivotal concept of "detachment." In the fifth chapter, I place the two masters in conversation with one another, identifying and defining five key points of conversation which, in chapter six, I imagine as "nodes."

The conversation that I have attempted to initiate between our two masters is a conversation which, as I have stated above, I believe can function as a "new matrix" for Christian-Muslim dialogue—a matrix that will challenge us to delve more deeply into the truths revealed in the ways we speak *of* God, all the while steering ourselves away from the temptation to speak *for* God. The identification and articulation of the five "points of conversation" between the two masters—points I later refer to as "nodes" of the new matrix—are one of the distinct contributions of this dissertation. They are, however, by no means, the only nodes that one could imagine emerging out of the conversation between these two masters. Indeed, as I mention above, as a single scholar/practitioner, I cannot create a new matrix myself. The best I can do is to provide others with a methodology and a vision, and encourage them to help "birth" such a matrix in the actuality of their own lived praxis.

BIBLIOGRAPHY

On Ibn al-ʿArabi:

Addas, Claude. *Ibn ʿArabi, ou, La quete du sourfre rouge, (Quest for the Red Sulphur: The Life of Ibn ʿArabi)*. translated from the French by Peter Kingsley, Cambridge: Islamic Texts Society, 1993.

——. *Ibn ʿArabi: The Voyage of No Return*. Cambridge: Islamic Texts Society, 2000.

——."The ship of Stone." *The Journal of the Muhyiddin Ibn ʿArabi Society,* 1996, Volume XIX, in the special issue entitled, "The Journey of The Heart."

Afifi, A. E. "Memorandum by Ibn ʿArabi of His Own Works." Introduction, in *the Bulletin of the Faculty of Arts*, Alexandria University, VIII, 1954.

——.*The Mystical Philosophy of Muhyid Din-Ibnul ʿArabi*. London: Cambridge University Press, 1939.

Al-Ghazali. *Al Munqid min al-dalal*. Lahor: Hayʾah al-Awqaf bi-Ḥukumat al-Bunjab, 1971.

Akkach, Samer. *Cosmology and Architecture in Premodern Islam, An Architectural Reading of Mystical Ideas*. Albany: State University of New York press, 2005.

al- Hakim Souad. "Ibn ʿArabi's twofold Perception of Women." *Journal of The Muhyiddin Ibn ʿArabi Society*. Vol. xxxix, 2006.

Almond, Ian. *Sufism and Deconstruction*. London and New York: Routledge, 2004.

——. "Divine Needs, Divine Illusions: Preliminary Remarks Toward a Comparative Study of Meister Eckhart and Ibn Al'Arabi." *Medieval Philosophy and Theology*. 10, 2001.

al-Qashani, Abd al-Razaq. *Sharh al-Qashani ʿala Fusus al-Hikam*. Cairo, 1321 A. H.

al-Shaʿrani, ʿAbd al-Wahhab. *al-Tabaqat al-Kubra*. Cairo, 1954, Vol. I.

Ates, A. "Ibn al-ʿArabi." *The Encyclopedia of Islam*. new ed., ed., Bernard Lewis et. Al., Leiden: E. J. Brill, 1971.

Bashier, Salman H. *Ibn al-ʿArabi's Barzakh, the Concept of the Limit and the Relationship between God and the World*. Albany: State University of New York Press, 2004.

Chittick, C. William. "Presence with God." *The Journal of the Muhyiddin Ibn ʿArabi Society*. Vol. XX, 1996.

——. *Ibn ʿArabi : Heir to the Prophets*. Oxford : Oneworld, 2005.

——. "Note on Ibn Al-'Arabi's Influence in the Subcontinent." *The Muslim World*. Vol. LXXXII, No. 3-4, July-October, 1992.

——. "Ibn al-'Arabi and His School." *Islamic Spirituality, Manifestation*. ed. by Seyyed Hossein Nasr, New York: Crossroad, 1991.

——. *The Self-Disclosure of God: Principles of Ibn al-'Arabi's Cosmology*. Albany: State University of New York Press 1998.

——. *Imaginal Worlds: Ibn al-'Arabi and the Problem of Religious Diversity*. Albany: State University of New York Press, 1994.

——. "On the Cosmology of Dhikr." in *Path to the Heart, Sufism and the Christian East*. Edited by James S. Cutsinger, World Wisdom, 2002.

——. *The Sufi Path of Knowledge: Ibn al-'Arabi's Metaphysics of Imagination*. Albany, N.Y. : State University of New York Press, 1989.

——. "The Five Divine Presence: From al-Qunawi to al-Qaysari." *Muslim World*. 72, 1982, 107-128.

——. "The Perfect Man as a Prototype of the Self in the Sufism of Jami'." *Studia Islamica*. 49, 1979, 135-158

——. "Mysticism versus Philosophy in Earlier Islamic History: The al-Tusi al-Qunawi Correspondence." *Religioua Studies*. 17, 1981, 87-104.

——. "*Wahdat al-Wujud* in Islamic Thought." *Bulletin of the Henry Martyn Institute of Islamic Studies*. 10, 1991, 7-27.

——. "Belief and Transformation: Sufi Teaching of Ibn al-'Arabi." *The American Theosophist*. 74, 1986.

——. "Rumi and Wahdat al-wujud." Amin Banani, Richard G Hovannisian, and Georges Sabagh. eds. *Poetry and Mysticism in Islam: the Heritage of Rumi*. New York : Cambridge University Press, 1994.

——. "Sadr al-Din al-Qunawi on the Oneness of Being." *International Philosophical Quarterly*. 21, 1981, 171-184.

Chodkiewicz, Michel. *Ocean Without Shore: Ibn 'Arabi, the Book, and the Law*. Albany, NY: State University of New York Press, 1993.

——. *Seal of the Saints: Prophethood and Sainthood in the Doctrines of Ibn Arabi*. trans. Liadain Sherrard, Islamic Text Society, Cambridge, 1993.

Corbin, Henry. *Creative Imagination in the Sufism of Ibn al-'Arabi*. Princeton: Princeton University Press, 1969, or *Alone with the Alone: Creative Imagination in the Sufism of Ibn 'Arabi*. with a new preface by Harold Bloom, 1998. (A new Translation of the Creative Imagination)

Coates, Peter. *Ibn 'Arabi and Modern Thought, The History of Taking Metaphysics Seriously*. Oxford: Anqa Publishing, 2002.

Dabashi, H. *Truth and Narrative: The Untimely Thought of Ayn al-Qudat al-Hamadhani*. Richmond: Curzon Press, 1999.

——. "Persian Sufism during the Seljuk Period." Lewinsohn, Leonard, ed. *The Heritage of Sufism, Classical Persian Sufism for Its Origin to Rumi (700-1300)*. Vol.I, Oxford: Oneworld, 1999.

Elmore, Gerald T. "The Uwaysi Spirit of the Spirit Autodidactic Sainthood as the "Breath of the Merciful." *Journal of Ibn Arabi Society*. Vol. XXVIII, 2000.

——. *Islamic Sainthood in The Fullness of Time, Ibn al-'Arabi's Book of the Fabulous Gryphon*. Leiden, Brill, 1999.

——. "On the Road to Santarem." *Journal of the Muhyiddin Ibn 'Arabi Society*. Vol. XXIV, 1998.

Ernst, Carl W. *Words of Ecstasy in Sufism*. Albany: State University of New York Press, 1985.

Esack, Farid. *Qur'an, Liberation, and Pluralism, An Islamic Perspective of Interreligious Solidarity against Oppression*. Oxford, Oneworld, 1997.

Hirtenstein, Stephen. *The Unlimited Merciful, The Spiritual Life and Thought of Ibn 'Arabi*. Oxford: Anqa Publishing, 1999.

Homerin, Emil. "Ibn Arabi in the People Assembly, Religion, Press, and Politics in Sadat's Egypt." *The Middle East Journal*. Vol. 40, 1986.

Houedard, Dom Sylvester. "Ibn 'Arabi's Contribution to the Wider Ecumenism." *Muhyiddin Ibn 'Arabi, A Commemorative Volume*. eds. Stephen Hirtenstein and Michael Tiernan, Shaftesbury: Element, 1993.

Ibn al-'Arabi, Muhyi al-Din. *The bezels of wisdom*. translation and introd. by R.W.J. Austin ; pref. by Titus Burckhardt, New York : Paulist Press, 1980.

——. *Sufis of Andalusia: the 'Ruh al-quds' and 'al-Durrat al-fakhirah' of Ibn 'Arabi*. translated with introduction and notes by R. W. J. Austin; with a foreword by Martin Lings, London, Allen and Unwin, 1971.

——. *Risalat ruh al-quds fi muhasabat al-nafs*. Damascus: Mu'assasat al-'Ilm li l-Tiba'ah wa-al-Nashr, 1964.

——. *al-Diwan al-akbar*. Bulaq, 1271H.

——. *Mir'at al-'Arifin*. Damascus: Maktabah Rafiq Hamdan al-Khassah, nd.

——. *Fusus al-Hikam*. ed. A. Afifi, Beirut: Dar al-Kutub al-'Arabi, 1946.

——. *Shajarat al-Kawn*. trans. A Jeffrey, Lahore: Aziz, 1980.

——. *al-Futuhat al-Makkiya*. ed. 'Uthman Yahya, Cairo: al-Hay'at al-Misriyat al-'Amma li al-Kitab, 1972- .Vol. 12 has date on cover: 1989. Includes bibliographical references and indexes Introductions in Arabic and French.

——. *Fusus al-Hikam*. by Caner Dagli, Kazi Press, Chicago, 2001.

——. *Journey to the Lord of Power*. trans. Rabia Terri harris, London: East West Publications, 1981.

——. *The Wisdon of the Prophets*. partial translation of the *Fusus al-Hikam*. from Arabic to French by T. Burckhardt, and from French to English by A. Culme-Seymour, Swyre Farm, Gloucestershire, 1975.

——. *The Tarjuman al-Ashwaq: A Collection of Mystical Odes by Muhyiddin Ibn al-Arabi*. trans. R. Nicholson, London, 1978.

——. *Ismail Hakki Bursevi's Translation of and Commentary on Fusus al-Hikam*. trans. B. Rauf, 4 vols, Oxford, 1986-91, Vol. 4.

Ibn Hazm. *On the Perfect Knowledge of Juridical Bases (Al-Ihkam fi usul al-ahkam)*. Cairo: 1345-47/1926-28, 8 books in 2 vols.

Izutsu, Toshihiko. *Sufism and Taoism, A comparative Study of Key Philosophical Concepts*. Berkeley, Los Angeles, London: University of California Press, 1983.

Izutsu, Toshihiku. "Ibn al-'Arabi," *The Encyclopedia of Religion*. Mircea Eliade, ed. -in chief, New York: MacMillan, 1987.

——. *Creation and the Timeless Order of Things, Essays in Islamic Mystical Philosophy*. Ashland, Oregon: White Cloud Press, 1994.

Jayyusi, S. K. *The Legacy of Muslim Spain*. Vol. I, Leiden: Brill, 2000.

Jeffrey Arthur. "Ibn al-'Arabi's Shajarat al-Kawn." *Studia Islamica*. 11, 1959.

Knysh, Alexander D. "Ibrahim al-Kurani (d. 1101/1690), An Apologist for Wahdat al-Wujud." *Journal of the Royal Asiatic Society*. 3rd series, 5, 1995, 39-47.

——. *Ibn 'Arabi in the Later Islamic Tradition: The Making of a Polemical Image in Mediaval Islam*. Albany: State University of New York Press, c1999

——. "'Orthodoxy' and 'Heresy' in Medieval Islam: An Essay in Reassessment." *The Muslim World*. Vol. LXXXIII, No. 1, Jan. 1993.

Lanzetta, Beverly J. *Other Side of Nothingness, Toward a Theology of Radical Openness*. Albany, State University of New York Press, 2001.

Lewinsohn, Leonard. ed. *The Heritage of Sufism, Classical Persian Sufism for Its Origin to Rumi (700-1300)*. Vol.I, Oxford: Oneworld, 1999.

Little, John T. "al-Insan al-Kamil: The Perfect man according to Ibn al-'Arabi." *The Muslim World*. Vol. vii, 1987.

Morris, James Winston. "How to study the Futuhat: Ibn 'Arabi's Own Advice." Stephen Hirtenstein and Michael Tiernan, eds. *Muhyiddin Ibn 'Arabi: A Commemorative Volume*. Shaftesbury, 1993.

——. "Ibn 'Arabi's 'Esoterisism': The Problem of Spiritual Authority." *Studia Islamica*. 71, 1990, pp. 37-64

——. "The Spiritual Ascension: Ibn 'Arabi and the Mi'raj." pts. 1 and 2, *Journal of the American Oriental Society*. 107, no 4, 1987: 108, no. 1, 1988, 69-77.

Murata, Sachico. *The Tao of Islam*. State University of New York Press, 1992.

Nasr, Seyyed Hossein. *Sufi Essays*. London, 1972.

——. *Three Muslim Sages*. Delmar, New York: Caravan Books, 1970.

Nicholson, Reynold A. "Lives of 'Umar Ibnu'i-Farid and Muhiyyu' ddin Ibnu'l-'Arabi. *J. R. A. S.* 1906.

——. *Studies in Islamic Mysticism.* Cambridge, 1921.

Palacios, Miguel Asin. *Ibn al-'Arabi, hayatuhu wa-madhhabuh.* tr. al-Isbaniyah 'Abd al-Rahsan Badawi , translation of El-*Islam Christianizado; estudio del "sufismo" a traves de las obras de Abenarabi de Murcia.* Cairo: Maktabat al-Anjlu al-Misriyah, 1965.

——. *Islam and the Divine Comedy.* translated and abridged by Harold Sunderland. Lahore : Qausain, 1977.

Sells, Michael Anthony. *Mystical languages of Unsaying.* Chicago: University of Chicago Press, 1994.

——. "Ibn 'Arabi's 'Polished Mirror': Perspective Shift and Meaning Event." *Studia Islamica.* 67, 1988, 121-149.

Shah-Kazemi, Reza. *Paths to Transcendence: According to Shankara, Ibn Arabi, and Meister Eckhart.* Bloomington: World Wisdom, 2006.

——. *The Other in the Light of the One, The Universality of the Qur'an and Interfaith Dialogue.* Cambridge: The Islamic Text Society, 2006.

Tahrali, Mustafa. "The Polarity of Expression in The Fusus al-Hikam." Hirtenstein and Tiernan, eds. *Muhyiddin Ibn 'Arabi: A Commemorative Volume.* Shaftesbury, Dorset ; Rockport, Mass. : Element, 1993.

Takeshita, Masataka. *Ibn 'Arabi's Theory of the Perfect Man and Its Place in the History of Islamic Thought.* Tokyo, 1987.

Winkel, Erick. *Islam and The Living Law, The Ibn al-Arabi Approach.* Oxford: Oxford University Press, 1997.

——. "Ibn al-Arabi's fiqh: Three Cases from the Futuhat." *Journal of the Muhyiddion Ibn 'Arabi Society.* 13, 1993, 54-74.

Winter, Michael. *Society and Religion in Early Ottoman Egypt.* New Brunswick, N.J.:
Transaction Books, 1982.

On Meister Eckhart:

Blakney, Raymond. *Meister Eckhart, a Modern Translation.* New York, London, Harper & Brothers, 1941.

Broneke, F. Vanden. "Meister Eckhart." *New Catholic Encyclopaedia.* Detroit, MI: Thomson, Gale Group; Washington, D.C. : in association with the Catholic University of America, 2003.

Caputo, John D. "Fundamental Themes in Meister Eckhart's Mysticism." *The Thomist.* 42, April, 1978.

——. "The Nothingness of the Intellect." *The Thomist.* Vol. XXXIX, January, 1975, No. I.

——. *The Mystical Element in Heidegger's Thought*. Fordham University Press, 1978.

——. "Mysticism and Transgression: Derrida and Meister Eckhart." *Derrida and Deconstruction*. ed. Hugh J Silverman, New York and London: Routledge, 1989.

Clark, James M. *The Great German Mystics: Eckhart, Tauler and Suso*. Oxford: basil Blackwell, 1949.

Clark, James M. ed. *Meister Eckhart: An Introduction to the Study of his Works with an Anthology of his Sermon*. London: Nelson and Sons, 1957.

Davies, Oliver, ed. *Meister Eckhart, Selected Writings*. Penguin Book, 1994.

Davies, Oliver. *Meister Eckhart: Mystical Theologian*. London: SPCK, 1991.

Denifle, Henrich. "Meister Eckharts Lateinische Schriften und die Grundanschauung seiner Lehre." *Archiv fur Literatur und Kirchengeschichte des Mittelarters* 2. 1886.

Eckhart, Meister. *Parisian Questions and Prologues*. Trans. and itro. Armand A. Maurier. Toronto: Pontifical Institute of Medieval Studies, 1974.

——. *Selected Treatises and Sermons Translated from Latin and German with an Introduction and Notes*. trans. and eds. James M. Clark and john V. Skinner,: London: Faber and Faber, 1958.

——. *Meister Eckhart: Die deutschen und lateinischen Werke*. ed. Josef Quint; 5 vols.; Stuttgart: Kohlhammer Verlag, 1936.

——. *Sermons and Treatises*. translated and edited by M.O'C. Walshe, Shaftesbury, Dorset, [England] : Element Books, 1978, 1987.

——. *The Essential Sermons, Commentaries, Treatises and Defence*. Edmund Colledge, and Bernard McGinn, (eds.) New York: Paulist Press, 1981.

——. *Teacher and Preacher*. ed., Bernard McGinn, Classics of Western Spirituality, New York: Paulist Press, 1986.

Forman, Robert. K. *Meister Eckhart, Mystic as Theologian*. Shaftesbury: Adorset, 1991.

Fox, Mattew, O. P. *Breakthrough: Meister Eckhart's Creation Spirituality in New Translation*. New York: Image Books a division of Dobleday and Company Inc, 1980.

Hollywood, Amy. *The Soul as Virgin Wife, Mechthild of Magdeburg, Marguerite Porete, and Meister Eckhart*. Notre Dame and London: University of Notre Dame Press, 1995.

Karrer, Otto. and H. Piesch. *Meister Eckharts Rechfertigungsschrift vom Jahre 1326, Einleitung, Uebersetzung und Anmerkungen*. Ehrfurt, 1927.

Kertz, Karl G. "Meister Eckhart's Teaching on the Birth of the Divine World of the Soul." *Traditio*. 15, 1959.

Kelley, F. *Meister Eckhart: On Divine Knowledge*. New Heaven, 1977.

Kieckhefer, Richard. "Meister Eckhart's Conception of Union with God." *Harvard Theological Review* 71. July-October, 1978.

Konrad Weiss. "Meister Eckharts Biblische Hermeneutik." *La Mystique Rhenane.* Paris, 1963.

Langer, Otto. *Mystische Erfahrung und spirituelle Theologie: zu Meister Eckharts Auseinandersetzung mit der Frauenfrömmigkeit seiner Zeit.* München: Artemis Verlag, 1987.

Lichtmann, Maria R. "The Way of Meister Eckhart." Valerie M. Lagorio. *Mysticism, Medieval and Modern.* Lewiston: Edwin Melen Press, nd.

McGinn, Bernard. "The God beyond God: Theology and Mysticism in the Thought of Meister Eckhart." *The Journal of Religion.* Vol. 61, No. I, January 1981.

———. "The Problem of Mystical Union in Eckhart, Seuse, and Tauler." *Miscellanea Medievalia, Meister Eckhart in Erfurt.* Berlin, New York: Walter de Gruyter, 2005.

———. "Ocean and Desert as Symbol of Mystical Absorption in the Christian Tradition." *Journal of Religion.* 74, 1994, 155-181.

———. "'Evil-Sounding, Rash, and Suspect of Heresy': Tensions between Mysticism and Magisterium in the History of The Church." *The Catholic Historical Review.* Vol. xc April, 2004 No. 2.

———. *The Mystical Thought of Meister Eckhart, The Man from Whom God Hid Nothing.* New York: The Crossroad Publishing Company, 2001.

———. "Eckhart's Condemnation Reconsidered." *The Thomist, A Speculative Quarterly Review.* Vol. 44, Washington D. C: The Thomist Press, 1980.

Mieth, Dietmar. "Meister Eckhart, The Power of Inner Liberation." *Toward a New Heaven and a New Earth.* ed., Fernando F. Segovia, New York: Maryknoll, Orbis Books, 2003.

Millem, Bruce. *The Unspoken Word, Negative Theology in Meister Eckhart's German Sermons.* Washington D. C.: The Catholic University of America Press, 2002.

Muller-Thym, Bernard J. *The Establishment of the University of Being in the Doctrine of Meister Eckhart of Hochheim.* Published for Institute of Medieval Studies by New York, London: Sheed and Ward, 1939.

O'Meara, Thomas, O.P. "The Presence of Meister Eckhart." *The Thomist.* 42, no. 2, 1978.

Pfeiffer, Franz. *Meister Eckhart.* trans. C de B. Evans, London, 1924.

Quint, Josef. *Textbuch zur Mystik des deutschen Mittelalters.* Halle: Niemeyer, 1952.

Royster, James E. "Personal Transformation in Ibn al-ʿArabi and Meister Eckhart." *Christian-Muslim Encounters.* Eds. Yvonne Y. Haddad and Wadi Y Haddad, Tallahassee: University Press of Florida, 1995.

Ruh, Kurt. *Die Mystik des deutschen Predigerordens und ihre Grundlegung durch die Hochscholastik.* Vol. 3 of *Geschichte der abendlandischen Mystik.* Munich: C H. Beck, 1996.

Schurmann, Reiner. *Meister Eckhart: Mystic and Philosoper: Translation with Commentary*. Bloomington: Indiana University Press, 1978.

Shah-Kazemi, Reza. *Paths to transcendence: according to Shankara, Ibn Arabi, and Meister Eckhart*. Bloomington: World Wisdom, 2006.

Shizuteru, Ueda. "'Nothingness' in Meister Eckhart and Zen Buddhism." *The Buddha Eye, an anthology of the Kyoto School*. ed. by Frederick Franck New York : Crossroad, 1982.

Soudek, Ernst H. "Meister Eckhart." *Dictionary of the Middle Ages*. ed. in chief, Joseph R. Strayer, Vol. 4, New York: Charles Scribner's Sons, 1982-89.

Suzuki, D. T. *Mysticism: Christian and Buddhist*. New York: Harper, 1957.

Tobin, Frank. *Meister Eckhart: Thought and Language*. Philadelphia: University of Pennsylvania Press, 1986.

Wackernagel, Wolfgang. "Two Thousand Years of Heresy: An Essay." *Diogenes*. (International Council for Philosophy and Humanistic Studies) no187 138-48 1999.

Woods, Richard, O.P. "In The Catholic Tradition, Meister Eckhart (1260-1328) Mystic under Fire." *Priest and People*. November, 1994.

——. *Eckhart's Way*. Collegeville, Minnesota: The Liturgical Press, 1990.

General:

al-Hakim, Souad. *Al-Mu'jam al-Sufi: Al Hikma fi Hudud al-Kalima*. Beirut, 1401/1981.

al-Qushayri. *al-Risalah al-Qushayriyah, li-Abi al-Qasim 'Abd al-Karim al Qushayri*. ed. 'Abd al-'alim Mahmud [wa-]Mahmud ibn al-Sharif, Cairo: Dar al-Kutub al-Hadithah, 1966.

Asad, Muhammad. *The Message of the Qur'an*. Gibraltar, 1984.

al-Tabari. *Jami' al-bayan 'an ta'wil ayat al-qur'an*. Vol. I, Beirut, 2001.

al-Tusi, Abi Nasr al-Sarraj. *al-Luma'*. ed., 'Abd al-Halim Mahmud, Taha 'Abd al-Baqi Surur, Cairo: Dar al-Kutub al-Hadithah, 1960.

Aykara, Thomas A. ed. *Meeting of Religions*. Bangalore: Dharmaram Publication, 1978.

Barraclough, Geofferey. *The Medieval Papacy*. New York: Harcourt, Brace & World, 1968.

Berger, Peter. ed. *The Desecularization of the World: Resurgent Religion and World Politics*. William B. Eerdmans, July 1999.

Bourdieu, Pierre. *Outline of a Theory of Practice*. Cambridge University Press: 1977.

Brient, Elizabeth. *The Immanence of the Infinite*. Washington DC: The Catholic University of America Press, 2002.

Caputo, John, D. *Radical Hermeneutics: Repetition, Deconstruction, and the Hermeneutic Project*. Bloomington : Indiana University Press, c1987.

Carl, W. Ernst. "Persecution and Circumspection in Shattari Sufism." *Islamic Mysticism Contested: Thirteen Centuries of Debate and Conflict.* Fred De Jong and Bern Radke, eds., Leiden: Brill, 1999, 416-435.

——.*Words of Ecstasy in Sufism.* Albany: State University of New York Press, 1985.

Chittick, William C. "Islamic Mysticism." Donald H. Bishop ed. *Mysticism and the Mystical Experience, East and West.* Susquehanna University Pres, London ad Toronto, 1995.

Cornell, Vincent. *Realm of the Saint: Power and Authority in Moroccan Sufism.* Austin: University of Texas Press, 1998.

Cupitt Don. *Mysticism after Modernity.* Oxford, 1998.

Cutsinger, James S. ed. *Path to the Heart, Sufism and the Christian East.* World Wisdom, 2002.

Derrida, Jacques. *Writing and Difference.* translated, with an introd. and additional notes by Alan Bass Chicago: University of Chicago Press, 1978.

Derrida, Jacques. *Dissemination.* trans. Barbara Johnson, London: Athlone Press, 1981.

Dunne, John S. *The Way of All The Earth, An Encounter with Eastern Religions.* London: Sheldon Press, 1972.

Esack, Farid. *Qur'an, Liberation and Pluralism, An Islamic Perspective of Interreligious Solidarity against Oppression.* Oxford, 1997.

Fakhry, Majid. *A History of Islamic Philosophy.* New York: Columbia University Press : Longman, 1983.

Rahman, Fazlur. "The Post-Formative Development in Islam: I." *Islamic Studies.* I, 4, 1962.

Forman, Robert. *Meister Eckhart, Mystic as Theologian.* Rockport: Element, 1991.

——. ed. *The Problem of Pure Consciousness.* New York: Oxford University Press, 1990.

Gasche, Rodolphe. *The Tain of the Mirror.* Cambridge: Harvard University Press, 1986.

Gilson, Étienne. *L'esprit de la philosophie médiévale.* Gifford lectures, Université d'Aberdeen, Première[-deuxième] série, Paris, J. Vrin, 1932.

——. *History of Christian Philosophy in the Middle Ages.* New York : Random House, 1955.

Goodwin, William F. "Mysticism and Ethics: an Examination of Radhakrishnan's Reply to Schweitzer's Critique of Indian Thought." *Ethics.* Vol 67, no. 1, October, 1956.

Guichard, Piere. "The Social History of Muslim Spain From the Conquest to the End of the Almohads Regime." S. K. Jayyusi. *The Legacy of Muslim Spain.* Vol. I, Leiden: Brill, 2000.

Heim, Mark. *The Depth of the Riches: A Trinitarian Theology of Religious Ends.* Grand Rapids, MI: William B. Eerdmans, 2001.

Hick, John. "Ineffability." *Religious Studies*. 36, United Kingdom: Cambridge University Press, 2000.

Hoffman, Valerie J. *Sufism, Mystics, and Saints in Modern Egypt*. University of South Carolina Press, 1995.

Hume, Martin A. S. *The Spanish people; their origin, growth, and influence*. New York, D. Appleton and company, 1914.

Hyman, Arthur and James J. Walsh, eds. *Philosophy in the Middle Ages: The Christian, Islamic and Jewish Traditions*. Indiana Polis: Hacked Pub. Co., 1973.

Ibn Aybak Safadi, Khalil. *al-Wafi bi al-Wafayat*. Vol. 4, Weisbaden, 1966.

Ibn Hazm. *Mulakhkhas ibtal al-qiyas wa 'l-ra'y wa'l –istihsan wa'l-taqlid wa'l-ta'lil*. Damascus, 1379/1960.

Izutzu, Toshihiku. *Creation and the Timeless Order of Things*. Ashland, Oregon, 1994.

Iqbal, Muhammad. *The reconstruction of religious thought in Islam*. London, Oxford Univ. Press, 1934.

Kasimow, Harold and Byron L. Sherwin, eds. *No Religion Is an Island: Abraham Heschel and Interreligious Dialogue*. Maryknoll, N. Y: Orbis, 1991.

Katz, Steven. "Language, Epistemology, and Mysticism." *Mysticism and Philosophical Analysis*. London: Sheldon Press, 1978.

Kepel, Gilles. *The Revenge of God: The Resurgence of Islam, Christianity and Judaism in the Modern World*. Pennsylvania: The Pennsylvania State University Press, 1993.

Knitter, Paul. *One Earth Many Religions, Multifaith Dialogue and Global Responsibility*. New York: Maryknoll Orbis Books, 1995.

——. *No Other Name? A Critical Survey of Christian Attitudes Toward the World Religions*. New York: Maryknoll Orbis Books, 1985.

——. "The World Religion and the Finality of Christ: A Critique of Hans Kung's On Being A Christian." *Interreligious Dialogue*. Richard W. Rousseau, ed., Ridge Row Press, 1981.

Knowles, David. *The Evolution of Medieval Thought*. eds. D.E. Luscombe and C.N.L. Brooke, London : Longman, 1988.

Kung, Hans, et al. *Christianity and The World Religions, Path of Dialogue with Islam, Hinduism and Buddhism*. New York: Doubleday, 1982.

Lane. *Arabic-English Lexicon*, Vol.2.

Lapidus, Ira M. *A History of Islamic Societies*. Cambridge: Cambridge University Press, 1988, second edition, 2002.

Leff, Gordon. *Heresy in the Late Middle Ages*. I, Manchester, 1967.

——. *The Dissolution of the Medieval Outlook, An Essay on Intellectual and Spiritual Change in the Fourteenth Century*. New York: New York University Press, 1976.

——. "Heresy and the Decline of the Medieval Church." *Religious Dissent in the Middle Ages*. edited by Jeffrey Burton Russell, New York: John Wiley and Son, 1971.

Levtzion, Nehemia and John O. Voll. "Introduction." *Eighteenth Century Renewal and Reform Movement in Islam*. Syracus: Syracuse University Press, 1987.

Lewisohn, Leonard. *The Heritage of Sufism*. Oxford; Boston, MA: Oneworld, c1999.

Macquarrie, John. "Christianity and Other Faiths." *Union Seminary Quarterly Review*. 20, 1964.

Masao, Abe. "The Impact of Dialogue with Christianity on my Self-Understanding as a Buddhist." Paper delivered at the American Academy of Religion Annual Meeting, Comparative Studies in Religion Section, December 6, 1987.

Memon, Muhammad Umar. *Ibn Taimiya's Struggle against popular Religion*, with an annotated translation of his *Kitab iqtida' as-sirat al-mustaqim mukhalafat ashab al-jahim*. The Hague : Mouton, 1976.

Menocal, Maria Rosa. *The Ornament of the World: How Muslims, Jews, and Christians Created a Culture of Tolerance in Medieval Spain*. Boston: Little, Brown & Co., 2002.

Merton, Thomas. *The Asian Journal of Thomas Merton*. New York:New Direction Book, 1973.

——. *Mystics and Zen Masters*. New York, 1967.

Netton, Ian Richard. *Allah Transcendent: Studies in the Structure and Semiotics of Islamic Philosophy, Theology, and Cosmology*. London ; New York : Routledge, 1989.

Nicholson, R. A. *The Mystics of Islam*. London and Boston: Routledge & Kegan Paul, 1963.

Norwich, Julian. *Showings*. trans. Edmund Colledge and James Walsh, New York: Paulist Press, 1978.

Ozment, Stevent. *The Age of Reform 1250-1550, An Intellectual And Religious History of Late Medieval And Reformation Europe*. New Heaven and London: Yale University Press, 1980.

Pinnock, Sarah K., ed. *The theology of Dorothee Soelle*. Harrisburg, PA: Trinity Press International, 2003.

Proudfoot, Wayne. *Religious Experience*. Berkeley: University of California Press, 1985.

Pseudo-Dionysious. *The Mystical Theology, in Pseudo-Dionysius: The Complete Works*. Colm Luibheid and paul Rorem, trans. New York: Paulist Press, 1987.

Radke, Bern and Fred De Jong, eds. *Islamic Mysticism Contested: Thirteen Centuries of Debate and Conflict*. Leiden: Boston : Brill, 1999.

Richardson, Alan. *A dictionary of Christian theology*. London, S.C.M. Press, 1969.

Rumi, Jalal al-Din. *Mathnawi.* trans. R. A. Nicholson, London, 1926.

Shah-Reza Kazemi. *The Other in the Light of the One, The Universality of the Qur'an and Interfaith Dialogue.* Cambridge: The Islamic Text Society, 2006.

Smart, Ninian. "Understanding Religious Experience." Katz, ed. *Mysticism and Philosophical Analysis.* New York: Oxford University Press, 1978.

Soelle, Dorothee. *The Silent Cry: Mysticism and Resistance.* translated by Barbara and Martin Rumscheidt., Minneapolis : Fortress Press, 2001.

——. *Theology for Skeptics: Reflections on God.* Minneapolis : Fortress Press, 1995.

Scholem, Gershom. *On Kabbalah and Its Symbolism (Zur Kabbala und ihrer Symbolik).* translated by Ralph Manheim, New York: Schocken Books, 1965.

Southern, R. W. *Western Society and the Church in the Middle Ages.* London: Penguin Books, 1970.

——. *Medieval Humanism and Other Studies.* Oxford: Basil Blackwell, 1970.

Stace, Walter T. *Mysticism and Philosophy.* London ; New York : Macmillan Press, 1960.

Tauler, Johannes. *Predigten.* Bd. I., Uebertragen und herausgegeben von Georg Hofmann, Einfuehrung von Alois M. Haas, Einsideln, 1979.

Tracy, David. *Plurality and Ambiguity: Hermeneutics, Religion, Hope.* San Francisco: Harper and Row, publishers, 1987.

——. *Blessed Rage for Order: The New Pluralism in Theology.* New York: Seabury, 1975.

Tuchman, Barbara W. *A Distant Mirror: The Calamitous 14th Century.* New York: Alfred A. Knopf, 1978.

van Buren, Mary Lou. "Spirituality in the Dialogue of Religions." Hinson E. Glenn ed., *Spirituality in Ecumenical Perspective.* Louisville, Ky.: Westminster/John Knox Press, 1993.

Vineeth, V.F., CM. "Interreligious Dialogue: Past and Present. A Critical Appraisal." *Journal of Dharma.* no 1, Vol. xix, Jan-March, 1994.

Watt, Montgomery. *Muslim Intellectual: A Study of al-Ghazali.* Edinburgh, University Press, 1963.

Weber, Max. *The Sociology of Religion.* Ephraim Fischoff, tr., fourth edition, (Boston, MA: Beacon Press, 1993.

Weismann, Itzchak. *Taste of Modernity, Sufism, Salafiyya, and Arabism in Late Ottoman Damascus.* Leiden, Boston, Koln: Brill, 2001.

Winter, Michael. *Society and Religion in Early Ottoman Egypt, Studies in the Writings of 'Abd al-Wahhab al-Sha'rani.* New Brunswick [N.J.]: Transaction Books, 1982.

Young, Frances. "A Cloud of Witness." *The Myth of God Incarnate.* John Hick, ed. London: SCM Press, 1977.

INDEX